Advanced Reporting

News gathering is a large, complicated, and often messy task that has traditionally been viewed by journalists as irretrievably idiosyncratic, best learned through trial and error. *Advanced Reporting* takes the opposite approach, focusing on reporting as a process of triangulation based on three essential activities: analyzing documents, making observations and conducting interviews. In this readable book, veteran journalism professor Miles Maguire shows how the best reporters use these three tools in a way that allows them to cross-check and authenticate facts, to reduce or eliminate unsupportable allegations and to take readers and viewers to a deeper level of insight and understanding.

This book will help to prepare students for a profession marked by increasing complexity and competition. To succeed in this environment, journalists must learn to make the most of digital media to intensify the impact of their work. At the same time, reporters must contend with a host of sophisticated public relations techniques while engaging with news audiences that no longer just consume journalism, but also collaborate in its creation. Discussion questions and exercises help students put theory into practice.

Miles Maguire is a professor of journalism at the University of Wisconsin Oshkosh, where he teaches writing, editing and reporting. He has worked as a beat writer, columnist, Washington bureau chief and monthly magazine editor, and his innovative approach to journalism has been recognized in programs such as the Knight-Batten Awards and the Great Ideas for Teachers (GIFT) competition sponsored by the Association for Education in Journalism and Mass Communication. His media scholarship and criticism have appeared in *Folio:, American Journalism Review, Newspaper Research Journal, Journalism & Mass Communication Quarterly, Journal of Media Economics, The International Journal on Media Management* and the *Journal of Information Technology & Politics.* He currently serves as an associate editor of *Literary Journalism Studies.*

Advanced Reporting

Essential Skills for 21st Century Journalism

Miles Maguire

Routledge
Taylor & Francis Group

NEW YORK AND LONDON

First published 2015
by Routledge
711 Third Avenue, New York, NY 10017

and by Routledge
2 Park Square, Milton Park, Abingdon, Oxon OX14 4RN

Routledge is an imprint of the Taylor & Francis Group, an informa business

Library of Congress Cataloging-in-Publication Data

Maguire, Miles.
   Advanced reporting : essential skills for 21st century journalism / Miles Maguire.
      p. cm.
   Includes bibliographical references and index.
  1. Journalism—Authorship.   2. Journalism—Technological innovations.
  3. Journalism—History—21st century.   4. Online journalism.
  5. Reporters and reporting.   I. Title.
   PN4775.M325   2014
   070.4'3—dc23
   2014001084

ISBN: 978-0-415-82427-9 (hbk)
ISBN: 978-0-415-82428-6 (pbk)
ISBN: 978-0-203-38540-1 (ebk)

Typeset in Stone Serif
by Apex CoVantage, LLC

To Roberta, with love and admiration—and much gratitude.

CONTENTS

FIGURES

PREFACE

I learned to research and write news articles the way lots of reporters learned—by having someone tell me to go somewhere and come back with a story.

There was no real direction, just the expectation that I would figure it out. One of the reasons I got no training, and this goes for thousands of other journalists like me, is a deeply ingrained belief within the profession that ultimately reporting can't be taught. Every situation is different, and so is every story. What works on one occasion may not work on another, and what works for one reporter may not work for anyone else.

While those statements are generally true, it's also true that all reporters base their work on just three specific acts: making observations, analyzing documents and interviewing sources. If you want to be a better reporter, the kind of journalist who can find the stories that matter and present them in a way that makes a difference, then you need to be good at those three methods of gathering information. And that's what this book is designed for.

This book takes the act of "reporting" and breaks it down into its foundational parts, showing how different tools and techniques can be applied in different situations, and most importantly showing how the combination of these different techniques is the key to developing accounts that will earn you credibility as a journalist and have an impact on your readers.

News gathering is a large, complicated, and often messy task that has traditionally been viewed by journalists as irretrievably idiosyncratic, best learned through trial and error. This book takes the opposite approach, presenting a comprehensive framework and methodology, a protocol, that journalists can apply to report the news in a way that is both transparent and authoritative.

Because of economic and technological changes, news organizations face a daunting set of challenges. Competition has never been more intense, for revenues and for reader attention, even while digital media and devices have led both to an explosion in the amount of available information and to a vast expansion in the ability of untrained reporters, the citizen journalists, to participate in the news gathering process.

Journalists who wish to stand out in this environment must be both highly efficient in their use of time and exceptionally authoritative, so that their reports on controversial topics will withstand the inevitable criticism. The methodology at the core of this book represents a way for student journalists to learn how to survive, and thrive, in the contemporary news environment. It provides a way of looking at the world that leads journalists to get better stories faster, and it shows how to gather the information that will make those stories resonate.

Unlike standard reporting textbooks, which explain what reporters do, this one explains how to do it—and how to do it better. A key element of the book is an emphasis on reporting as a process of triangulation in which the information gained through one of three essential tools is cross-checked and analyzed in light of facts gathered with the other two tools. The book also addresses the complexity of contemporary news reporting, especially the impact of technology, and examines the sophisticated public relations techniques with which reporters must contend.

ACKNOWLEDGMENTS

A book about reporting is inevitably dependent on examples of outstanding journalism, and I am grateful to the organizations that granted permission to reprint material in this text. These groups include Investigative Reporters and Editors, the Nieman Foundation for Journalism at Harvard, the Society of Environmental Journalists and *The Tuscaloosa News*. I also wish to thank several individuals for their assistance, especially Anne Whiteside and Karen Falcon, the daughters of Thomas Whiteside, who provided me with the photograph of their father that appears as Figure 13.1, and Dan Grech, who granted permission to reprint his tipsheet for covering trauma and trauma victims.

Some of the research for this book was conducted under a chapter adviser grant from Kappa Tau Alpha. The University of Wisconsin Oshkosh Office of Grants and Faculty Development provided assistance for several previous research projects that helped shape my thinking on this topic.

Much of the material in Chapter 1 first appeared as "Connecting the DOT: A Protocol for the Perception and Practice of Journalism," in *From Theory to Practice: How to Assess and Apply Impartiality in News and Current Affairs*, edited by Leon Barkho and published by Intellect Ltd. in 2013.

Finally, I wish to thank my students and those campus colleagues who have helped me on this project.

PART ONE

The Elements of Reporting

CHAPTER 1

Connecting the DOT

Finding stories that matter and reporting them with impact should be the primary goals of any journalist. But good intentions will not make you a good reporter. You need to know the essential tools that top-notch journalists use to gather information, applying them in a structured way to produce articles with high credibility. This chapter will introduce you to a methodology for news reporting based on analyzing documents, making observations and talking to sources. It will then describe how that methodology works by integrating the information that you uncover in a way that will help you produce compelling stories, whether you are working on a routine assignment or a major project.

Bob Woodward, whose work on the Watergate investigation led to the resignation of President Richard M. Nixon, has won nearly every major award in American journalism and been described by his contemporaries as one of the best reporters of all time. But shortly after he started working at *The Washington Post* in 1971, he came perilously close to making the kind of mistake that would have made his editors doubt his reliability and might well have kept him off the Watergate story.

Woodward is legendary for his ability to develop and work human sources, and after just a few months at the paper he had found one at the District of Columbia Department of Health who was funneling him copies of restaurant inspections. One day the source came through with the makings of a sure-thing Page 1 story: extreme sanitary violations at a place that Woodward instantly recognized as a landmark dining establishment for Washington's elite: the Mayflower Coffee Shop.

As Woodward recounts in a video interview posted on YouTube (Woodward, 2009), the Mayflower is a storied establishment just a few blocks from the *Post* and not far from the White House. For decades it enjoyed a reputation as the finest hotel in Washington, the site of gala events for celebrities and political leaders as well as private meetings among lobbyists, journalists, industrialists and all manner of movers-and-shakers.

The tip that Woodward had received was a journalist's dream—an airtight story that was based on solid documentary evidence that could be easily buttressed with quotations drawn from on-the-record interviews. Without leaving his chair, he was able to write up a sensational story (both in the sense of very good and in the sense of impossible to ignore) using the two strongest and most reliable methods of information gathering: analyzing documents and interviewing sources. As an added bonus for his editors, the story was so neatly laid out for him that Woodward was able to finish his article long before the deadline for the next day's paper.

A ROOKIE MISTAKE—AVERTED

Lucky for Woodward, one of his editors insisted that he not take the rest of the day off as a reward for his efforts but instead employ the gift of time to make use of the third of what Woodward describes as the three "channels" that bring the news to a reporter: direct observation. Dutifully Woodward set off down 16th Street toward the Mayflower and started making inquiries. Much to his surprise he learned that there was no Mayflower Coffee Shop at the Mayflower Hotel. He took a look back at the inspection report and noticed that the address of the Mayflower Coffee Shop was farther north, at another famous Washington hotel, the Statler-Hilton. He made his way there and came upon a prominent "closed for repairs" sign at the Statler's eatery. Looking around, he found a restaurant manager and confirmed with him that the repairs that were being made were indeed at the behest of the Department of Health to address violations of the city's sanitation code.

Woodward quickly returned to the *Post*'s newsroom and asked for his story back, telling his editor that he had "a few minor corrections" to make. The moral of the story, Woodward says, is that a reporter cannot rely on just one or two of the news gathering tools. His use of documents and interviews had gotten him a Page 1 story, but "without me . . . going to the scene we probably would have had to run a front page correction also," Woodward recalls.

Looking back, decades after that incident, Woodward can clearly describe how journalists use three basic tools of reporting in a process of triangulation—taking information that arrives in one form and checking it against information that arrives in other ways. But this process wasn't written down somewhere for him to read and absorb. Woodward had a savvy editor who made him keep reporting even after he thought he had finished his story. But not all rookie reporters can expect to get the same treatment as they learn the ropes. In many of today's newsrooms, the ranks of editors have been thinned, and the ones who are left have taken on more duties, leaving them little time to pass on their years of wisdom to those who are just starting out. Given the accelerating pace of the 24-hour-a-day news cycle, reporters with little experience will likely find themselves on their own as they climb a steep learning curve for how to cover the news.

A ROADMAP FOR REPORTERS

That's why this book was written: to provide a roadmap and a methodology that journalists, or people who want to be journalists, can use to find the stories that matter and report them in a way that has an impact on readers. In today's competitive environment, journalists can't afford to waste any time. They need to move quickly to stay ahead of the news, and when a story breaks, they need to know how to go about gathering information so that they can provide comprehensive and authoritative coverage.

To help students meet this challenge, this book focuses on the three specific tasks that, according to Canadian journalism scholar G. Stuart Adam, are at the core of a reporter's pursuit of authoritative facts: "acts of observation, analysis of documents and interviewing" (Adam, 2006, 357). Whether consciously or not, the best reporters use these three tools in a way that allows them to cross-check and authenticate facts, to reduce or eliminate unsupportable allegations, and to lead them to a deeper level of insight and understanding. The topflight journalists may use these tools with greater sophistication and efficiency than less experienced colleagues, but they are exactly the same tools that are available both to the Pulitzer Prize winner and to the rookie reporter assembling an overnight police roundup based on blotter entries, questions posed to the department's press officer and, when time allows and circumstances warrant, a visit to the scene of a crime.

For lack of a better term, and at the risk of appearing glib, the methodology in this book is called "Connecting the DOT" (see Figure 1.1). The first two letters of this acronym come from two of the three elements, documentary analysis and observations made in the field. The acronym is completed by substituting the word "talking" for "interviewing." This switch accomplishes two things: It creates an easy to remember term, and it underscores the fact that when it comes to getting information from human sources, there are alternatives to the question-based interview approach that may lead to better results. But it's really the first word in the phrase, "connecting," that is most significant. It is meant to underscore a way of approaching the news that is based on a mindful comparison of facts and purported facts as a way of getting closer to a true account of events. Rather than pretending to be a mere conveyor of information, a reporter who is connecting with the news in this way is using a "not quite scientific" method based on testing and retesting theories and suppositions with the evidence that is provided through documents, observation and talk.

Connecting the DOT

Journalists connect the DOT by using three tools—documents, observation and talk—to look at a news topic in different ways and from different perspectives. The best reporters know how to use these tools to cross-check and authenticate facts, to reduce or eliminate unsupportable allegations, and to arrive at a deeper level of insight and understanding.

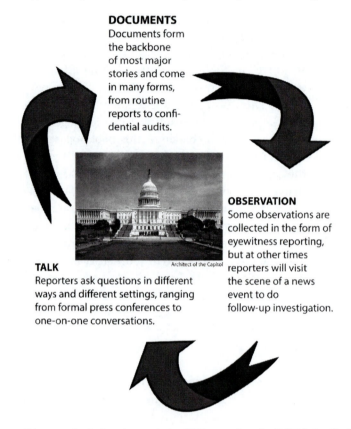

DOCUMENTS
Documents form the backbone of most major stories and come in many forms, from routine reports to confidential audits.

OBSERVATION
Some observations are collected in the form of eyewitness reporting, but at other times reporters will visit the scene of a news event to do follow-up investigation.

TALK
Reporters ask questions in different ways and different settings, ranging from formal press conferences to one-on-one conversations.

Architect of the Capitol

FIGURE 1.1 *Diagram depicting the process of "Connecting the DOT." Credit: Miles Maguire*

A FLEXIBLE METHODOLOGY

In the following chapters, you will learn more details about each of the core activities of DOT. Subsequent chapters show how to work with DOT tools from the first day of the semester on simple assignments, such as a weather story, and then how to expand your use of these tools as you progress to more complex articles. As you learn to "connect" the information you have gathered, you will also start to explore the more subtle aspects of reporting, including situations that present ethical concerns, defenses that can be used to deal with propaganda and public relations, and the challenges of pursuing stories that may upset well-connected people, powerful institutions or deeply held community values.

One reason why journalists may not consciously think about using documents, observation and talk as a unified methodology is the way that the practice of reporting has evolved. Sociologist Michael Schudson describes how reporting before the Civil War was largely a matter of "stenography, observations, and sketches" (2008, 81). In the second half of the 19th century, a second technique was added: interviewing, which helped to identify "journalism as a distinct occupation," according to Schudson. Just as interviewing was not widely accepted as a legitimate journalistic tool initially, the profession took some time to overcome its concerns about documents. Curtis D. MacDougall's seminal 1938 textbook, *Interpretative Reporting,* places far greater weight on cultivating human sources than on consulting documents and even warns about the dangers posed by relying on careless writing often found in a police blotter. But the central role of documentary analysis, as opposed to the mere reprinting of official notices, was well established by the end of World War II and exemplified in the Pulitzer Prize for national reporting that James Reston won for his coverage of the Dumbarton Oaks conference. Reston's key scoop explained the negotiating positions of the major world powers as they discussed the formation of what would become the United Nations. Reston explains in his memoirs that this story came about because a source, who was Chinese, "opened up a big briefcase and handed me the whole prize, neatly translated into English" (1991, 134).

Whether they are writing for print, lining up interview subjects for a news broadcast or developing multimedia packages for the Web, professional journalists are aware that all reporting is ultimately based on a narrow set of activities that are performed, to varying degrees, in just about every assignment. These three reporting tools—documents, observation and talk—do in fact represent a widely used methodology, although they are not acknowledged as such. This book's conception of DOT as a methodology goes a step further, showing how the three tools are most successful when used dynamically, not as individual reporting techniques but as part of a unified approach that seeks out contradictions and makes plain the places where fact-gathering has come up short.

HOW NEWS COMES TO BE KNOWN

Each element of DOT represents its own way of knowing, what philosophers call "epistemology," and each comes with intrinsic strengths and weaknesses. Documents, assuming that they are based on the work of fair-minded and disinterested researchers, reflect an accumulation of knowledge, but they provide no guarantee of accuracy and may embody hidden or unconscious bias. Information gained through firsthand experience has the benefits of immediacy and authenticity, but it is also limited, in no small part because of its specificity of perspective. Talk with human sources can lead to colorful details and unexpected insights, but verbal communication is fraught with the possibility of misunderstanding and omission. As reporters gain experience with these tools, they also learn about their limitations as well as their ability to function iteratively. A document may contain names that lead to human sources; an interview may inspire a site visit to inspect a particular locale; as part of an observation, a reporter may meet additional sources, who may in turn provoke additional documentary research. Ultimately, however, these reporting tools require different underlying skills and appeal to different personality types. That's why many reporters specialize in one kind of reporting and why the three elements of DOT are rarely viewed as a holistic methodology.

THE DIFFICULTY OF DOCUMENTS

Documents, for example, can be dull, difficult to get and hard to understand. For those three reasons, some professional journalists shun the idea of using documents in their research. They think that documents are just too time-consuming and too much work. But many of the most accomplished journalists, including those with a string of major prizes to their names, have made documents central to the way they work (see Figure 1.2). At the same time, it must be acknowledged that documents are not always reliable and may not even be true.

FIGURE 1.2   *The documents that reporters use come in many different forms, including government studies and reports. Credit: Miles Maguire*

Documents come in many forms, everything from incident reports filed by police officers to email messages, classified reports, audits, photographs, databases, books and newspaper articles. A good definition of a document comes from William C. Gaines, a Pulitzer Prize-winning reporter for the *Chicago Tribune* who went on to become a journalism professor at the University of Illinois: "A document is information that is preserved" (2007, 24). Using this broad definition, we can see that documents do not have to be on paper or even in a traditional medium. As Gaines puts it, "The document could be written in stone—like a tombstone or a cornerstone of a building. It could be a dental chart or a flag. The contents are the document." It could also be a voice or video recording.

For starters, here are three reasons why documents deserve so much attention. The most important is that documents are authoritative. As pioneering investigative reporter Paul N. Williams has noted, "Documents are often the best evidence—far better than prejudiced recollections or oral accounts—of what happened" (1978, 37). The second key argument in favor of using documents is that they stick to their story. What's written on the page doesn't shift over time, in contrast to what human sources say, or even what a reporter remembers from observations. Sources may want to revise their quotes, perhaps because of pressure from another party or simply because of further self-reflection. This can cause a great dilemma for a reporter—which version of events is the right one to use? The one that provides a colorful, if misleading, story? Or the one that may be closer to the truth but may also reflect a desire to keep embarrassing information out of print? The document, by contrast, keeps stating the same information again and again.

A third reason to emphasize documents is that at least some of them will form a very effective deterrent against libel suits. A document can bolster a reporter's claim that what was published was true, which has been an absolute defense against libel accusations under U.S. law (Pember and Calvert, 2010). In addition, official police arrest records or transcripts of court testimony are considered by the American legal system to be privileged, meaning that they can be quoted, as long as they are quoted accurately, in news stories. Even if the information in these privileged documents turns out to be false, its origin as an official government statement serves as a shield against libel. While many of the most commonly used documents can provide journalists with this peace of mind, it's important to remember that it does not apply to all kinds of documents, particularly private correspondence that turns out to be a forgery.

FIRSTHAND OBSERVATIONS

Unlike documents, which at least in theory provide the same information to all comers, observations are highly individualistic and depend on a range of factors, including vantage point and the skill of the observer. For a reporter, the act of observation serves at least two purposes. First of all, the reporter wants to gain as complete an understanding as possible of a story or situation, and second the reporter is gathering specifics that can be incorporated into a news article. In the end these two goals come together as the reporter seeks to strengthen the credibility of a finished account by demonstrating an authoritative understanding buttressed with compelling visual images and other physical details.

It is certainly true that many stories, particularly breaking stories, have to be reported by phone. Sometimes a looming deadline means that a reporter cannot go out to a crime scene or a government meeting or the home of a grieving family. For many routine stories, the investment of time in making observations about well-known locations or sources cannot really be justified. But far too often reporters skip over the crucial step of firsthand inspection.

One form of observation is the eyewitness account, which may occur from the baseball press box or from a war zone or during an emergency or an ensuing rescue or cleanup operation (see Figure 1.3). As valuable as the observations gathered in this way can be, they can also be difficult, if not impossible, to obtain. Some news events can be anticipated, and reporters can make sure that they are on hand when a successful candidate gives a victory speech or when a rescued hostage is escorted to safety. But there are other occasions, when the news happens too quickly or when authorities keep reporters at a distance, that will not lend themselves to direct viewing by journalists.

FIGURE 1.3 *To make observations about fighting conditions, reporters sometimes accompany soldiers onto the battlefield. Credit: Sgt. Sean Casey/U.S. Army*

Reporters need to make every effort to be on the front lines of the news, but they should also keep in mind that observations do not only occur in dramatic settings. There is another kind of observation, a firsthand inspection that may occur after the fact or on the ground prior to the implementation of a new policy or program. Such efforts are, admittedly, similar to a fishing expedition in that there is no real control over the results. You might come up empty-handed, but you may also come away with a big haul of information in the form of insights, sources and leads that you would not have gotten otherwise. You never know unless you give it a try.

For readers, an article lacking observational details should be a signal that the reporter is engaging with the material in a limited and perhaps superficial way, relying too heavily on abstractions and secondhand information. An intensive act of observation requires a level of engagement on the part of the reporter that almost necessarily will lead to better reporting.

IMPORTANCE OF INTERVIEWS

For all the valuable background that documents can provide and despite the critical role of direct observation, it is in talking to sources that reporters do their most important work. Human sources can provide confirmation about key details and can also walk a reporter through an explanation, with digressions as necessary, in a way that a documentary source cannot. Human sources also dispense the golden quotes that reporters need to emphasize key points about a topic or to reveal character traits about a person (see Figure 1.4).

FIGURE 1.4 *Reporters talk to public officials and other sources to get quotes and background information. Credit: Marilee Caliendo/Federal Emergency Management Agency*

In general a source who is named and identified in a way that reveals the potential for bias is believed to give more credible information than either unnamed sources or sources whose partisan or corporate affiliations are not revealed. Some journalists take a quantitative approach to sources, insisting on two or more sources in a story. Such an approach, however, can create a false sense of security in that the sources may not have arrived at their positions on their own and could be, knowingly or unknowingly, echoing the same point, rather than providing independent confirmation of a fact.

One of the dangers of working with human sources is that it is very easy to be misled. Some sources may actively seek to mislead, but there are also many sources who may accurately and honestly say something that turns out to be wrong. A reporter needs to cross-check one source against another and against what is found in documentary and observational research.

AN INTEGRATED APPROACH TO NEWS REPORTING

For close to a century, journalists, scholars and critics have urged the profession to adopt an approach that more closely resembles the way that scientists pursue knowledge through a process of experimentation and testing. But the idea of adapting the scientific method to journalism has never really taken hold, in large part because of the major differences between science and journalism. Science generally operates in a systematic way with an emphasis on controlled conditions, whereas journalism is driven by news developments, the course of which is often difficult if not impossible to predict. Journalists sometimes consciously adopt specific aspects of the scientific method, such as hypothesis formation and statistical analysis, but such approaches have not proved to be universally necessary or desirable.

That said, it is still true that top journalists follow certain patterns that can be described and emulated, even if they cannot be reduced to a step-by-step formula. This general pattern is what this textbook refers to as "Connecting the DOT," and it is based on a recognition that getting to the factual basis, or "truth," of a situation is a significant undertaking that requires diligence, thoroughness and care. Some characteristics of this approach include the following:

1. Reporting rarely happens along a straight line, even when such a line connects two opposite perspectives. To get as complete an account as possible, reporters generally proceed with a circular motion, examining a topic from multiple angles until, if they get lucky, the circle turns into a spiral and a story emerges.

2. Information comes not only from different directions but in different forms, meaning that a story is not complete until reporters have

done their best to combine what they have found from documents, observation and talk.

3. While more information is better than less information, reporting is not so much a process of addition as it is of filtration, in which some pieces of information are tested against other pieces of information so that less reliable or less valuable data points can be screened out.

4. As they gather information, the best reporters are consciously looking for gaps, which may occur because of imperfections in their own understanding or because of inconsistencies in the way policies are followed, resources are distributed or outcomes are arrived at.

5. At the base of every news story is some kind of inconsistency or anomaly (see Chapter 2 for a fuller discussion of this point), and the most successful news reports are those that highlight and explain these disruptions by making connections among pieces of information that were previously unknown or little understood.

On any given day journalists around the world pursue thousands of different stories of varying complexity, on a range of topics and under differing deadline constraints. The steps that a political reporter working for a print publication in Washington follows are not going to be exactly the same as the ones that a fashion reporter writing from Los Angeles for a website will follow. But on their best days, and with their best stories, they will make the kinds of connections described above.

Experienced reporters would agree that their stories result from a combination of documents, observation and talk, and the idea of stressing the key roles of these information techniques isn't really new. A nonprofit journalism organization (Fleeson, 2000) and even the U.S. Department of State have published reporting guides based on these concepts (Potter, 2006). But what this textbook emphasizes is the need to go beyond simply gathering and relaying information. Instead the focus is on gathering information and assessing it before passing it along.

Too often reporters follow the more standard practice of seeking "convergent validation," what has been defined as "using a combination of methodologies to examine the same phenomenon" (Killenberg, 2008, 32). However, this bias toward validation, sometimes called the "discipline of verification" (Kovach and Rosenstiel, 2001, 25), can be a source of error, particularly when reporters attempt to build a case toward a particular conclusion by emphasizing areas of overlap and consistency. Connecting the DOT implies an opposite approach, using one kind of information to highlight contrasts and inconsistencies until a fuller picture emerges.

SELF-REFLECTION IN REPORTING

Rare is the reporter who is equally skilled in, or equally inclined to use, all three reporting techniques. Thus a byproduct of the DOT methodology is that it would make journalists move away from their natural strengths and reconsider how thoroughly they actually understand what they are reporting. Nearly a century ago the journalist and political commentator Walter Lippmann (1920, 83) argued:

> You can judge the general reliability of any observer most easily by the estimate he puts upon the reliability of his own report. If you have no facts of your own to check him, the best rough measurement is to wait and see whether he is aware of any limitations in himself.

But rare is the reporter who provides such an estimate. After all, journalists are trained to report what they know, not what they don't know. If reporters were expected to make explicit their use of documents, observation and talk—and the limitations therein—readers would have an easier time judging the quality of the effort that went into a report.

"DOT" IN PRACTICE

From the journalist's perspective, the use of a methodology that requires reflection as well as the resourcefulness to sort through different types of information may seem onerous. But in truth it is not, because good journalists have been doing these things for years, starting with print and continuing into the online era. The two accounts that follow illustrate this point.

In 1969 investigative journalist Seymour Hersh wrote an article bringing to light the massacre of hundreds of civilians by U.S. forces in and around the Vietnamese hamlet of Mylai, for which he won the 1970 Pulitzer Prize for International Reporting. Writing in the *Saturday Review,* the reporter gave a blow-by-blow account of his efforts to nail down the facts of the case in an essay called "How I Broke the Mylai 4 Story" (Hersh, 1970). A review of that essay shows clearly that the blockbuster story was the result of a mixture of documents, observation and talk.

Among the documents that Hersh used was a newspaper clipping from *The New York Times,* and indeed "clippings" of previously published work, which are usually found in electronic form these days, are among the most important, and certainly the first, documents that a reporter consults. Clippings provide valuable background information and also point the reporter to the edge of the news by revealing what has already been written. In Hersh's case the clipping told him that the Associated Press had moved a story about six weeks earlier reporting that an Army officer, First Lt. William L. Calley, had been "charged with murder in the deaths of an unspecified number of civilians in Vietnam" (Associated Press, 1969, 38). Perhaps surprisingly no one until Hersh had sensed that this was a much larger story.

But to get the larger story, Hersh had to get to Calley, which involved a trip to Fort Benning, Georgia, where the officer was awaiting trial. Hersh turned to other documentary sources once he was there, including the base telephone directory, the register at the bachelor officers' quarters and other military directories at the base. Two key documents that came into play were a slightly out-of-date telephone directory (which unlike the then-current directory included a listing for Calley) and a short personnel sheet that Hersh talked a disgruntled GI into purloining from Calley's official file. As in this case, documents are often a good starting point, but they are typically only a starting point. For example, Hersh used a Washington directory to follow up on a tip that Calley's lawyer was named Latimer. The only Latimer in that directory was not the right one, but he pointed Hersh to another lawyer named Latimer, who was based in Salt Lake City and who turned out to be representing Calley.

CONFIRMATION FROM A LAWYER

Calley's lawyer confirmed that the officer was still at Fort Benning, and Hersh recognized that to get an interview he would have to visit the sprawling base and go "blindly looking for him." Hersh would need to use his powers of observation to track down his subject. Once Hersh learned of the apartment complex where Calley was living, he headed to the site, only to discover that it consisted of about 250 units. Hersh had no choice but to go looking door-to-door. When he was about to give up for the night, he next went to a nearby parking lot and started flagging down cars to ask the drivers if they knew Bill Calley. His break finally came when he spotted some men working on a car in a distant corner of the parking lot. One of them knew Calley, chatted with Hersh over drinks in his apartment and ultimately made the introduction just as Hersh was getting ready to walk back to his car and call it a night. Hersh's powers of observation also came into play when he sat down to write the story and used his opening words to create a visual image of the accused mass murderer, which he recounted in his magazine article: "Lt. William L. Calley Jr., twenty-six, is a mild-mannered, boyish-looking Vietnam combat veteran with the nickname of 'Rusty'" (1970, 49).

In the end the key was talking to Calley. The soldier confirmed some key details and provided "some essential quotes" (Hersh, 1970, 49). But before he got to Calley, there were many others he had to talk to, from the original tipster who called the reporter on the phone all the way to the officer who finally connected Hersh to the accused. Hersh estimates that when he first started working on the story he made 50 to 75 calls over several days. Before he left Washington, Hersh spoke with Congressional staffers and Pentagon officers, some of them helpful, some of them not. Talking with Calley's law-yer in Salt Lake City gave him the specifics of the case. At Fort Benning, Hersh talked with the officers in charge of keeping prisoners in the base stockade, a sergeant manning the front desk at the Judge Advocate General's office, Calley's military lawyer and Calley's commanding officer. Another person he talked to was an unhappy GI, who had just been busted from sergeant to private and who snatched part of Calley's personnel file so that Hersh could catch up with some of Calley's former housemates. These officers were the ones who finally told Hersh that Calley was living on base at the senior bach-elor officers' quarters, which allowed the reporter to make contact.

DIGGING FOR THE STORY OF "DILBIT"

In 2013 the Pulitzer for national reporting went to an online news site that did not let the limitations of a small staff keep it away from pursuing a big story. The news site is known as InsideClimate News (ICN), and the Pulitzer jury gave it the prize for "rigorous reports on flawed regulation of the nation's oil pipelines, focusing on potential ecological dangers posed by diluted bitumen (or 'dilbit'), a controversial form of oil."

The process of getting the news by "connecting the DOT" is dynamic, a pattern that is clearly seen in the story of how ICN put together its dilbit report. The following account is taken from the Pulitzer website, which, beginning in 2013, has included the entry information for prize win-ners, including the cover letters that explain how a nominated work came together (Columbia, 2013). Reviewing these cover letters is an excellent way to learn how journalists deal with the challenges of pursuing complicated projects.

The heart of ICN's coverage was an investigation of a pipeline spill in Michigan, but the story began when reporters headed to Nebraska to see where the Keystone XL pipeline was to be built and to hear what landowners there had to say. What they heard was a concern about what would happen if the pipeline failed and polluted the Ogallala aquifer.

What the consequences of such an event would be was a good question, but it turned out there weren't many answers because not much scientific research had been done on the subject. To illuminate the issue the reporters decided to turn their attention to a pipeline accident in Marshall, Michigan, which had allowed almost a million gallons of polluted material into the Kalamazoo River but had gotten little media attention previously because of timing—it happened in July 2010, shortly after the massive Deepwater Horizon blowout in the Gulf of Mexico was capped.

By visiting the spill site, talking to residents and reviewing federal records, the ICN reporters were able to identify and highlight several aspects of the incident that were particularly noteworthy. For example, they found that the pipeline had ruptured at a point where there was a known defect that had been documented in federal records but had not been addressed.

But perhaps the most significant fact they brought into focus was that a dilbit spill was very unlike a conventional oil spill and that techniques used to contain conventional spills would not work with dilbit, a substance that was expected to play an increasingly large role in U.S. energy consumption.

The reporters, Lisa Song, Elizabeth McGowan and David Hasemyer, did not stop there, but continued to pursue the topic, highlighting additional inconsistencies that they discovered. Subsequent stories focused attention on weaknesses in the leak-detection technology that the pipeline industry says reduces the need for tougher oversight. A key finding was that the general public is more likely to detect a leak than the automated systems the industry installs. Another unsettling fact that the website uncovered was that a section of the replacement pipeline was to run through the Lake Michigan watershed, which provides water to 10 million people, and would do so without employing the best available leak-detection technology.

"Despite our relatively small readership, our stories have had a big impact," wrote Susan White, ICN's executive editor, in her letter to the Pulitzer judges. She noted that following ICN's stories the company involved had agreed to abide by local law in Michigan and that the issues raised by her website were much more widely known: "Thanks to our work, the word 'dilbit' and the Kalamazoo spill are now part of the ongoing national debate over the Keystone XL" (White, 2013).

Take particular note that the site's reporting team did not move in a straight line, nor did it content itself with simply presenting "both sides of the issue." On-the-ground reporting at the site of the Michigan pipeline spill was critical, but there was much more background information that needed to be brought to bear. The reporters turned to government reports, industry websites and even petroleum engineering textbooks so that they could get a grasp of the situation and focus their readers' attention on the gaps that they were seeing between the risks that were posed by the pipeline and the way that those risks were perceived and understood by residents and government regulators alike (Song, 2013).

It would be a mistake, however, to conclude from the stories of Mylai and of dilbit that the use of documents, observation and talk in an integrated, iterative fashion is something that is left only to major projects or stories that have prize potential. The use of this kind of a methodology should be an everyday practice, in no small part because it could address some of the major issues that confront the journalism profession. These interrelated concerns include the low opinion that the public has about the press and its credibility, the difficulty of deciding who is or is not a journalist and the increasing importance of finding a way to get better stories and report them more thoroughly, to produce journalism with impact.

PRESS PERFORMANCE AND PERCEPTIONS

A 2013 survey by the Pew Research Center for the People & the Press showed that only 26 percent of Americans believe that news organizations usually get the facts straight, a steep decline from the 55 percent that believed in press accuracy when the survey was started fewer than 30 years ago (Pew, 2013). The 2013 survey showed other troubling signs of the public's declining confidence in journalism, with 75 percent saying that the news media are often influenced by the powerful, 76 percent saying they tend to favor one side, 71 percent saying they try to cover up mistakes, 58 percent saying they are politically biased and 35 percent saying they hurt democracy. This last survey result is particularly worrisome given that a conceit among Western journalists is that they form an indispensable pillar of democratic society. The late media critic and theorist James Carey has argued, "When democracy falters, journalism falters, and when journalism goes awry, democracy goes awry" (Carey, 2001,19).

DEFINITIONAL ISSUES

Among both media scholars and working journalists, there has been great consternation about how to define the essential core of reporting, but the issue remains far from resolution. Because of the ubiquity of television news, many people derive their idea of reporting from the image of the crime- or accident-scene standup, where a microphone-wielding person provides the initial, sketchy details of some event and concludes by announcing, "This is so-and-so reporting live from . . . . " Newer forms of technology, especially cell phones equipped with keyboards and cameras, mean news reports can be generated by anyone carrying such a device. Such information surely has its place in news coverage, but it should not enjoy the same status as work prepared according to professional protocols that specify the techniques of reporting, their appropriate selection and application, or the minimum level of skill in the use of such techniques. Reporters who are conscious of their craft should arguably be placed in a different category than those who claim to be journalists but do not follow those craft conventions.

Journalists and other observers have been similarly frustrated in distinguishing between reporters who adhere to traditional standards of objectivity and those who appear willing to take part in partisan debate. Howell Raines, a former *New York Times* executive editor, argued that the Fox News Channel has "overturned standards of fairness and objectivity that have guided American print and broadcast journalists since World War II" (Raines, 2010, B3) while most mainstream journalists have turned a blind eye. When the Obama White House attempted to cut Fox out of a particular news story in apparent retaliation for its partisan news coverage, it set off a revolt within the presidential press corps. A correspondent for a competing network described Fox as "one of our sister organizations" (Rutenberg, 2009). By generally accepted and outwardly observable indicators of journalistic practice, Fox is indistinguishable from other news operations—Fox fields individuals identified as reporters who gather quotes, appear in video footage that is assembled into stories and narrate information before a camera. In other words, absent the recognition of a methodology such as DOT, Fox news personalities are entitled to claim the occupation of "journalist" as much as anyone else who performs the tasks of gathering and disseminating information.

LOOKING FOR IMPACT

For a variety of reasons, which will be discussed in some detail in Chapter 13, the journalism profession has grown increasingly concerned in recent years with the question of impact, what it means and how to achieve it. Because of economic and technological changes, journalistic impact has gone from a vaguely defined and unevenly pursued goal to a top priority at many news organizations. Impacts can be felt in different ways, and reporters have been acclaimed for all manner of achievements. Some of these are very specific, such as clearing the names of convicts or spurring the prosecution of criminals who had long gone unpunished, but more often the impact is more diffuse, such as promoting a shift to healthier eating habits. As we will see in the rest of this book, stories that have an impact are almost always built by combining documents, observation and talk into a persuasive account of an event or explanation of a trend.

In the face of the technological onslaught that has turned news values and hierarchies on their heads, journalism's vague and sometimes contradictory canons about what constitutes acceptable practice no longer suffice. Tom Rosenstiel, the executive director of the American Press Institute, has argued that the "trust me era" is over and that readers and viewers have adopted the attitude of "show me" instead (2009). The DOT methodology provides a way for reporters to go about gathering news in a systematic manner that is both flexible and efficient and then to lay out their findings so that news audiences can connect with and come to rely on the news accounts that they receive.

EXERCISES

1. Find a news article from your favorite newspaper or from your favorite writer and try to work backward to see how the reporter put the story together, looking especially at the use of documents, observation and talk. Also consider whether the information has been

gathered through a process of addition, in which information has been strung together, or through a process of filtration, in which comparisons are made and context is provided.

2. Review two articles from the front page (or Internet homepage) of your local newspaper and grade them on their use of documents, observation and talk. How well have the reporters connected the information they gathered? Does one article have more impact or greater credibility?

3. Looking over the front page of a national newspaper, such as *The New York Times*, analyze each article you find there in terms of which of the three DOT elements plays the biggest role. Start by focusing on the lead paragraph and try to trace the source of the information there to a document, a firsthand observation or an interview with a human source. In doing so, look to see how careful reporters are about explaining where their information comes from.

REFERENCES

Adam, G. Stuart. "Notes Towards a Definition of Journalism," in *Journalism: The Democratic Craft*, edited by G. Stuart Adam and Roy Peter Clark, 344–370. New York: Oxford University Press, 2006.

Associated Press, "Army Accuses Lieutenant in Vietnam Deaths in 1968," *The New York Times*, September 7, 1969.

Carey, James W. "Lawyers, Voyeurs, and Vigilantes," in *What's Next: Problems & Prospects of Journalism*, edited by Robert Giles and Robert W. Snyder, New Brunswick, N.J.: Transaction Publishers, 2001.

Columbia University, "The 2013 Pulitzer Prize Winners, National Reporting, Citation," accessed October 6, 2013, at http://www.pulitzer.org/citation/2013-National-Reporting.

Fleeson, Lucinda S. *Dig Deep and Aim High: A Training Model for Teaching Investigative Reporting*, Washington: International Center for Journalists, 2000, accessed December 1, 2013, at http://www.icfj.org/sites/default/files/Dig_Deep.pdf.

Gaines, William C. *Investigative Journalism: Proven Strategies for Reporting the Story*, Washington: CQ Press, 2007.

Hersh, Seymour M. "How I Broke the Mylai 4 Story," *Saturday Review*, July 11, 1970, 46–49.

Killenberg, George M. *Public Affairs Reporting Now: News of, by and for the People*, Burlington, Mass.: Focal Press, 2008.

Kovach, Bill, and Tom Rosenstiel. *The Elements of Journalism: What Newspeople Should Know and the Public Should Expect*, New York: Crown, 2001.

Lippmann, Walter. *Liberty and the News*, New York: Harcourt, Brace and Howe, 1920.

MacDougall, Curtis D. *Interpretative Reporting*, New York: MacMillan, 1938.

Pember, Don R., and Clay Calvert. *Mass Media Law*, 17th ed., New York: McGraw-Hill, 2010.

Pew Research Center for the People & the Press, "Amid Criticism, Support for Media's 'Watchdog' Role Stands Out," August 8, 2013, accessed November 25, 2013, at http://www.people-press.org/files/legacy-pdf/8-8-2013%20Media%20Attitudes%20Release.pdf.

Potter, Deborah. *Handbook of Independent Journalism,* Washington: U.S. Department of State, 2006, accessed December 1, 2013, at http://photos.state.gov/libraries/amgov/30145/publications-english/handbook_journalism.pdf.

Raines, Howell. "Why Don't Honest Journalists Take on Roger Ailes and Fox News?" *The Washington Post,* March 14, 2010.

Reston, James. *Deadline: A Memoir,* New York: Random House, 1991.

Rosenstiel, Tom. "Fighting for Survival: The State of the News Media 2009," speech delivered at the University of Southern California, YouTube video, 1:32:09. Posted September 8, 2009, at http://www.youtube.com/watch?v=sJHVhqEZ4PE.

Rutenberg, Jim. "Behind the War Between White House and Fox," *The New York Times,* October 23, 2009, accessed August 1, 2013, at http://www.nytimes.com/2009/10/23/us/politics/23fox.html?_r=1.

Schudson, Michael. *The Sociology of News,* New York: W.W. Norton, 2008.

Song, Lisa. Interview by Massachusetts Institute of Technology Graduate Program in Science Writing, "Spotlight on: Lisa Song," May 2013, accessed September 7, 2013, at http://sciwrite.mit.edu/news/spotlight-on-lisa-song-09.

White, Susan. "Cover Letter for Entry," January 24, 2013, accessed October 8, 2013, at http://www.pulitzer.org/files/2013/national-reporting/insideclimatenewsentryletter.pdf.

Williams, Paul N. *Investigative Reporting and Editing,* Englewood Cliffs, N.J.: Prentice-Hall, 1978.

Woodward, Bob. "Tips from Bob Woodward on Investigative Journalism." PostTV/*The Washington Post,* YouTube video, 5:09. Posted June 25, 2009, at http://www.youtube.com/watch?v=VVKGUctuoXE.

CHAPTER 2

Defining News

News is what's not supposed to be.

Two airliners full of civilian passengers are not supposed to crash into a pair of high-rise office towers. Those towers are not supposed to collapse. Waiting emergency rooms are not supposed to go unused because nearly all of the casualties from the collapse are fatalities, buried in the rubble.

Open the pages of your local newspaper, turn the channel to TV news, log on to the Internet. Again and again you will find that what's been published, broadcast or posted as news is, to one degree or another, something that's not supposed to be.

A bicyclist out for some exercise on a country road is not supposed to get hit by a drunken driver. An elected official is not supposed to be exchanging steamy emails with a woman who is not his wife. A military contractor is not supposed to charge $600 for a toilet cover.

Using this definition of the news does not mean the news has to be bad.

Think about the 7-year-old girl who is so appreciative of the help that military personnel provide to her neighborhood after a devastating hurricane that she starts a nonprofit organization that sends care packages to soldiers deployed to a war zone. That's not supposed to happen. Or think about the quarterback who takes the field the day after learning about the untimely death of his father, the man who coached him in his formative high school years, and goes out and throws for nearly 400 yards and completes four touchdown passes. That's not supposed to be.

All of these stories are true; all of them have made the news. Understanding why they made the news provides a clue as to what goes into being a good reporter, someone who is good at finding stories—or having stories find you. This chapter explores some of the theories that journalists and journalism scholars have used to explain the thought processes that have been used to discover and develop news stories. Advances in information technology have called into question some of these traditional approaches, and this chapter will identify steps that reporters can take to adapt to the contemporary news landscape. It will also introduce a simple system of classification for the two major kinds of news accounts that you will write, event stories and enterprise stories, explaining how different elements of the DOT methodology will come into play in different kinds of circumstances. This chapter will conclude with a discussion of some of the habits of mind that good journalists develop as they gain experience in finding and reporting stories that will engage their readers.

INFORMATION OVERLOAD

Most of what happens on any given day isn't news. But that doesn't mean that it won't be posted, blogged or Tweeted—adding to the crush of information that weighs upon news audiences. But the big stories somehow stand out, and the best reporters are the ones who know how to find those stories and bring their most important aspects into the foreground. Being in the right place at the right time will always be a factor in journalistic success, but good reporters develop a way of approaching the news that helps them find good stories based on an understanding of what separates the remarkable from the routine.

Right from the start it's important to be clear that a reporter is not simply a recorder and that the reporting process is not simply a matter of reflecting back the world as it is. The world is too messy and complicated for that, and a reporter who sets out only to transcribe the news as encountered step by step and word for word would wind up with an unintelligible mass (and mess) of disconnected facts and impressions. The job of the reporter is to gather information, but the job also requires condensing that information and rearranging it to make it more accessible to the news audience. During the course of covering a story, a reporter also needs to be open to the possibility that the "real" story is not the one that first cropped up. Perhaps another angle on the subject would yield more and better insights for readers.

A theme of this book is that the journalistic myth about reporters being born not made is simply not true. You can learn how to be a reporter (or a better reporter), and the things you need to learn how to do are relatively few. One of the things you need to learn to do is to look for the news. The first step is figuring out what to look for, and the examples above provide an important clue—you look for things that are out of place, things that don't fit with expectations or the normal course of life.

There's a word for things that look out of place—anomaly. Its Greek roots mean "not the same," and the word itself is just a fancy way of saying that something doesn't fit in, that it isn't supposed to be. An ability to spot things that are out of place, that don't fit in with their surroundings, is just another way of describing the "nose for news" that a good reporter has to have. The difference is that a nose for news is an inborn trait while the ability to spot an anomaly is a skill that can be acquired, and sharpened over time. It's easy to confuse the two.

Bill Marimow, a two-time Pulitzer Prize winner who has worked as vice president for news at National Public Radio and as editor of *The Baltimore Sun* and *The Philadelphia Inquirer,* described a story he wrote while a reporter at the *Inquirer* as coming from "pure intuition." The story put a stop to an effort by City Council members to sweeten their pensions at a time when the city was in a fiscal crisis. In an interview for a book about investigative reporting, Marimow said the story was "based solely on a reporter's experience and instincts and nothing else" (Ettema and Glasser, 1998, 23).

But a closer look at the reasoning for why he decided to pursue the story reveals that it was an anomaly that sparked his interest. Essentially he was sitting among a dozen reporters listening to the routine reading of new bills during a council meeting, and the title of one of the proposals caught his attention: "Amending Elected Officials' Pension Plan A." Apparently his fellow reporters were snoozing through the bill reading, but anyone who was on the lookout for anomalies—for things that are not supposed to be—would surely have wanted to know what the council was up to in making changes to its pension plan.

Marimow said it was intuition that prompted him to dig deeper, but he also said it was a matter of recognizing two things that did not normally go together. He told the authors of the book: "Whenever I heard 'pensions' and 'elected officials' when I was covering the council, I said, 'Interesting'" (Ettema and Glasser, 1988, 24). That's because pension payouts are supposed to be the routine result of objective mathematical formulas while the role of elected officials is to make subjective decisions based on specific sets of circumstances. If elected officials are voting on pensions, it is always going to be because they want to substitute their judgment for a preset calculation, and it's a good bet that they are exercising their judgment in a way that will advance their personal interests. In other words, they are taking a process that is supposed to work one way and turning it around so that it is something that is not supposed to be.

This is not to say that Marimow did not bring something special to the situation that allowed him to scoop the competition when the story was right in front of their noses. But that something special was not simply some kind of instinctual magic; it was a way of looking at the world coupled with sufficient background knowledge to know when something was out of place. The lesson to be learned here, particularly for inexperienced reporters, is really two-fold. The first part is that if you want to get good stories, you need to practice looking for anomalies. But the truth is that you may not be able to spot anomalies unless you know enough about a subject to see things that are not supposed to be. The second part of the lesson, then, is that taking the time to immerse yourself in a topic—through documentary research, firsthand observation and talking to sources—is an essential step toward becoming a first-rate journalist.

THE IMPORTANCE OF JUDGMENT

That reporting is necessarily interpretive does not mean that reporters are free to make things up or to distort the facts they find. Instead they are bound to try to come as close as possible to the fact-based truth. To do so, however, they will have to make decisions and judgments. They will have to decide, for example, what kinds of documents might be available for a particular story and how to go about getting them. They will also have to decide whether firsthand observation would help their understanding of a story and where might be the best vantage point. Some of their biggest decisions will be whom to use as sources and how to get them to talk. The starting point of this whole process is the basic judgment about what constitutes news, what makes something worthy of attention and news coverage.

Anyone who is a regular consumer of news may have some trouble with the idea of news being what's not supposed to be. After all, aren't news reports full of regularly scheduled events, like sports competitions and elections? If those things happen the way they are supposed to, then why do we think of them as news?

The easiest way to answer that question is to consider what constitutes the normal course of affairs. Elections are not held every day, and even in frequently played sports like basketball or baseball, the same two teams don't play every day. An event in itself is a deviation from some norm and therefore provides an opportunity to find news.

But there's another way of looking at sporting events and elections that may help to illuminate why news draws our attention in the first place. This insight comes from Michael Schudson, the sociologist at Columbia University who has written extensively about the role of journalism in U.S. democracy. In Schudson's view, citizens follow the news as a way of controlling their environment. "All of us want to tame the anarchy of events," he writes. "The entire insurance industry rests on this desire. So does the legal institution of contract," he adds, citing numerous other examples of widely adopted practices, such as long-term mortgages and systems of table etiquette, that are used to ward off disorder (2008, 88–89).

News, also, is a way of controlling the uncontrollable because reporters don't simply transmit information but organize it in a way that helps to make sense of what has happened, whether that happening was as unusual as a terrorist attack or as regular as a change in weather conditions. Sporting events and elections represent moments in which outcomes are in question, and the specific results are what is of interest because they are what are out of the ordinary. The results mark the taming of at least short-term anarchy by putting the competitors, whether basketball players or Senate candidates, back into order.

The idea of news as an anomaly is not really new, but it is not the typical definition of news that has found its way into most reporting textbooks over the years. As you learn to apply the DOT methodology in your reporting, you will likely see some advantages to approaching the news in this way, but that doesn't mean that it isn't important to be familiar with more traditional approaches to news or to more contemporary ones that are evolving with the ongoing changes in communications technology.

Many journalism textbooks define news based on certain observable characteristics. The six that are commonly used are timeliness, singularity, prominence, proximity, impact and conflict. Using a fairly common experience, driving a car, we can see how these qualities may be present and help determine whether something would be considered news.

- **Timeliness** refers to how recently something has happened. The idea is that news should be new and that something that has just happened, or is still happening—even if relatively minor—would be of interest to news audiences. A good example of this might be a traffic jam during rush hour. It could be something that happens every day. Yet many news outlets, particularly radio and television, devote significant resources to reporting on traffic conditions because at the time they are happening they can be extremely important to commuters.

- **Singularity**, also sometimes called oddity or uniqueness, signifies that something is extremely unusual and rare, and therefore of interest. Say this morning's traffic jam was caused not just by the usual heavy volume of cars but because a cargo truck overturned and spilled 40,000 pounds of ice cream or 2,100 cases of beer or 14 million bees or millions of dollars in coins. The traffic delays may not be appreciably greater because of this event, but the incident would surely be seen as news.

- **Proximity** is a fancy word for nearness and reflects the fact that people are more likely to take notice of something that happens close by than of something that happens at a distance. All major cities, and many small ones, have traffic tie-ups at busy times at the beginning and end of the work day. But the traffic jam that most matters is the one that you are in or are hoping to avoid. The ones that are happening all over the country almost certainly don't matter to you.

- **Prominence**, in the context of discussing news, is a measure of how well known the people involved are, whether they are celebrities in some sense. Imagine that a famous athlete or a movie star is caught speeding or driving drunk. It's their celebrity that turns a routine, thousand-times-a-day kind of event into a headline.

- **Impact** refers to the outcome or consequences of an event. A traffic accident that is no more than a fender-bender may reduce highway traffic to a crawl, but it is unlikely to make it into the nightly news or into the print or online news columns. On the other hand, an accident with life-threatening injuries will draw notice—though not as much attention as a crash in which a person (or perhaps more than one) is killed.

- **Conflict** comes in all different sizes and levels of intensity, from policy disputes between political rivals to sporting events to shooting wars. It seems to be a basic element of human existence, which may be why readers and viewers are drawn to it, since it gives them a chance to form opinions about how a conflict should play out and then see if they are right about the resolution. A common traffic jam is the result of a basic conflict, as too many vehicles attempt to occupy a limited amount of space. But a traffic story would get more interesting, newsier, if more obvious kinds of conflict appear—such as a road rage incident involving two drivers.

Some journalists and journalism scholars use slightly different lists, sometimes with more and sometimes with fewer news factors. But the real question about this approach is whether it is merely a descriptive theory of journalistic thinking or whether reporters and editors actually go through the process of using these elements as they decide what stories to cover each day.

Many media researchers think this news factor approach is more the former than the latter, that the actual process of identifying news and writing about it may include other considerations and probably is not as nice and neat as this list of six elements of news implies. Johan Galtung and Mari Holmboe Ruge, of the Peace Research Institute in Oslo, Norway, published a path-breaking article that compared news coverage to the tuning of a short-wave radio receiver, arguing that journalists choose from a potentially infinite number of signals to select just a handful of ones to pay attention to (1965). Starting with this metaphor, the Norwegian scholars developed a list of a dozen factors that they thought could help explain how journalists decide what occurrences they will turn into news stories.

Their first observation was that items selected for news coverage were more likely to have the same frequency as the medium in which they appear. Thus a daily newspaper would have a tendency to focus its coverage on events that began and ended in the course of a day. More complicated stories, or ones that take a longer time to develop, would more naturally be covered in formats that appear less frequently, such as weekly newspapers, monthly magazines or even books. Although the Norwegian researchers were writing long before the introduction of the Internet and microblogging services like Twitter, it's easy to see how this insight applies to advanced communications technology, which by its nature would put greater emphasis on providing a constant stream of many discrete developments. Some of these items might have dramatic consequences and great significance, but the overwhelming majority of these would, just by the laws of counting, have to be trivial.

One of the advantages of the Norwegian model of news is that it emphasizes the cultural context in which news decisions are made, the environment in which events are recognized as news and presented as news. By contrast, the six-factor approach to news suggests that these factors are universally recognized and that news coverage is determined by the facts of an event rather than by the choices of reporters and editors about what to cover and how. The goal of objective news coverage is a worthy one, even if it is elusive. For reporters to be objective, however, they need to be aware of their own inbred biases, or at least that they might be subject to inbred biases. A good reporter needs to have empathy and specifically the ability to feel how others might be affected by a given event.

One of the worst examples of journalists assuming their values were universal can be found in the coverage of African-Americans by the mainstream media during most of the 20th century. Blacks were not considered worthy of attention by many journalists, and so both their accomplishments and their ill treatment received little coverage. When race riots swept the country in the mid-1960s, many newspapers were left groping for explanations because they had paid so little attention to what was happening in their own backyards (National Advisory Commission on Civil Disorders, 1968).

HOW THE WORLD HAS CHANGED

In the early days of American journalism, news was scarce. Some newspapers intentionally left blank spaces so that their readers could write in additional information for subsequent readers. Another strategy for filling space was to lift entire articles from out-of-town papers and reprint them without concern for the copyright of the original publisher. Today's environment is entirely different, as news organizations and their customers are overwhelmed by a seemingly endless flow of news that is accessible around the clock through many different channels of communication. As someone once joked, "The Information Revolution is over—Information won!"

In the 21st century a journalist has to find a way to stand out in this world of information overload. Simply passing along news is no longer enough, because news audiences have many ways to discover news on their own. When a story breaks, the news is typically available in many different places at no cost to the consumer. A reporter needs to learn how to differentiate among the many different events that can pass as news and to find the ones that will stand out because of their intrinsic interest and ultimate impact.

At its most fundamental level, news depends on being new, and as a result journalists have always placed great emphasis on immediacy, on providing the first account of an event, what is sometimes called a "scoop." Without a doubt the most active consumers of news are always on the alert and looking for their favorite media outlets to bring them the word about the latest developments. Thus a news organization that has a reputation for bringing news as soon as it is available can attract a loyal audience. For reporters, however, an overemphasis on immediacy has to be balanced with other considerations. The first is competition, which can be especially intense in the current media environment. When, on June 28, 2012, the U.S. Supreme Court issued its ruling on the Affordable Care Act, better known as Obamacare, news organizations were racing to be first. The Associated Press initially thought that it had been first to break the news that the Supreme Court had upheld the law, but journalists at Bloomberg, a news service that specializes in financial news, produced computer screen shots showing that its first report appeared 24 seconds before the AP's (Romenesko, 2012). A later review showed that Bloomberg had, indeed, "scooped" the rest of the world by getting the news out just 52 seconds after Chief Justice John Roberts started to describe the court's decision (Goldstein, 2012).

Coverage of this case also demonstrates the danger of focusing too strongly on immediacy, at least when you are covering breaking news. Winning the race to be first is surely the mark of a superior journalist, but coming in second or third is not the only downside of making immediacy the overriding goal. The real danger of losing the race to be first is winning the race to be wrong. That's what happened to two major news organizations, CNN and Fox News, both of which reported that the law had been declared unconstitutional. The confusion was that the Supreme Court did say that the law was unconstitutional when considered under the commerce clause of the Constitution, but then it added that Congress had acted within its powers under a different part of the Constitution, the section that allows for it to levy taxes for various purposes.

Fortunately there is another way for a reporter to score a scoop besides being the first by a millisecond or two with the news of a breaking story. The alternative is what is known as a "conceptual scoop," which has been defined as "a new way of connecting dots into big pictures" (Starobin, 1996, 21). The conceptual scoop is based on looking at information that is open and available but then grouping it so that its significance becomes clear. A good example of a conceptual scoop is the 2006 story in *The Boston Globe* about the way that President George Bush was signing legislation into law while simultaneously asserting his authority to ignore the parts that he disagreed with (Savage, 2006). Referring to the Watergate source who helped *The*

Washington Post investigate that scandal, NPR media correspondent David Folkenflik has noted that many news organizations are producing "stories that rely as much on deep thought as on Deep Throat" (2007).

Kevin Kelly, who was the executive editor of *Wired* magazine from its founding in 1992 until 1999, argues that current communication networks function essentially as one big copying machine so that original work is quickly passed along and devalued. Thus the reporting strategies that worked in the 20th century will no longer bring the kinds of economic returns that will support the sophisticated kind of journalism that a complex society requires. In a previous era a reporter might be able to produce an exclusive report that could be sold and resold and possibly repackaged in different forms that could also be sold and resold. Today, such a report would quickly be copied and recopied, with the value quickly dropping to zero. "The previous round of wealth in this economy was built on selling precious copies," writes Kelly. Thanks to the Internet there is no such thing as a precious copy. Today, "once anything that can be copied is brought into contact with [the] Internet, it will be copied, and those copies never leave" (Kelly, 2008).

In Kelly's view, journalists—and other producers of content—need to recognize that their original works will be copied to the point of becoming worthless. The only solution that he sees is to concentrate on qualities that cannot be diluted through duplication, one of which is trust. Because audiences would rather rely on news organizations that they can trust, trust is something that will increase in value even while copies are cutting the value of most other things. This is one of the reasons to use a methodology like the one in this book. It will lead to trustworthy reports, and it will give your readers a way of assessing the level of trust that your work deserves.

Kelly identifies several other qualities that he believes will create value in the current media environment, dominated as it is by digital distribution over the Internet. Several of these have direct relevance to reporting, including personalization, accessibility and interpretation. The first two may be easier to connect to news reporting since clearly reporters should understand the audiences they work for and be prepared to make their work available across different media platforms. Interpretation, on the other hand, may sound more like editorializing, injecting opinions rather than presenting facts. But as Kelly points out, raw information often has little value unless it can be explained. By providing context and meaning, reporters are doing their readers a big service and can do that without losing their objectivity.

The idea of objectivity is so firmly rooted in journalistic values that students of reporting may find it difficult to accept the proposition that their own judgments and subjective assessments can and should play a critical role in their work. But such a reaction betrays a fundamental, although common, misunderstanding about objectivity as it relates to journalistic practice. Bill Kovach and Tom Rosenstiel have called the way objectivity is typically applied "one of the great confusions of journalism." They explain that the objectivity ideal was introduced in the 1920s not to suggest that journalists should be without bias but rather to acknowledge that bias is unavoidable. "Objectivity called for journalists to develop a consistent method of testing information— a transparent approach to evidence—precisely so that personal and cultural biases would not undermine the accuracy of their work" (Kovach and Rosenstiel, 2001, 72). The DOT methodology is one way to advance this idea.

TYPES OF NEWS STORIES

It has been often observed that no matter how much news happens on a given day, journalists will find a way to fill exactly the space allotted— whether in a daily newspaper, on a website or on a television or radio broadcast. The way they do this is by not limiting their definition of news to something that has just happened. While journalists often emphasize this kind of breaking news, finding it to be both exciting to cover and engrossing for news audiences, they cannot count on there being enough on any given day to fill their newspapers, websites or broadcasts. They therefore know that in addition to covering events, they also need to engage in what is called "enterprise" journalism, reporting that is initiated by a journalist as opposed to reporting that is a reaction to some specific happening, what is often called "spot" reporting. Reporters are always on the lookout for specific events that they can cover and turn into spot stories while also paying attention to trends or patterns that they can highlight in an enterprise effort.

Most of the stories that win journalism prizes are examples of enterprise stories, but some of the biggest, most memorable stories are spot stories. In the Pulitzer competition, for example, there is just one category for breaking news, but the work that is cited there includes stories that have had profound effects on the country. Winners include *The Wall Street Journal* for its coverage of the September 11 terrorist attacks, *The Times-Picayune* of New Orleans for its coverage of Hurricane Katrina, and *The Washington Post* for its coverage of the shootings that left 33 people dead at Virginia Tech. Enterprise reporting can show up in many different categories, such as investigative, public service and explanatory. Some examples include the *Post*'s coverage of Watergate and the *Los Angeles Times*' 2011 exposé of small town officials paying themselves stratospheric salaries. Other examples of Pulitzer-winning enterprise stories can be found in the category of feature writing, such as a 2006 story about a Marine major whose job it was to notify the next of kin in the case of warzone fatality.

These two different kinds of stories are very different in some ways, and yet they share fundamental similarities. They are not made up—they arise out of actual occurrences. They also depend on the use of the same fact-gathering tools—documents, observation, talk. But these tools are likely to be used in different proportions. Because of the speed at which they must be reported, spot stories are more likely to be built on the kinds of facts that can be gathered quickly, either through direct observation or through interviews with human sources. Documentary sources will, of course, be consulted, but mostly for verification or fact-checking. Enterprise stories will usually depend more heavily on documents, especially at the initial stages, but they will also require interviews and most often some kind of direct observation. Since event-driven stories are closer to the traditional concept of news, we'll first examine those before moving on to enterprise news stories.

EVENT STORIES

Reporters would do well to bear in mind that there are at least three different kinds of events, which can be classified according to what might be called "news intent," that is, whether the event is intended to attract attention or affect public opinion. While all three kinds of events have news value and deserve some form of coverage, they differ in important ways and particularly in how they can distort a journalist's perceptions and ability to render an objective account.

The first kind of event that reporters cover is a naturally occurring event, one that happens on its own and often because of impersonal forces, such as a wildfire started by lightning (see Figure 2.1), or with no consideration

FIGURE 2.1 *An example of a spontaneous news event was the 2012 fire in New Mexico's Gila National Forest that was started by lightning and grew to 300 square miles. Credit: Brandon Oberhardt/U.S. Forest Service Gila National Forest*

of media coverage, such as a fatal traffic accident or a petty crime. These are often fast-breaking, on-the-spot stories that present deadline challenges that may restrict a reporter's ability to do as much fact gathering as one would like. On the other hand, such news events do not come with pressures to favor one side or the other.

The second kind of event is scheduled in advance and therefore lacks a degree of spontaneity. Such events typically include sponsors, partisan supporters or simply committed advocates on one side or the other. Examples include courtroom cases, some legislative proceedings (such as debates and votes) and cultural events, such as artistic performances or sports competitions. Because these events are planned, reporters have time to prepare themselves with documentary research and interviews so that they are well aware of the contrasting points of view they are likely to encounter. Thus forewarned and forearmed, reporters can more easily maintain an objective stance. Such events require a balanced approach, but fortunately the opportunity to obtain both sides of the story—from plaintiffs and defendants, from liberals and conservatives, from members of the winning and the losing team—is almost built into the situation.

The third kind of event is what lawyer, professor and history scholar Daniel J. Boorstin called the "pseudo-event" (1962). These are events that might be viewed as news for the sake of news, events that have been carefully constructed to attract attention and to promote a specific public relations message. Reporters find that each day they are confronted with a flood of pseudo-events and need to take special precautions because to one degree or another all such events are attempts at manipulation.

One of the most common types of pseudo-event is a presidential announcement from the White House (see Figure 2.2), but the classic example is the one that Boorstin described based on the writings of Edward L. Bernays, a relative of Sigmund Freud who is sometimes called "the father of public relations." In this example, the owners of a hotel wish to improve business by boosting the facility's reputation. The solution, offered by a PR specialist, has nothing to do with improving the hotel's quality or services but instead with attracting attention by hosting a celebration of the hotel's 30th anniversary, a celebration that is attended by local notables, photographed and reported on. This is manmade news, not naturally occurring news, but it works. According to Boorstin, "Once the celebration has been held, the celebration itself becomes evidence that the hotel really is a distinguished institution. The occasion actually gives the hotel the prestige to which it is pretending" (1962, 10).

Boorstin goes on to identify the characteristics of a pseudo-event. First, it is planned rather than allowed to arise out of the natural flow of human activity. Second, it is intended to be the subject of a news report and so is designed for the convenience of journalists, who are assisted in their

FIGURE 2.2 *Politicians use pseudo-events, such as this announcement by President Barack Obama in the White House Rose Garden, to get attention and shape public opinion. Credit: White House*

coverage by receiving press releases that have been written in advance to create the impression that the event took place in some previous timeframe.

The third characteristic cited by Boorstin is an especially odd one in the context of supposedly objective journalism, and that is ambiguity. The pseudo-event, because it has been constructed, has an ill-defined relationship to the reality on which it is based. Motivations are particularly unclear and unresolved, which Boorstin argues is critical to maintaining some level of public interest.

The fourth characteristic, which also seems contrary to the idea of fact-based journalism, is that a pseudo-event functions as a kind of self-fulfilling prophecy, assuming and projecting an air of significance simply by virtue of its existence. In this way pseudo-events undermine the supposed independence of reporters by distorting their news judgment. Pseudo-events get covered because they have been publicized, and for a variety of reasons, ranging from competitive pressures to a lack of something better to write about, reporters often feel pressure to treat a pseudo-event as a suitable stand-in for reality.

The Boorstin-Bernays example of the hotel anniversary celebration does not begin to suggest how widely the pseudo-event has become accepted as a staple of serious journalism. On every beat, from the arts to business to politics to sports, reporters are regularly invited to cover pseudo-events: gallery openings, annual shareholder meetings, legislative hearings, post-game press conferences. In each case, the reporter is a kind of guest and is forced to function within a system of constraints, a kind of etiquette that reporters violate at the peril of not being invited back the next time. At the same time this unspoken code of behavior, under which reporters are not supposed to emphasize the contrived nature of the event, can exact a toll over time and diminish a reporter's effectiveness.

No reporter can function without pseudo-events, which will often, although not always, allow for real news to be made. Such events also provide access to officials and other potential sources who might not otherwise be reachable for quotes. But journalists should not ignore the essentially manipulative function of a pseudo-event and do the best they can to alert their readers to ways in which it can distort reality. Pseudo-events are, by definition, designed to be covered, and so they make easy pickings. But those pickings are too easy sometimes, and reporters who are seduced into spending too much time at pseudo-events are undoubtedly missing real stories that are occurring elsewhere.

ENTERPRISE STORIES

Enterprise reporting can cover a full range of stories, from the trivial to the earth-shattering, and across every possible beat: sports, politics, culture, crime. During the course of their careers, most reporters will handle both kinds of stories, although they may find themselves more comfortable doing mostly spot stories or mostly enterprise stories. In some ways spot stories can be easier to cover, because the salient facts that have to be included are usually very obvious and do not require a great deal of news judgment. At the same time, spot stories are often the most important stories of a given day, and so editors may choose to keep inexperienced reporters away from them, for fear that they will make some kind of mistake in a story that has to be completed on deadline and that is likely to draw increased attention from readers. As a result, rookie reporters may find themselves assigned to trend stories. One advantage of working on a trend story is that it is likely to be less competitive and less critical to a news organization's ongoing coverage. On the other hand, it may require more sophisticated thinking and analysis so that the most important elements are properly highlighted. (See Chapter 9 for a discussion of how to write a trend story.)

Enterprise stories are rooted in events, but they are also removed from those events, some more than others. In certain ways an enterprise story is an optional story—it doesn't have to be done and in many cases it will "belong" to a particular reporter or news organization. For example, if there is a major fire in your town or a multiple homicide, every news organization around will feel compelled to cover it at least in headline fashion, capturing and transmitting the most significant details. But from there different reporters will go in different directions. Some will move on altogether, but others may decide to come back for a "second day" story that recapitulates the main points of the first day story but then emphasizes some other angle or angles. In the case of a fire, the first day's coverage would naturally include the Five W's to the extent that such information was available: Who was involved? What exactly happened? When did the fire start? Where did it occur? Why did it happen? On the second day, a reporter might decide to delve into just one of these areas, developing profiles of the victims, for example, or interviewing arson investigators to find out the causes of the blaze.

Another approach to enterprise coverage is to write in anticipation of some event. If a major movie star has a film that is about to be released, some publications might find that an appropriate time to assign a profile story about the star. In advance of major events, such as political conventions or championship games, other kinds of enterprise stories may appear, such as backgrounders on the location of the event or chronologies of what is expected to happen during the upcoming event. (See Chapter 9 for a discussion of preview stories.) Geography can also provide a useful perspective, as reporters often look at trends that are developing nationally or events that have happened in another region and use them as a starting point for local reporting. In the end most enterprise stories present themselves to reporters who are looking for them, and looking specifically for the things that are out of place, that aren't supposed to be.

HABITS OF MIND

It's easy to say that reporting in the 21st century news environment requires journalists to think in new ways. But the challenge is actually bigger than that. The challenge is to develop an agility of mind that allows you to think in different ways at the same time. Here are some habits of mind that you should try to cultivate.

1. **Search for patterns—and for the lack of a pattern**. The story that the *Globe* published about President Bush's signing statements came about because the reporter, Charlie Savage, was able to see a pattern, a pattern that pointed to an underlying inconsistency between approving legislation and simultaneously saying it wasn't fully binding. By contrast Bill Marimow saw the opposite of a pattern in his report on Philadelphia pensions; what he saw was a break in the usual pattern of how things are done. In other words, you need to be able to see patterns and also be able to see the significance when there isn't a pattern or when a pattern is broken.

2. **Look microscopically—and see globally**. The best reporters love to dig into the details of a topic they know well, whether it's political polling or sports statistics or popular culture. But they also know that most readers aren't interested in minutia, until they understand why it matters in their lives and in a global perspective.

3. **Break the story—and put it into context**. Pat Steigman, the editor-in-chief at ESPN.com, says that the billions of page views that his site attracts each month come down to two very different things: immediate scoops and deep analysis. "All of those little stories, all of those scoops that we break every single day, add up," he says. But that's not enough. "People come to ESPN . . . for the perspective," he adds. Readers say, "What does this mean? OK—here's the news. Interpret this for me. Put this in perspective. How important is this in the grand scheme of things?" (2012).

4. **Probe the past—and imagine the future**. The typical news story is an account of something that has happened in the recent past. But knowledgeable journalists are always looking ahead, over the horizon, to see what the implications might be.

5. **Accept every possibility—and doubt everything**. Reporters are often urged to be skeptical, but it may be more important to be the opposite—to be open to a full range of possibilities, at least initially. Skepticism will encourage you to question the truth of what you are being told, and that's important. Reporters need to question and check the facts. But openness can also help you think about the news if you are open in a certain way. At the start of the reporting process, a reporter needs to be willing to believe things that most people would dismiss out of hand. Take the case of a school district that issues a press release saying that standardized test results prove that local children are learning their lessons well. Be willing to believe that—but also be willing to believe the opposite, that the test scores have been selectively presented to cover up serious deficiencies. That's being skeptical. Being open is going even further, believing that it is at least possible that standardized tests may not reflect all of the kinds of learning that occur in a classroom and may not even be a good predictor of how well students will do in later schooling. Don't be satisfied staying at the starting point of your story. Look beyond to see what else might be there.

The main advantage of trying to maintain these seemingly contradictory ways of looking at the world is that this approach is more likely to lead you to consider alternative perspectives and help you get closer to the truth. If you are truly, deeply skeptical, you run the risk of doubting everything, and not everything is false. Skeptical reporters sometimes become cynical reporters, and this darkness colors their work, eventually undermining it and them. The opposite approach means keeping your eyes and your mind open.

If you use the DOT methodology properly, the unsettled phase of your reporting, when you are between the opposite ways of thinking described above, will not go on indefinitely. A big part of DOT is extensive information gathering using tools that often lead to facts, which may or may not add up. But as you go along, you will start to find ways to make sense of the inconsistencies that you encounter. Ultimately you will be able, in Schudson's words, "to tame the anarchy of events."

EXERCISES

1. Pick two recent news stories, one of them a spot story covering an event and the other an enterprise story, that is, a story that reflects the insight and originality of the reporter. For each article identify the part that's "not supposed to be." Is one story stronger than the other from the standpoint of newsworthiness?

2. Any two journalists, or any two people for that matter, are likely to have differing opinions about what is and what is not supposed to be. Aside from some obvious cases, like an eight-alarm fire, two given reporters might look at the same set of facts and see a story or not see a story, based at least in part on their personal expectations of what is "normal." Take a few minutes to think about what your personal baseline is for normal. On any given day, what are some things that are and are not supposed to take place in your community, on your job, at the place where you spend most of your time outside of your home?

3. Most of us know a lot about something, maybe a sports team, a TV show, an entertainer or a hobby. Identify some topic on which you have deep knowledge and think about how you acquired that knowledge. Did it come from focused reading? Conversation with friends? Random experience? What do you think is the best way to acquire deep knowledge about a topic?

REFERENCES

Boorstin, Daniel J. *The Image: or What Happened to the American Dream,* New York: Antheneum, 1962.

Ettema, James S., and Theodore L. Glasser. *Custodians of Conscience: Investigative Journalism and Public Virtue,* New York: Columbia University Press, 1998.

Folkenflik, David. "As Media Multiply, So Do 'Conceptual Scoops,'" NPR.org, June 19, 2007, accessed December 3, 2013, at http://www.npr.org/templates/story/story.php?storyId=11194195.

Galtung, Johan, and Mari Holmboe Ruge. "The Structure of Foreign News," *Journal of Peace Research* 2, no. 1 (1965): 64–91.

Goldstein, Tom. "We're Getting Wildly Different Assessments," *SCOTUSblog*, July 7, 2012, accessed December 3, 2013, at http://www.scotusblog.com/2012/07/were-getting-wildly-differing-assessments/.

Kelly, Kevin. "Better than Free," *The Technium* (blog) *Kevin Kelly*, January 31, 2008, accessed December 3, 2013, at http://www.kk.org/thetechnium/archives/2008/01/better_than_fre.php.

Kovach, Bill, and Tom Rosenstiel. *The Elements of Journalism: What Newspeople Should Know and the Public Should Expect,* New York: Crown Publishers, 2001.

National Advisory Commission on Civil Disorders. *Report of the National Advisory Commission on Civil Disorders,* Washington: Government Printing Office, 1968.

Romenesko, Jim. "Bloomberg News: We Were First With Health Care Ruling," *Jimromenesko.com,* June 28, 2012, accessed December 3, 2013, at http://jimromenesko.com/2012/06/28/bloomberg-news-we-were-first-with-health-care-ruling/.

Savage, Charlie. "Bush Challenges Hundreds of Laws," *Boston Globe,* April 30, 2006, accessed December 3, 2012, at http://www.boston.com/news/nation/articles/2006/04/30/bush_challenges_hundreds_of_laws/.

Schudson, Michael. *Why Democracies Need an Unlovable Press,* Cambridge, Mass.: Polity Press, 2008.

Starobin, Paul. "The Conceptual Scoop," *Columbia Journalism Review,* January/February 1996, 21–25.

Steigman, Pat. "Keynote," 2012 annual conference of the Northeast Wisconsin Scholastic Press Association, April 25, 2012, University of Wisconsin Oshkosh, Oshkosh, Wis., accessed December 13, 2012, at http://www.uwosh.edu/journalism/newspa/resources.

CHAPTER 3

Digging into Documents

Since journalism is sometimes called history in a hurry, it's easy for reporters to think that they don't have time to stop and read, especially with all the information that comes streaming across their desks and computer screens. They may think they will move faster if they pick up the phone or go out and ask their questions in person. But if they want to get the most out of an interview, or want to scoop the competition, they will learn to turn to documents first. Veteran journalists know well that whatever time is invested in reading a document is likely to bring a big payoff later in the reporting process. In this chapter you will learn how to obtain documents and how to mine them for information—and why so many prize-winning journalists attribute their success to having what they refer to as a "documents state of mind."

Think back to the summer of 2011, when the federal government was veering dangerously close to defaulting on its debt as the Obama administration and congressional leaders engaged in intensive, politically charged discussions about the budget. On both sides, Republican and Democratic, politicians were eager to spin the story their way. Not surprisingly, the Washington press corps was having trouble getting past the rhetoric to learn the specific points of the negotiations. At a White House briefing on July 26, reporters were peppering Press Secretary Jay Carney with questions, and then one of them revealed her frustration about not getting anything in writing. "When we were in the Roosevelt Room," she said, "there was paper that we asked for that we weren't actually physically handed. So was that—are you going to give that to us?" (White House, 2011).

"Paper" may sound like an innocuous term, but it is the coin of the realm in Washington's journalism circles, where reporters, lobbyists and aides barter for information. Getting quotes and access to top officials is important, but to really nail a story so that it can't be disputed or downplayed in the next news cycle, reporters know they have to "get paper," documents that represent pay dirt: real numbers, specific legislative language, hard facts that can't later be denied.

Sometimes reporters find themselves overwhelmed with routine and rightfully ignored kinds of documents: press releases, talking points, position papers. But big stories often depend on paper, and the budget talks are a good example as Carney, the White House spokesman, made clear. There would be no paper from the White House, he explained, because as soon as one side revealed any specifics in writing, talks would break down under pressure from both political friends and enemies. "That's how it works," Carney said to the reporters assembled in the West Wing briefing room. "You know that's how it works" (White House, 2011). Inside Washington, documents are key, and transcripts of government briefings are full of pleas for, and promises of, "paper."

"WHATEVER YOU NEED IS WRITTEN DOWN"

Despite the frustrations of working to get documents and the challenges that they can present once they are in hand, they have played a critical role for many highly successful journalists. Walt Bogdanich, a three-time Pulitzer Prize winner who now works for *The New York Times,* has very simple advice for student journalists who want to write big, blockbuster stories: "Learn public records," he says. "Imagine that whatever you need is written down someplace. And believe me, in my experience, I found that to be the case. You just have to figure out where" (2008).

If this seems like an extravagant claim, a closer look at Bogdanich's body of work shows just how many places he has found the documents he needed. Bogdanich picked up his first Pulitzer in 1988 for what the judges described as "his chilling series of reports on faulty testing by American medical laboratories" (Columbia, 1988). At the time those labs were taking in $20 billion a year, and their shortcomings were not exactly unknown. As Bogdanich's first article on the topic noted, Congress had "declared war" on the problem 20 years earlier (1987, A1).

To dramatize the seriousness of the problem in a way that was completely convincing and that could not be refuted by the labs he had been investigating, the reporter turned to documents. In the first three paragraphs of his first article on the subject, Bogdanich references four different documents: an autopsy, two sets of test results and a legal settlement. In the hands of a master like Bogdanich, the documents don't make for difficult reading. He has mined them for the key details: a 34-year-old mother of two who dies in the early morning hours without ever learning that the cancer that killed her might have been treated if only the unlicensed, unregulated laboratory that analyzed her Pap smears had recognized that they revealed the presence of the deadly disease.

For the balance of the article, documents continue to come into play. Bogdanich cites a report from the Senate Labor and Human Resources Committee; a study by researchers at the Harvard Medical School and the Boston

Hospital for Women; a report from the U.S. Air Force; a grand jury indictment; tests conducted by the Center for Disease Control; records from the Pennsylvania agency that monitors labs in doctors' offices; a lawsuit by a woman who was twice told, erroneously, that she was pregnant; regulatory orders from the federal Health Care Financing Administration; reports from the Joint Commission on Accreditation of Hospitals; complaints sent to the Federal Drug Administration; and scholarly articles published in the *Journal of the American Medical Association*.

"I believe that I will always find what I am looking for written down somewhere," Bogdanich says. "And if after a day of digging and looking, I still haven't found it, then I believe I will find it tomorrow" (2013).

In 2005 Bogdanich won a second Pulitzer, this time for a series of articles called "Death on the Tracks," which revealed serious safety failings at railroad crossings. Again documents played a crucial role in Bogdanich's reporting as he demonstrated one of the great truths about documentary research—that deep within a massive pile of eye-numbing and duplicative records a journalist can find the gemlike details that make a story jump off the page. Documents are the repository of specific facts and explicit descriptions that frequently are impossible for reporters to witness and that can be extremely difficult to draw out from human sources in the context of an interview.

A DETAILED ACCOUNT

Bogdanich began his series with a searing account of a collision between a locomotive and a trucker hauling newly harvested potatoes. He notes the exact instant it happened, 5:45 p.m.; the environmental conditions, with an "autumn sun dipping toward the horizon"; the weight of the train, 4,700 tons; its operator, the Union Pacific; and the outcome, describing how the driver was struck with "the force of an explosion, ripping apart his body" (Bogdanich, 2004).

In this series Bogdanich took his use of documents a step further, enlisting the help of computerized tools to help him make sense of years' worth of federal records. Computerized data analysis allowed him to highlight important facets of the safety situation. More importantly, the use of what's called computer-assisted reporting, which is discussed in greater detail later in this chapter, allowed Bogdanich to make sweeping but authoritative statements.

Bogdanich's third Pulitzer, which he shared with *Times* colleague Jake Hooker, was for a 2008 series called "The Toxic Pipeline," in which the reporters traced how a cheap, but poisonous, counterfeit ingredient used in household drugs was making its way from Chinese factories into products on pharmacy shelves, with deadly results. Documents, particularly those that are used in international trade to track shipments, allowed the reporters to map the movement of the faked chemical across the globe. The documents also gave the reporters the "kicker" they used at the end of their first article to highlight a sad irony about the case, which involved thousands of deaths in several different countries where public health officials had struggled to figure out why people were getting so sick before they recognized that it was adulterated chemical compounds that were causing the problem. The shipping documents referred to the counterfeit ingredient with the letters "TD," which the reporters discovered was a reference to the Chinese word for substitute. As they observed in the final lines of their article, the explanation for the mystery illness had been "hiding in plain sight" all along in the paperwork that had been used to send the product around the world (Bogdanich and Hooper, 2007).

Former CBS News anchor Dan Rather learned to his great chagrin, in an incident described more fully below, that documents are not always reliable and may not even be true. But there are many reasons why documents are so highly prized, including the three that are discussed in Chapter 1: their authority, their consistency and their legal status. One of the nice things about documents is that they say what they have to say right from the start, unlike a human source who has to be cultivated and perhaps asked the same question four or five different ways before revealing the facts that the reporter is seeking. A document does not employ evasive tactics or withhold key facts until cornered with just the right query. Like human sources and personal observations, documents have their shortcomings and cannot be relied on without additional reporting. But they form a very useful base for that additional reporting, a process that often includes review and reconsideration of what a reporter has found in a document the first time through.

One of the best reasons for prizing documents is a competitive one. Because many journalists don't seek out documents or spend time deciphering them, those reporters who do know how to work documents will often find themselves ahead of the curve on a given story. Working with documents, and the keepers of documents, over time, will give a reporter an edge when a story is breaking and key information is waiting to be found in a written record. If you know how to look and where to look for documents, you can beat your competition to the punch, and even if you don't get the story first, you can probably provide a fuller, more accurate account by including documentary information. There are many more kinds of documents available than you might think. One analysis identified 75 different kinds of records that are generated by local government alone, a figure that does not include records from the local school system, which generates another 20 kinds of documents. Federal agencies are similarly the source or repository of many kinds of documents, some of which may originate with a private company but are then made widely available through a public database (Williams, 1978).

CLASSIFICATIONS OF DOCUMENTS

Using the definition of documents discussed in Chapter 1, "information that is preserved," there are several ways of classifying documents and thinking about how to get them and use them. A very basic distinction is between primary and secondary documents. Primary documents are those that are the original source of information, such as a birth certificate or a building permit. A secondary document is a document about a document, such as a previously published news article or an online press release that includes a link to a spreadsheet with detailed data. Secondary documents can provide a trove of leads, but they should rarely show up in a news article. Only under the rarest and most extenuating circumstances should a journalist repeat what another publication has already reported, such as a scoop by a competitor that can't be confirmed but can't be ignored. Instead use secondary documents to get to primary documents, and do your own reporting. One form of secondary documents, specialty publications such as trade magazines or academic journals, can be especially useful in providing names of potential sources as well as perspectives that would otherwise be hard to come by. Military officers or industry insiders sometimes open up and say things to what they perceive as "friendly" publications, making candid comments that they might be reluctant to say to a reporter they don't know or for a general news audience.

It's also a good idea to keep in mind that there are public documents, which you have an absolute right to inspect, and private documents, such as confidential government files or personal correspondence, which may present legal and ethical issues. Just because a document is legally restricted doesn't mean that a reporter shouldn't try to get it and use it. The rules for keeping records secret have been regularly abused by government officials seeking to gain cover for mistakes and misdeeds. Even documents that have been illegally obtained have been published by newspapers without leading to criminal convictions. But that doesn't mean that a vague assertion of "the public's right to know" will protect a journalist who uses filched documents or ones that constitute an invasion of privacy. Be careful.

DOCUMENTS IN ACTION

To understand the power and the versatility of documents, let's look at some case histories. I.F. Stone, although sometimes derided as a dangerous Communist sympathizer, is a good model for reporters working in the Internet era because he was an entrepreneurial journalist who for many years self-published a weekly newsletter, a sort of pre-computer blog. Unlike many of today's bloggers who do little of their own digging, Stone was a one-man reporting band who delivered plenty of opinion to his readers but based it on extensive research. He was famous for his skill in ferreting out government documents. Ironically he described his "best scoop" (Patner, 1988) as coming not from some obscure, hard-to-get-a-hold-of insider's report but from a series of briefs published in *The New York Times* that apparently were overlooked by nearly everyone else. The backdrop to his scoop was a debate over nuclear weapons and, more specifically, whether a proposed ban on testing could be enforced in the Soviet Union using a network of seismic monitors that the Soviets, in a potential diplomatic breakthrough, had proposed to install.

Nuclear experts in the United States government who were opposed to the Soviet plan argued that monitoring underground tests wouldn't work because the shocks would not be felt beyond a relatively short distance from the test site. To support this argument a now-defunct federal agency known as the Atomic Energy Commission issued an official account of a September 1957 underground test in Nevada. In its press release the AEC said the shock waves were felt no more than 250 miles away, which was in line with the official prediction that was made at the time of the test explosion.

What the officials at the AEC had not figured on was that Stone had been paying attention to the news reports that were published right after the test. These included small items in the *Times* called "shirttails," short paragraphs from the wire services appended to a longer, staff-written story. These shirttails had recorded that seismic monitoring stations in Rome and in Tokyo, far more than 250 miles away from the test site, had detected the test. Stone used these shirttails in a couple of ways. First, they allowed him to go back to the AEC and challenge its account. But he also used these snippets as the springboard for doing additional reporting, finding another federal agency that could confirm that the test was indeed detected by U.S. government seismic equipment as far away as Alaska, almost 10 times farther away than the AEC had said.

Stone's reporting forced the AEC to issue a correction to its official statement about the Nevada test, a correction that undercut the agency's effort to head off a ban on nuclear testing. Sitting before a congressional committee a few weeks later, the head of the AEC had to admit that it was Stone's reporting that had forced the agency to back away from its original untrue statement.

"You see," Stone later said, "a scoop isn't a matter of luck, you work, you dig, you make calls, and you grab the discrepancy, the loose thread, and you pull. And you have to have been paying attention in the first place. That's not luck" (Patner, 1988, 57).

The Watergate investigative duo of Bob Woodward and Carl Bernstein are rightly acclaimed for their shoe-leather reporting, their extensive efforts to track down and interview human sources. But it was documentary evidence that provided the first direct link between the burglary of the

Democratic National Committee offices in the Watergate complex and the White House. The evidence appeared in the third *Post* article on Watergate, which was headlined "White House Consultant Linked to Bugging Suspects." The link came in the form of address books found on two of the Watergate burglars. In the address books was the name Howard Hunt annotated with "W. House" and "W.H." Make no mistake, Woodward did substantial reporting and interviewing by phone before putting that story into print, but he shared a byline on that story with Eugene Bachinski, a police reporter for the *Post* who was able to get one of his sources to let him look at the evidence files on the case, which contained the address books (Woodward, 2005).

When the story broke about U.S. soldiers abusing inmates at Abu Ghraib prison in Iraq (see Figure 3.1), the reaction was swift and strong. Secretary of Defense Donald Rumsfeld offered his resignation to the president on two different occasions (King, 2005). Archbishop Giovanni Lajolo, the foreign secretary of the Vatican, said the mistreatment of prisoners was "a more serious blow to the United States than Sept. 11. Except that the blow was not inflicted by terrorists but by Americans against themselves" (Associated Press, 2004). President George Bush apologized "for the humiliation suffered by the Iraqi prisoners and the humiliation suffered by their families" (Bumiller and Schmitt, 2004).

But some media critics questioned why it had taken the story so long to break. The ombudsman at the *Post* said his paper was "slow off the mark on this story" (Getler, 2004, B06), and the *Columbia Journalism Review* noted

FIGURE 3.1 *The documentary evidence provided by photographs of prisoner mistreatment at Abu Ghraib prison set off outrage around the world, which prompted Defense Secretary Donald Rumsfeld to offer his resignation on two occasions.*

that the story could have come out sooner because "regrettably and unnecessarily, the facts lay at the outer edge of journalism's radar screen for too long" (2004, 6).

But the reason why those facts lay untouched for so long is actually fairly simple: What propelled the facts of Abu Ghraib onto the air waves in a *60 Minutes II* report by Dan Rather and into the pages of *The New Yorker* a few days later in a story written by Seymour Hersh was documentation, in the form of graphic photographs and an official Army investigative study. The photographs were impossible to ignore, and the Army findings moved the facts of the story past the point of debate. As one account put it, "Without the photographs there would have been no scandal." But at the same time, the pictures "are not the story." The story of extreme and systemic misconduct at Abu Ghraib came to light only when "a flood of previously secret policy papers, memoranda, interrogation rules, military correspondence, investigative findings and sworn statements began to be made publicly available" (Gourevitch and Morris, 2008, 264–85).

While the rewards of using documents can be great, the truth is that documentary research is a process that is rarely straightforward. One of the biggest challenges is just figuring out what records are available, and sometimes it is almost a matter of coincidence, or even luck, that leads a reporter to the existence of written evidence. See Chapter 10 for the story of how the Boys Town investigation came together based on just such a coincidence. On rare occasions documents may appear unexpectedly before you, as they did for journalists Barton Gellman and Glenn Greenwald, who were on the receiving end of blockbuster revelations about intelligence gathering by the National Security Administration and whose reporting would not have carried nearly as much weight absent the documents on which their stories were based (Weinger, 2013).

A "DOCUMENTS STATE OF MIND"

In many cases documents form the rock-solid basis of compelling news articles, but getting to that basis is not an easy or straightforward task. The starting point is to build an awareness of what kinds of documents are either routinely available or potentially obtainable, if you know where to go and whom to ask. But veteran journalists say that what is even more important is the conviction that, in Walt Bogdanich's words, "whatever you need is written down someplace." This belief that records exist to answer almost any reporting question is sometimes called having a "documents state of mind," a phrase that is associated with the investigative team of Donald L. Barlett and James B. Steele. Over the course of 40 years, the pair has shown how obtaining and analyzing documents can lead to powerful stories with startling insights into the complexities of the modern economic, political, and social systems. As newspaper reporters at *The Philadelphia Inquirer,* they won a Pulitzer Prize in 1971 and again in 1989. Moving on to *Time* magazine, they won two National Magazine Awards, in 1999 and 2001. They have won dozens of the other national awards as well, in large part because of their willingness to take the time to read technical, complicated documents like the federal tax code.

"Every project is going to encounter certain kinds of documents that we've never had any contact with before, so that's compelled us to adopt what we call 'a documents state of mind,'" says Steele. "It's a certain discipline you try to apply to yourself. We assume documents are out there until we're proven wrong, and we try to think systematically about where we might find something that would deal with the issue" (Ettema and Glasser, 1998, 39–40).

Oftentimes individual pieces of information can be overlooked or considered trivial, but when they are gathered over time or accumulated across different locations, they become a vibrant repository ready to reveal patterns or trends that can provide useful insights or can help to point up an event that is out of the ordinary and, hence, newsworthy.

To understand how much information is available, a student might engage in a thought experiment, trying to identify the various kinds of data and documents that track even the routine events in a person's life. Starting with breakfast, for example, there are federal statistics on food prices, food safety, and nutrition. (At last count there were more than 30 million federal Web pages, and so you can be sure that there are government statistics on many other things as well.) Step outside for your morning commute and think about documents that deal with air quality, climate and traffic congestion. As you pass through your neighborhood, consider how local governments keep track of things like the buying and selling of houses, the frequency and type of crimes committed on any given street, and even the names of household pets. An institution like a university is subject to numerous reporting requirements, and you can find information on everything from campus crime to educational costs, course difficulty, teacher effectiveness and the costs of recruiting student athletes. Students with a part-time job can use documents to research prevailing wage rates, workplace safety, and the ownership structures of their employers. And if they end their days by visiting a local restaurant or bar, they might want to look into whether health inspectors have found sanitary violations, who holds the liquor license and how much the establishment pays in property taxes.

When students think about documents, especially government documents, one of the first things that come to mind is FOIA—the federal Freedom of Information Act. That's a mistake. Using this law to make formal requests for government information is sometimes necessary, even to the point of seeking a court order to compel the release of documents. But this should be a final option, not a first step. The main reason is time. FOIA gives agencies a month to respond to your request, and the response that comes back may be that the agency needs even more time. Some requests are filled sooner than that, but agencies are inundated with formal demands for records, and the requests can go unfilled for years. Once you send off a formal letter, you will trigger a process that may needlessly complicate your efforts because the agency has to open a formal file and track how it handles your request.

FORMAL VS. INFORMAL REQUESTS FOR INFORMATION

Particularly at the state and local level, a friendly conversation over the phone may be a faster way to get the job done. Don't be adversarial or absolutist, and don't try to make too much of the First Amendment. It's only human nature for government employees to protect their positions and their agencies, so you don't want to come across as threatening. You also need to recognize that there are exemptions within the law that allow agencies to withhold certain kinds of information. Certain kinds of information may be harder, purely for technical reasons, for an agency to retrieve, and if you really don't need everything that an agency has on file, you may only be hurting yourself, and slowing down your reporting, by demanding to see all of it. By talking through your options with an agency representative, you may get to see what you need even if it's not everything that you have a legal right to. Also keep in mind that your right to gain access to government records is your right as a citizen, not as a journalist. If you try to make too much of your status as a journalist, you may end up just creating needless complications.

While you certainly shouldn't hide or disguise your occupation, you don't have to volunteer it in all cases. Some bureaucrats may be put off by the idea that a reporter is trying to intrude into their job duties. They may be more willing to respond to what they see as a routine request from a private citizen than as an official request from a news organization. A request for government information is within the scope of rights enjoyed by all citizens—not something special that is reserved to accredited journalists. On the other hand, if you do have to make a formal FOIA request, there may be some advantages to doing so as a journalist since you can ask for fees to be reduced or waived. From a competitive standpoint, journalists need to keep in mind that FOIA requests are themselves public documents, so one other possible downside of filing a formal request is that it may tip off other news organizations to what otherwise could turn into a scoop.

Another way to avoid having an information request end up in the fog of FOIA is to scour the Internet first. Many government agencies make enormous amounts of information—everything from detailed reports to extensive datasets—available for free download. This information also extends beyond the public sector, as thousands of publicly traded companies are required to make regular reports about their operations, including salaries of top executives, available through the Securities and Exchange Commission's EDGAR website.

Despite your efforts to cajole information from government agencies or to push for access to public records through an administrative appeals process, there may be times when filing a lawsuit is necessary to compel the government to release records. This can be an expensive undertaking, and a court may ultimately decide that the government is properly withholding information. For example, the American Civil Liberties Union filed a FOIA request in 2003, followed by a lawsuit in 2004, to learn more about the treatment of prisoners in overseas detention centers. The efforts have been successful to the extent that thousands of pages of documents have been released, but an appeal court ruled in 2012 that certain other records can be legally withheld because they relate to intelligence techniques (American Civil Liberties Union, 2012).

GOING BEYOND GOOGLE

Most students are familiar with basic search engines, such as Google or Bing. But they should also be aware that there are ways of conducting advanced searches that might help them get better results. For example, if students are looking for data that might be contained in an Excel spreadsheet, they could specify that search results include the ".xls" file extension to limit the returns to that kind of document. To learn more, you can do a Web search on the term "Internet search strategies" and follow the links that you find.

Standard search engines can take you a long way, but it turns out that there is far more information on the Web than these services have historically been able to reach. This is the part of the digital world known as the "deep Web" or "invisible Web," and it exists for a variety of reasons, including subscription barriers; a lack of links; the use of media, such as video, that do not lend themselves to search; and the existence of databases whose content cannot be accessed except through specific queries. You can search on the term "deep Web" to find ways to investigate this hidden information, but staying on top of Internet search possibilities is an ongoing challenge because of the way that the Web is constantly changing.

The federal Freedom of Information Act applies only to agencies of the national government, mostly in the executive branch. But document-savvy reporters know that there are vast amounts of information readily available through the other two branches, the legislative and judicial. In each case, the key is knowing what kinds of information are produced and being willing to spend time just nosing around.

Particularly at the federal level, a great deal of legislative activity is devoted to hearings, which is where many kinds of information come bubbling to the surface either in prepared testimony or in the question-and-answer sessions that follow. Sometimes breaking stories are written based on these hearings but not always. The transcripts can often yield valuable background information, including some that may contextualize, or even contradict, more recent statements from officials or other experts. One problem with accessing hearing transcripts is that it is up to the individual committees to decide when and whether to publish them, a process that can take years. One useful tool for exploring transcripts and other kinds of federal records is the Government Printing Office's Federal Digital System, a searchable online depository of documents. It includes the *Congressional Record*, the *Federal Register*, and opinions of federal courts.

GOVERNMENT WATCHDOGS

The Government Accountability Office (GAO), commonly referred to as the "watchdog branch of Congress" and formerly known as the General Accounting Office, produces close to 1,000 reports a year, some of them prompted by congressional inquiries and some of them part of its ongoing oversight responsibilities. GAO reports are intended to be authoritative and nonpartisan, which means that they are fact-based and reliable. While they often render judgments about a program or an agency, they also include rebuttals from whoever is being criticized. This leads to the second reason why journalists should keep an eye out for relevant reports—they will include names, titles and contact information for potential sources. Perhaps the most important quality about GAO reports is that they are written to be understood by members of Congress, who are supposed to be, but often are not, experts in the fields for which they are setting policy. In other words, GAO reports are also perfect for journalists who are expected to be "instant experts" because they present information even on complex subjects in a way that a nonspecialist can understand.

GAO has counterparts at the state level, investigators who work at the behest of legislators, sometimes in an agency called a reference bureau or an audit bureau (some states have both). These researchers get the kind of access and cooperation that journalists can only dream about and often turn up instances of sloppy record-keeping and other kinds of errors that cost taxpayers. Their reports are typically made available over the Internet, but they go largely unread, in part because they can be voluminous in scope and full of many minute details, some of which are, in all honesty, not necessarily significant. Like GAO reports, these state audit reports are written in noninflammatory, almost bland, language. But a reporter needs to recognize that this writing style is a kind of camouflage for sometimes surprising findings.

Although the reports are long, they can easily be mined for useful details by using the "Find" function on a computer screen. Auditors look at an organization from the inside out, a perspective that reporters are usually denied. Auditors focus on actual operational issues and indicators of management quality, the kind of things that government executives often work to obscure. Auditors typically don't conduct full-scale investigations, so what they report may understate the seriousness of a problem. Even if auditors don't identify a problem that is newsworthy in itself, their work may suggest an area where further journalistic investigation is warranted.

To demonstrate how a student reporter can use an audit report, let's consider a recently completed audit of a state government in the Midwest. The audit covers all agencies of that state, with one section focusing on its university system. Within the university section, the report contains audit findings from the individual campuses that make up the state's university system. One paragraph on a particular campus includes this ominous sounding statement: "we identified concerns related to internal controls over student payroll processing, the return of student financial assistance funds, federal reporting within the Fiscal Operations Report and Application to Participate (FISAP), enrollment reporting, and reconciliation procedures" (Wisconsin Legislative Audit Bureau, 2012, 69). Later in the same paragraph, the auditors note continuing problems, from a previous year's audit, with reimbursements.

In other words, right off the bat, the reporter can see a juicy story developing, with official investigators citing concerns with half a dozen different functions at the university, including hot-button issues like student payrolls and financial assistance. But a closer look may reveal that perhaps there is less here than meets the eye. The auditors have "concerns," but the amounts of money involved are relatively small, in the hundreds of dollars. Maybe there is smoke, but no fire.

The reporter has a couple of options at this point. One is to decide to do nothing. But by ignoring the information in the audit, a journalist in this case would be walking away from one of the most important roles of the profession—to serve as a watchdog over public agencies. Just by reporting what the auditors have found, a journalist is likely to spur action by public officials that might otherwise not occur. In addition, a reporter who shows the willingness to look at a topic in this kind of audit-level detail will earn the grudging respect, if not the affection, of top-ranking officials and may have an easier time getting phone calls returned and questions answered in the future.

Some further thinking about the audit report may also help the reporter see other possible stories. While it's true in this case that the auditors did not identify large amounts of money that were handled inappropriately, it's also true that the auditors only looked at a handful of cases. Perhaps the reporter can extrapolate the hundreds of dollars of questioned costs to the full amount that might be at risk across the entire student body. Maybe the real amount of money involved isn't $300, but $300,000. Then you have a story.

This is an example of how a document has to be read, and re-read. While documents don't change what they say, a reporter's views about the significance of a document can change as additional perspectives and possibilities are considered. This kind of reflection about documentary information is vital. Sometimes the value of documents is not so much what they contain, but the way that they can inspire reporters to take a closer look at something that is mentioned only in passing. In this case the auditors had raised questions about student payroll processing. Maybe the story isn't some scandal about student payrolls, but maybe there is a story about students who are also employees of the university. How many are there? What kinds of jobs are available? Which jobs pay the most, or have the best or worst working conditions? A student reporter asking these kinds of questions out of the blue might get only vague responses. But using the audit report as a kind of roadmap, the reporter could ask more knowledgeable questions, knowing, for example, that the university has a specific system for processing student paychecks and that it had just been reviewed for accuracy. It's not hard to imagine a university official attempting to stymie a student reporter who wants to know how many students work for the university by saying that the number of student employees fluctuates over the course of the semester. But having read the audit report, the student reporter knows a better way to frame the question, by asking how many students received paychecks in a given pay cycle. That's a question an administrator would not be able to dodge.

The judiciary is the third branch of government, and in the United States it operates in two parallel spheres, a system of state courts and a system of federal courts. Unless documents are sealed by court order, legal records are open for inspection and copying, and they are frequently a source of fascinating and minutely detailed information. Court files are often the place where criminal investigation records first come to light, and they often include information that is withheld while police complete their interviews with witnesses and potential suspects. Like a deep mine, civil cases can similarly provide rich seams of information because they typically go through a phase called "discovery" in which each side is allowed to demand facts and data from the other side.

While reporters often have to go to great lengths to get certain kinds of documents from the responsible officials, there is another class of documents that journalists should not overlook and that are typically under the control of government employees who will go out of their way to be helpful. These employees are public reference librarians, and the kind of documents they are eager to share are books. Larger cities and counties often have extensive collections of books, and sometimes other kinds of documents, that are freely available to reporters. Books may seem to be too far behind the news to contain relevant material for a reporter, but they can contain valuable background information that can help a reporter gain deeper insights into an issue. In addition to books, librarians can be helpful in tracking down specialized journals, which they have access to in hard copy or through electronic databases such as EBSCO and JSTOR.

COMPUTER-ASSISTED REPORTING

Up until now we have been considering documents mostly in their traditional, narrative-based form, documents that are mostly words and use words to tell their stories. But another form of document, the database, has become an increasingly popular tool for journalists on many different beats. Some of these databases are maintained by government agencies or other organizations; in other cases journalists construct their own databases from their own research or by combining separate datasets.

Databases usually contain large amounts of numerical information, and journalists typically use computerized tools to analyze them, everything from simple spreadsheet programs to powerful statistical packages that can perform many different kinds of quantitative tests. Because computers are an integral part of this kind of journalism, it is sometimes called computer-assisted reporting (CAR).

An organization, the National Institute for Computer-Assisted Reporting, was founded in 1989 and continues to provide specialized training in how to turn electronic data into news stories. Since 2005 the group, which is part of a larger organization called Investigative Reporters and Editors, has awarded prizes for journalism that uses computers and the techniques of social science research. First prize for 2011 went to the Scripps Howard News Service for a series of articles on unsolved murders across the country, stories that demonstrate how a journalist relying on documentary research and data analysis can highlight trends that may be truly a matter of life and death. The reporter, Thomas Hargrove, created a database of 185,000 unsolved murders across the country, using FBI records as a starting point but adding to them when he discovered that thousands of additional murders had not been properly reported to the FBI. To gain information on those killings he had to file public records requests with police agencies around the United States. Once he had all the information in hand, Hargrove then found a way to identify indicators of likely serial murders based on statistical analysis of the data, which led investigators to go back over cold cases to see if they could find the perpetrators.

DANGERS IN DOCUMENTS

As powerful as documents can be in bolstering a story, they can also have the opposite effect, as former CBS News anchor Dan Rather learned the hard way in a story concerning the military record of then President George W. Bush. The story, which aired on Sept. 8, 2004, just weeks before the presidential election, relied heavily on a series of memos allegedly written by Bush's commanding officer in the Texas Air National Guard that purportedly showed dereliction of duty and disobedience of direct orders by the future commander-in-chief. By early the next morning, just over 12 hours after the report had been broadcast, the memos were being called into question by political bloggers. Initially CBS held firm but eventually acknowledged that it could not verify the authenticity of the documents. By the end of November, Rather had announced his intention to retire. A few months later CBS fired several news executives and asked others to resign.

Surprisingly it was not the substance of the report that was called into question, even by the White House. A Bush spokesman said the White House initially assumed that the documents were authentic (Hagan, 2012). But it was the documentation that came under fire and that eventually undermined the story. The information in the documents may have been true, as several human sources attested, but the memos themselves were very likely forgeries, and eventually that's what dominated the headlines.

The lesson here is not merely to distrust documents, although like all other sources they must be approached with circumspection. The lesson is that certain kinds of documents, especially ones that are not official work products and that are not obtained through official channels, must be verified carefully. Methods of verification of private documents include talking to human sources who have knowledge about the information in the documents and matching information in the private documents, such as dates or other specifics, with information that can be independently authenticated.

While these accounts demonstrate the role that documents play in shaking loose major stories, it would be a mistake to conclude that documents are only important in the context of investigations or other special projects. Documents are crucial in routine coverage and serve as an essential tool for reporters in all kinds of day-to-day stories: crime, city government, sports and so on. A reporter who needs to double-check the spelling of a name or an address or an age can make some phones calls or perhaps do an Internet search to find the needed information. But in many cases that information can be found in a document that is associated with the story and that should have been obtained as part of the reporter's news-gathering routine.

Making documents part of that routine is a vital first step in developing the skills of a reporter. One habit that every reporter needs to adopt at the start of every story assignment is to check previously published articles on a given topic. Reporters need to know what has already been written and can find useful leads in these stories, such as the names of potential sources. Electronic publishing has made this process easier, especially if you work at a publication that doesn't maintain a print library with such files. Another possibility, although one that may cost some money, is the use of electronic databases, such as ProQuest or LexisNexis. Student journalists will often find these services available for free through their campus library.

GETTING INFORMATION TO COME TO YOU

Digging for documents is clearly central to what the best journalists do, but they also need to work the system in reverse—that is, to direct information flows to them so that news is coming in their direction without them having to seek that out. In the days before the Internet, this tactic meant that a reporter assigned to a new beat would spend some time contacting organizations to get placed on their mailing lists for distribution of press releases and other announcements. Today, that process is automated in many cases, and reporters should sign up for email notifications, at least to the extent that they don't swamp their email inboxes with more messages than they can productively look through. Targeted email alerts using keywords, such those available through major search engines, can be a useful tool for having the news come to you. Another possible approach is to sign up for listservs on specialized topics.

In the age of social media, a Twitter account can serve a similar purpose. It's a good idea to follow possible sources or even competing reporters through your Twitter account. You can use a "dashboard" application, such as TweetDeck or HootSuite, to organize your social media feeds and set up Twitter lists to help you manage the flow of information that you will be receiving.

EXERCISES

1. You can't expect every document that you pick up to be a gold mine, but you do need to get some practice reading them. Go to the GAO website and do a search by some geographic keyword, such as the name of your hometown or your current city or state of residence. Next sort by date, new to old, and review the first three documents that you find there. Do the same thing using a topical search term, such as "higher education" or "sports." Could any of these reports be

the starting point for a local story? How would you go about getting more information to complete the reporting process?

2. Who gets the best grades at your school? Which department grades the hardest? These questions can be answered by asking your university's institutional research office for reports on these and other topics related to student performance. You may be able to find some of this information on your university's website.

3. Your classmates might wonder which local landlords have the worst records with the housing inspector or which local bars draw the most attention from the police. You can request the necessary documentation at your city hall to answer these questions.

4. Documents and data are often used in hard news articles, but they can also be used for features. If your city or county licenses pets, it almost certainly has an electronic database of names. Ask to have a copy sent to you as a spreadsheet and sort through it to see which names are most popular. Or ask your campus parking office for a list of parking violations, including locations where tickets are written. Use this information to write a story about where drivers are most likely to get ticketed.

REFERENCES

American Civil Liberties Union. "Appeals Court Rules That CIA Can Keep Waterboarding Descriptions Secret," ACLU.org, May 21, 2012, accessed December 5, 2013, at https://www.aclu.org/national-security/appeals-court-rules-cia-can-keep-waterboarding-descriptions-secret.

Associated Press. "Vatican Calls Prison Abuse a Bigger Blow to U.S. Than Sept. 11," *USA Today*, May 12, 2004, accessed December 5, 2013, at http://usatoday30.usatoday.com/news/world/iraq/2004-05-12-vatican-iraqi-abuse_x.htm.

Bogdanich, Walt. "Medical Labs, Trusted as Largely Error-Free, Are Far From Infallible," *Wall Street Journal*, February 2, 1987.

—— "In Deaths at Rail Crossings, Missing Evidence and Silence," *The New York Times*, July 11, 2004, accessed December 5, 2013, at http://www.nytimes.com/2004/07/11/national/11RAILS.html.

——"Walt Bogdanich, 3-Time Pulitzer Prize Winning Investigative Reporter," *ColumbiaJournalism*, blogtalkradio.com, December 5, 2008, accessed December 5, 2013, at http://www.blogtalkradio.com/columbiajournalism/2008/12/05/walt-bogdanich-3-time-pulitzer-prize-winning-investigative-reporter.

——Telephone interview with the author, September 3, 2013.

Bogdanich, Walt, and Jake Hooper. "From China to Panama, a Trail of Poisoned Medicine," *The New York Times*, May 6, 2007, accessed December 5, 2013, at http://www.nytimes.com/2007/05/06/world/americas/06poison.html?pagewanted=all.

Bumiller, Elisabeth, and Eric Schmitt. "The Struggle for Iraq: Prison Scandal; President Sorry for Iraq Abuse; Backs Rumsfeld," *The New York Times*, May 7, 2004, accessed December 5, 2013, at http://www.nytimes.com/2004/05/07/world/struggle-for-iraq-prison-scandal-president-sorry-for-iraq-abuse-backs-rumsfeld.html?pagewanted=all&src=pm.

Columbia Journalism Review, "Out of Sight, Out of Mind," July 2004.

Columbia University. "1988 Winners and Finalists," *The Pulitzer Prizes*, Pulitzer. org, accessed December 5, 2013, at http://www.pulitzer.org/awards/1988.

Ettema, James S., and Theodore L. Glasser, *Custodians of Conscience: Investigative Journalism and Public Virtue*, New York: Columbia University Press, 1998.

Getler, Michael. "The Images Are Getting Darker," *The Washington Post*, May 9, 2004.

Gourevitch, Philip, and Errol Morris. *Standard Operating Procedure*, New York: Penguin, 2008.

Hagan, Joe. "Truth or Consequences," *Texas Monthly*, May 2012, accessed December 5, 2013, at http://www.texasmonthly.com/story/truth-or-consequences? fullpage=1.

Investigative Reporters and Editors, "Philip Meyer Journalism Award," ire.org, January 30, 2012, accessed December 5, 2013, at http://ire.org/media/ uploads/files/documents/awards/2011_phil_meyer_announcement.pdf.

King, Larry. "Interviews with Donald Rumsfeld, Dr. Phil," *CNN Larry King Live*, February 3, 2005, transcript accessed December 5, 2013, at http://transcripts. cnn.com/TRANSCRIPTS/0502/03/lkl.01.html.

Patner, Andrew. *I.F. Stone: A Portrait*, New York: Pantheon Books, 1988.

Weinger, Mackenzie."Barton Gellman, Glenn Greenwald Feud over NSA Leaker," *Politico*, June 10, 2013, accessed December 5, 2013, at http://www.politico. com/story/2013/06/edward-snowden-nsa-leaker-glenn-greenwald-barton- gellman-92505.html.

White House. "Press Briefing by Press Secretary Jay Carney, 7/26/2011," July 26, 2011, accessed December 5, 2013, at http://www.whitehouse.gov/the-press- office/2011/07/26/press-briefing-press-secretary-jay-carney-7262011.

Williams, Paul N. *Investigative Reporting and Editing*, Englewood Cliffs, N.J.: Prentice- Hall, 1978.

Wisconsin Legislative Audit Bureau. *State of Wisconsin FY 2010–11 Single Audit*, Report 12–6, March 2012.

Woodward, Bob. *The Secret Man: The Story of Watergate's Deep Throat*, New York: Simon & Schuster, 2005, 56–68.

CHAPTER 4

The Eyes Have It

What we know is based mostly on what we see. Scientists estimate that 80 percent of the information that a human has about the world comes from visual stimuli (Booher, 2003), and this physiological fact of human perception is reflected in many common sayings: "seeing is believing" or "a picture is worth a thousand words." Great writers, whether poets or playwrights or journalists, are acutely aware of the importance of vision and work hard to make their writing appeal to the sense of sight. For a reporter, the act of observation serves at least two purposes. First of all, the reporter wants to gain as complete an understanding of a story or situation, and second the reporter is gathering details that can be incorporated into a news article. In the end these two goals come together as the reporter seeks to strengthen the credibility of a finished account by demonstrating an authoritative understanding buttressed with compelling visual images.

The act of visual observation is central to some of journalism's most cherished ideas about its role in society, as eyewitness to crucial events and watchdog over powerful interests and institutions. It could even be argued that observation is the most basic part of being a reporter. But in practice observation can be problematic. While observation may be absolutely critical on some beats, such as sports or fashion, there are many subjects, in areas such as finance and government, where stories get written on a regular basis without much need for direct observation of key players. There is also an aspect of random chance to observation—sometimes a reporter has to be in the right place at the right time to get a good angle on an event—that may get in the way of reporters spending time honing their observation skills. Two other factors also come into play and tend to diminish the idea of observation as a key skill. The first of these is time. Observation can yield powerful and persuasive detail about a source or a situation, but getting those details will likely take a significant investment of time. Another concern is based on the limitations that are inherent in observation—reporters only see what is in front of them and may be missing key details that are out of their line of sight. Finally, there are ethical considerations that can arise under certain circumstances. For example, reporters should be concerned about questions of bias if the observation process leads them to become too closely engaged with what they are reporting on. Observations are often most fruitful when those being observed aren't aware that they are being watched, but undercover reporting that entails deception can taint a story and overwhelm a reporter's findings of wrongdoing with sympathy for someone who has been tricked into revealing improper practices or providing incriminating information.

Despite these issues, which will be discussed later in this chapter, there is no question of the power of a firsthand report. In some cases, vivid description based on observation can help to distinguish a reporter from other journalists, serving to improve a writer's reputation and career prospects. Walter Cronkite, the pioneering television journalist and CBS news anchor who went on to be called "the most trusted man in America," got a big break in 1943 when he was selected to ride along with a bomber crew in a mission over Nazi Germany. His firsthand account for the UPI wire service appeared in newspapers across the United States and identified him as a rising star. It includes this memorable description: "The first impression of a daylight bombing mission is a hodge-podge of disconnected scenes like a poorly edited home movie, bombs falling past you from the formation above, a crippled bomber with smoke pouring from one engine thousands of feet above, a tiny speck in the sky that grows closer and finally becomes a Focke-Wulf peeling off above you somewhere and plummeting down, shooting its way through the formation" (Brinkley, 2012, 100). Although best remembered as the familiar face of television evening news, Cronkite was truly a "cross-platform" journalist who also worked in radio and print and never lost his awareness of the power that comes from reporting from the field. As the CBS News anchor in 1968, Cronkite decided he needed to travel personally to Vietnam for a direct look at the fighting there. His pessimistic reports on what he saw are thought to have played a significant role in turning public opinion against the war (Brinkley, 2012).

SMALL DETAILS, BIG RESULTS

A skilled reporter knows the power of small details to convey a message that can lead to big results. Two *Washington Post* reporters, Dana Priest and Anne Hull, spent four months at Walter Reed Army Medical Center so that they could document the shockingly callous treatment the country's "wounded warriors" were receiving after suffering serious injuries fighting in Iraq and Afghanistan. The resulting series of articles began with a description of where one patient was living, including observations of a greasy smell in the air, black mold, vermin infestations and stained furniture. The room belonged to Jeremy Duncan, an Army specialist, and the reporters noted,

"When the wounded combat engineer stands in his shower and looks up, he can see the bathtub on the floor above through a rotted hole" (Priest and Hull, 2007).

The aftereffects of the Pulitzer Prize-winning series were equally striking. Within a matter of weeks, key officials ranging from the commander of the hospital to the secretary of the army had lost their jobs. The government immediately started work on cleaning up the facility, and Congress, after a series of hearings and commission reports, added hundreds of millions of dollars to the budget for healthcare for veterans.

What Cronkite, Hull and Priest were doing in reporting based on direct observation is part of a long tradition in the history of U.S. journalism. An early figure in that tradition who stands out for the impact of her observations is Nellie Bly, the intrepid "girl reporter" for Joseph Pulitzer's *New York World*. At a time of growing concern about the conditions of the psychiatric hospital on Blackwell's Island in the East River, a so-called insane asylum, Bly contrived to get herself committed there and then spent 10 days documenting the problems that she saw, including ill treatment of patients with no underlying mental illnesses and of foreign-born women who apparently had been committed because they could not express themselves in English. Her graphic accounts, which appeared in 1887, were credited with helping to bring about reforms. Bly's next big story was her trip around the world, as she successfully showed it possible to beat the standard established in Jules Verne's *Around the World in 80 Days*. Her first-person accounts of her travels increased circulation sales for the *World* and further solidified her reputation (Kroeger, 1994).

Throughout the 19th century, the journalistic sketch, based on direct observations of a place or an event, was a staple of newspaper coverage, practiced by a range of writers that included some, like Charles Dickens and Walt Whitman, who would become better known for their literary inventions. In fact some of the strongest advice on how to get better at observation comes from a newspaperman turned novelist, the Nobel Prize-winning author Ernest Hemingway. Hemingway, who started contributing to the *Kansas City Star* after high school and later reported on the Spanish Civil War and both World War I and II, provided pointers to a young writer in an *Esquire* magazine article, "Monologue to a Maestro: A High Seas Letter." At one point the young man, who was helping out on Hemingway's fishing boat, asks how he should go about training himself to be a better writer. Hemingway's response emphasizes the importance of gathering significant details that can be used to engage the reader: "Whether it was the rising of the line from the water and the way it tightened like a fiddle string until drops started from it, or the way he smashed and threw water when he jumped. Remember what the noises were and what was said" (Hemingway, 1935, 219).

THE IMPORTANCE OF PRACTICE

For Hemingway the key to developing observational skill was to work at it. In this same essay he urges the beginning writer to practice making observations in the most routine situations by, for example, making a mental note of everything in a room and then trying to recall everything that was there, including objects that may have set off emotional responses. Almost every situation provides an opportunity to get better at making observations, Hemingway says, including watching how different people get in and out of cars.

Ved Metha, an Indian-born journalist who's been blind since the age of 4, spent more than 30 years as a writer at *The New Yorker* and has written two dozen books. He compensated for his lack of eyesight by developing an acute sense of hearing and by spending long hours with his interview subjects so as to form in his mind a clear impression that he could set down on the page. He knew that if he wanted to be accepted as a writer, not just a blind writer, he had to be able to include visual details: "I had to write like anybody else—compete with them on their terms" (Jaggi, 2001). He got so good at including visual details that some came to doubt that he was really blind. Norman Mailer once challenged him to a boxing match to settle the dispute.

Mehta insisted that it was possible, even though blind, to write for a sighted audience. He gave the example of a profile he wrote of a British historian in which he said the man had a cigarette dangling from the corner of his lower lip. How did Mehta know? Because of the way that the man spoke. "I converted a sound impression into a visual image," Mehta told a writer for *The Guardian* in 2001 (Jaggi, 2001). The lesson here is that even if you don't have a chance to see something with your own eyes, you can still include detailed visual information. When direct observation is not possible or practical, reporters can return to the DOT methodological framework and seek out visual data from documents or from interviews with witnesses.

Two related fields where observation is considered a crucial research technique are sociology and anthropology, and some journalists have consciously borrowed from those disciplines, including Richard Critchfield, the first reporter to win a fellowship from the John D. and Catherine T. MacArthur Foundation, what is popularly known as a "genius grant." Such grants, which are now worth more than half a million dollars, are given in recognition of exceptional creativity and promise, but have gained an aura of mystery because MacArthur does not explain in precise detail how or why it chooses the recipients of its awards.

But based on a review of Critchfield's publication record, it is safe to assume that his fellowship was the result of a dramatic shift he made in his reporting and writing techniques after the release of a book on the Vietnam War, in which he argued that the underlying political dynamics of the country were far more complicated than the American people understood and may have involved high-level infiltration of North Vietnamese agents into the South Vietnamese government. "I left Vietnam in November 1967, convinced that our defeat was not a failure of power but a failure of knowledge," he wrote in the *Washington Journalism Review*. "Not only did we—the press, American academics, diplomats, the CIA—fail to learn enough about the Vietnamese communists and their strategy of subversion, we also failed to learn enough about the ordinary Vietnamese peasant out in his village and his Confucian culture" (Critchfield, 1985, 30).

CRITCHFIELD'S "VILLAGE REPORTING"

To remedy this lack of knowledge about ordinary life at the basic level of social organization, Critchfield decided he needed to spend more time in direct observation and dedicated himself to what he called "village reporting." He spent much of the rest of his career engaged in a form of immersion journalism that borrowed heavily from the ethnographic techniques of anthropologist Oscar Lewis. While most reporters limit themselves to direct observation, watching from outside a group without taking part in the group's activities, Critchfield became what is known as a participant observer, joining villagers in their daily work routines.

Although Critchfield believed that his close interaction with sources from different cultures provided him with special insights into their character and concerns, he was later criticized for not clearly seeing the nature of the communities he was observing. Instead he was accused of capturing details that conformed with his predetermined notions, an idea that he vigorously disputed. Whatever the validity of that argument, Critchfield's case demonstrates one of the great potential pitfalls of believing what you are seeing. Successful observation depends on being prepared for what might be encountered, but at the same time reporters need to avoid the temptation of selecting out only certain details. As the sociologist Joan Ferrante has written, "The challenge of observation lies in knowing what to look for while remaining open to other considerations; success results from identifying what is worth observing" (2012, 45).

As you work to develop your skill in this area, you may want to consider the technique used by social scientists called "structured observation" (Bailey, 2007). This is a systematic approach to observation with a heavy emphasis on planning. Instead of just showing up at a story and hoping to gather some visual impressions while there, a reporter using structured observation arrives with a clear idea of what to look for and how to record it for later use.

Arriving at a crime or accident scene, the reporter should look over the site with an aim of understanding how the events took place, where any witnesses were situated, how the incident developed. The reporter should also be sensitive to the color, size and shape of any objects that are significant, whether a weapon or a motor vehicle or an article of clothing. Jotting notes on paper is a time-honored way of capturing visual images, but reporters should also consider the use of technology, such as a digital voice recorder to memorialize their impressions while they are still fresh or a camera-equipped cell phone to capture images.

John Burroughs, the American nature writer, built his reputation on his ability to make acute observations about the environment. The keys to being a good observer, he said, were the ability to focus and the willingness to direct one's attention away from internal feelings and instead direct it toward the material world that can be perceived through the senses. Although practice may not make you a perfect observer, it will make you a better one. Burroughs suggests adopting the technique used to teach criminal investigators how to spot potential clues. In this method police detectives are told to walk quickly past a showroom window and then stop on the other side and describe everything that was on display.

Burroughs was well aware that observational skill, like other human traits, is not evenly distributed across the population. He said that some people had eyes that actually worked while others could see no better than if they had painted pieces of stone on their faces. He likened the vast majority of people to soldiers in an army, most of whom "fire vaguely in the direction of the enemy, and if they hit, it is more a matter of chance than of accurate aim. But here and there is the keen-eyed observer; he is the sharpshooter; his eye selects and discriminates, his purpose goes to the mark" (Burroughs, 2001, 3–15).

Burroughs may have meant his marksman metaphor as a jest, but one organization that takes observation very seriously is the military, particularly in its training of those sharpshooters known as snipers. Journalists may or may not identify with members of the military, but for those who wish to become better observers, there are some lessons to be learned from the sections of the U.S. Army field manual that deal with sniper training, especially since one of the roles of snipers is to serve as forward observers, reporting back on what they see. (The following sections of this chapter are based on the 1994 edition of the field manual, which is the most recent edition that is widely available outside of the military.)

HOW THE MILITARY TRAINS OBSERVERS

For an Army observation team, the act of gathering visual information is not a casual activity left to chance or the personal tendencies of individual soldiers. Instead the Army has given observation a formal structure, parts of which may make sense for a journalist to adopt. For example, the military divides the act of observation into four parts: awareness, understanding, recording and response. These can occur either sequentially or concurrently.

Awareness, according to the Army, refers to a conscious focus on specific circumstances, including factors that can distort perceptions. Good observers, then, are aware of, and try to compensate for, conditions that can lead to misinterpretation, such as distractions, incomplete observations or bad weather. They also pay attention to their personal limitations, such as their state of fatigue (the Army recommends no more than 10 or 15 minutes of intense observation followed by a similar period of rest), their awareness of individual sensory capability (such as shortcomings in hearing or vision) and the strength of their imagination, which "may cause possible exaggerations or inaccuracy" (U.S. Army, 1994, 4/30).

But, just like sociologists and anthropologists, military observers are also expected to prepare themselves for what they are to observe so that they can understand what they are seeing. According to the Army, "understanding is derived from education, training, practice and experience." Such understanding improves an observation team's "knowledge about what should be observed, broadens its ability to view and consider all aspects, and aids in its evaluation of information" (U.S. Army, 4/30–31).

The next step in the Army's methodology is to record what has been observed. With digital tools like cameras and voice recorders readily available, observers can make use of what the military calls "mechanical aids" for capturing information, but "the most accessible method is memory" (U.S. Army, 4/31). Being alert and knowing what is important to record are key, but there are other factors that can aid in remembering what has been observed. These include training, practice and experience. Other considerations include similarities to previous observations, the amount of time that passes between observing and recording, and the communication skill of the observer. (See Exercise 4 for the Keep in Memory game that is used in military training.)

The final phase of the military observation process is response, which "may be as simple as recording events in a sniper data book, making a communications call or firing a well-aimed shot" (U.S. Army, 4/31). For a journalist, the shot would be metaphorical and not literal, but actions similar to what the Army describes are the likely conclusion to a reporter's observation process.

In addition to identifying the discrete elements of observation, the military also specifies that observation can be, and should be, conducted in two different modes: the hasty search and the detailed search. The purpose of the hasty search is to focus on those features of the scene that stand out the most, starting with the immediate foreground and then moving out from there. For a reporter arriving at an accident scene, this process might translate into cataloging the number and placement of vehicles involved as well as the locations of ambulances, police cars and fire engines.

The next step would be to conduct a detailed search, which is a systematic sweep of the area, covering 180 degrees at a time. These sweeps should start with the immediate foreground and then move out, with sufficient overlap to make sure that no area is missed in the observation. For a reporter in the scene described above, this might translate into checking the road surface for broken glass and skid marks as well as taking note of details such as the makes and models of the vehicles in the accident as well as their exterior colors and any apparent damage.

Of course, before journalists can make observations, they must find a way to put themselves in position to see the news. The techniques that are used for this purpose range from the cultivation of sources who can provide access to news situations to various forms of undercover reporting. An in-between strategy is to seek out and visit so-called third places (Harwood, 2001), which are locations where people gather outside of the home, considered a first place, or outside of a formal setting such as a workplace or a classroom, considered second places. Examples of third places include public parks, bus stops, self-service laundries, open air markets, barbershops and taverns.

One advantage of going to such places to observe is the chance to hear people talking about issues and concerns at an early stage and to get a jump on a story or a trend. A reporter who goes to third places can blend in and learn to see the world from the perspective of an average reader. But sooner or later journalists who hang out in third places will have to identify themselves and their professions, which may have the effect of shutting down the conversation or severely restricting what is said. To avoid this, reporters typically try to approach third places in an informal way and work at developing a rapport with the people they meet before revealing that they are journalists. Third-place observation can be used to enrich a story with little-noticed details and fresh perspectives, but its value comes from its open-endedness, which is also its greatest drawback. There is no guarantee that going to a place where ordinary people go will tell you anything out of the ordinary.

THE UNDERCOVER DEBATE

By contrast, undercover reporting will more likely take a journalist where news is happening. This approach can yield a type of information that simply is not accessible through other means, but it raises challenging ethical questions that are not fully resolved among professional journalists. Hull and Priest, *The Washington Post* reporters who exposed the scandalous conditions at Walter Reed, knew that they had to have firsthand information about the physical deterioration at the facility, but they also knew that going through official channels and requesting a tour by the public affairs officer would not have worked. In a presentation at the Nieman Foundation's 2008

Conference on Narrative Journalism, the two talked about how they worked to gain access to the facility and then to protect their identities while knowing that it would be unacceptable from an ethical standpoint for them to lie if they were asked directly who they were or for whom they worked.

"We needed to see things to substantiate the allegations that some of these people suggested were happening there," Hull said (Hull and Priest, 2008). Getting in a position to make these observations was a multistep process. The reporters' first move was simply to find a way to spend some unstructured time on the base (see Figure 4.1). They discovered that there was a hotel on base that was full of wounded soldiers, and sometimes their families, and that in that hotel there was a bar, where the soldiers would hang out and drink. At first the reporters did nothing but watch, not even taking notes, just trying to take in the scene they called "surreal." From there they discovered other places to meet soldiers and to strike up conversations, but they knew that it was critical that their movements go undetected by base authorities.

This involved developing what the military calls "situational awareness." They adopted a mode of appearance and movement so that they wouldn't stand out. If they were in a room and saw someone coming who might notice that they were unfamiliar faces who perhaps shouldn't be there, they would get up and leave. They also left notebooks and cameras behind,

FIGURE 4.1 *Two* Washington Post *reporters published a powerful expose of conditions at Walter Reed Army Medical Center after they devised a plan to spend time at the facility without alerting authorities about their presence. Credit: Carol M. Highsmith/ Library of Congress Carol M. Highsmith Archive*

for fear that they would be stopped and searched and would then have to answer uncomfortable questions about what they were up to and for whom.

As they spent more time at Walter Reed, they heard of a place called Building 18, which had especially abhorrent conditions, and the description of which became the lead of their series. They knew that they had to find a way to observe the conditions there, but it wasn't a place they could just walk into. Patience and listening, according to Priest, were the keys to making the connections with sources who ultimately gave them entrée to Building 18. "I was determined to get there because it was just all there, the contrast—we support the troops, but we let them live with mold. It just seemed, again, almost too unbelievable to be true," she recalled at the Nieman conference. "So the questions became how are we going to verify what's in Building 18, and then, how are we going to get into Building 18?" Little by little, by making sure to include in every interview a question about whether the source had ever been to Building 18 or knew someone who lived there, the reporters finally found a resident who would help them get there and see for themselves.

The standard that Hull and Priest followed in terms of not revealing their identity is one that is widely accepted in the profession, namely that reporters do not have to announce themselves as reporters but, if asked outright, they cannot engage in deception or pretend to be something that they are not. In some cases journalists have gone so far as to create a new professional identity for themselves by leaving out information about their journalistic background.

Ted Conover wanted to write about what it was like to work inside a prison, but authorities would not give him permission to come in and do research. His solution to this problem was to apply for a job as a corrections officer in New York, a position that he got after leaving off key information on his application, such as the fact that he was already the author of three books on immersion journalism. The book that resulted from the 10-plus months he worked at Sing Sing was called *Newjack: Guarding Sing Sing* (Conover, 2000) and received rave reviews and won the National Book Critics Circle Award for general nonfiction.

But other journalists who have disguised their identities to get stories have been roundly criticized for their methods. In 2007 Ken Silverstein, the Washington editor of *Harper's Magazine,* set out to expose the corruptive way that foreign money could influence U.S. policymaking in Washington by posing as a representative of the repressive regime in Turkmenistan. He was able to set off a bidding war between two Washington lobbying firms and in that way capture direct evidence of the degree to which supposedly reputable individuals are willing to compromise American moral standards and alter public perceptions for the sake of a healthy payoff (Silverstein, 2007). Silverstein's argument was that going undercover was the only way to gather evidence of just what Washington lobbyists were willing to do on behalf of foreign governments. But prominent press critics and leading journalists accused him of engaging in an untrustworthy form of behavior that would do more harm to the reputation of reporters than of lobbyists (Lisheron, 2007).

Criticisms of Silverstein and *Harper's* echoed those that had been leveled three decades before against the *Chicago Sun-Times* after it opened a bar and placed a couple of its reporters there, working as bartenders so that they would get direct evidence of the routine corruption that had developed in city government. From their post, the reporters developed a 25-part series that showed payoffs, shakedowns, kickbacks and other kinds of fraud. Their work looked like it was certain to win a Pulitzer, but this expectation was derailed by members of the prize board who were uncomfortable with the tactics that the newspaper had used. In the course of the debate over whether this kind of undercover activity was acceptable for journalists to engage in, James Reston, the longtime Washington bureau chief for *The New York Times* and briefly its editor, drew the line that continues to distinguish between the kind of behavior that is considered ethically defensible and not. According to a report in the *Columbia Journalism Review,* Reston argued that reporters could engage in pretense, a passive form of disguise in which they allow others to draw incorrect conclusions about their identities, but should not engage in active deception, in which they go out of their way to mislead about who they are or what they are doing (Robinson, 1979).

Whether the benefits of undercover reporting outweigh the potential liabilities is likely to be an ongoing point of dispute, but what is not in dispute is that some forms of observation require a significant investment of time. In one of the most extreme examples of time invested in observation, a journalist named Adrian Nicole LeBlanc spent more than a decade chronicling the lives of what might be described as the extended family of a New York drug dealer, whose brief career was the starting point for her reporting. The book that resulted, *Random Family: Love, Drugs, Trouble, and Coming of Age in the Bronx* (LeBlanc, 2003), was a best-seller and helped to earn LeBlanc a "genius grant" from the MacArthur Foundation. There are few journalists who would be able to duplicate this kind of extended reporting over such a long period.

Aside from time requirements, the other major limitation of observational reporting is one that may seem counterintuitive. While it stands to reason that eyewitness, on-the-scene reporting is the gold standard of journalism, it is also true that observers see only what they see and may be unable to provide a broader context. Reporters who rely too much on observation may end up conveying information to their readers that is completely true and yet just as completely misleading.

THE LIMITS OF OBSERVATION

Consider the second battle of Fallujah, which occurred in November 2004 and involved a combined force of Marines, U.S. soldiers and Iraqi fighters. The Marines fought courageously and took the brunt of the casualties on the coalition side. Dexter Filkins, then of *The New York Times,* spent eight days embedded with a company of Marines as the troops fought their way street-by-street through the city. His up-close reports on the fighting won him a George Polk Award, whose judges said, "his riveting, first-hand account of an eight-day attack on Iraqi insurgents . . . conveyed the hellish intensity of urban warfare underway in Iraq" (Long Island University, 2005).

Writing in a Page 1 article after the worst of the fighting, Filkins said that "Falluja was a qualitatively different experience, a leap into a different kind of battle." He predicted that what he had gone through was a glimpse of things to come: "a grinding struggle to root out guerrillas entrenched in a city, on streets marked in a language few American soldiers could comprehend" (Filkins, 2004, A20).

What Filkins couldn't have known, however, was that Army units fighting their way through Fallujah had a very different experience because they had used a different set of tactics. While the Marines fought on foot, the Army used tanks to blast their way through streets that the Marines thought were too narrow for mechanized armor.

"If we ran into a problem with a building, we didn't go running into the building; we ran up to the tank and had them take it out," an Army sergeant recalled after the battle. The Army's tactics were so effective that at times its soldiers had to stop and wait for the Marines to catch up (Matthews, 2006, 77).

Filkins' reporting reflected remarkable personal courage, and his articles gave readers a vivid and dramatic view of the fighting in Fallujah. But because they were based on only his personal observations, they provided a skewed and incomplete picture of the battle. Readers were left with the idea that the only way to fight urban guerrillas was the way that the Marines had fought, when in fact Army units going through the same city and up against the same enemy had shown there was another way to win, and with many fewer casualties.

"MAKE ME SEE"

Gene Roberts was one of the most influential editors of the 20th century. He ran *The Philadelphia Inquirer* for 18 years, picking up 17 Pulitzer Prizes along the way, and later served as the No. 2 editor at *The New York Times* for four years. He often told the story of the editor who influenced him the most, an imposing country editor named Henry Belk who, like Mehta, was blind and who, like Mehta, insisted on the all-important role of visual detail in journalism.

Belk's continuing criticism of Roberts' prose was that it had a deficiency in description. Belk would edit copy by having the writer read it to him aloud. "You aren't making me see," Belk would say to Roberts. "Make me see." To force Roberts to practice this skill, he made him finish his regular column with a paragraph called "Today's Prettiest Sight." Roberts dreaded it but later conceded that this assignment was great training. "There is no truer blueprint for successful writing than making your reader see. It is the essence of great writing and great reporting" (Roberts, 1996, 4).

When you are out in the field, unsure of what your final draft will say, you should be alert to every detail and try to jot down every observation you can make. But when it comes time to write, you must, in the words of William Zinsser, be "intensely selective." If you are trying to capture the distinctive nature of a person or a place, you need to direct your reader's attention to that which is truly distinctive. He adds: "If you are describing a beach, don't write that 'the shore was scattered with rocks' or that 'occasionally a seagull flew over.' Shores have a tendency to be scattered with rocks and to be flown over by seagulls" (Zinsser, 1985, 98).

Close attention to detail needs to be matched by close attention to language, Zinsser says. "Strive for fresh words and images," he advises in his classic *On Writing Well*. Journalists are not expected to be poets, necessarily, but that doesn't mean they shouldn't work hard to use just the right words. Consider the following passage from the December 1952 issue of *The National Geographic*. It comes from a profile about La Jolla, California, by Deena Clark.

> Low tide exposed clusters of star-bright mussels, glistening like bouquets of purple sea flowers on the shiny wet ledges. On the sandy floors of the tide pools, tiny minnows cast their shadows, like photographic negatives of the original little fish (Clark, 1952, 758).

This is a deceptively simple and carefully crafted paragraph that mimics, and reinforces, in sound the description that it contains. The effect is achieved on one level by the selection of words that denote light or its absence: exposed, star-bright, glistening, shiny, shadows, photographic negatives, original (in the visual sense). The eye in the reader's imagination is drawn particularly to the contrast between the minnows and their shadows. The contrast is also manifested through aural cues. Go back over the sentences and notice how the sound of a long I is repeated in the first two-thirds of the selection: tide, bright, shiny, tide, tiny, like. Then listen for how a short I, a mirror sound image of the long vowel, recurs in five of the last seven words: photographic, negatives, original, little, fish.

For most of us, this kind of writing does not come naturally. It takes work to develop this level of craft. If you want to be able to pick just the right word for your description, chances are that you will need to spend some time with words, working to expand your vocabulary and to familiarize yourself with the options available to you. It will be time well spent.

There is, of course, a danger in getting too good at visual imagery, the danger of falling so much in love with a description that you allow it to depart from the facts. Do not invent visual details just for the sake of creating a compelling image. A reporter who is challenged on a quote can usually fall back on notes to defend the accuracy of the story and can usually argue the complaint to a standstill. But a reporter who is challenged about a physical fact of description won't find such ambiguity as an ally. In one famous case, the disgraced *New York Times* reporter Jayson Blair invented tobacco fields and cattle pastures to create the ambience that he felt was appropriate for a profile of a rescued prisoner of war returning to her West Virginia home.

The fields and pastures did not exist, and the report made the paper the butt of jokes within the soldier's family, as the *Times* acknowledged in an exhaustive front-page account of Blair's many deceptions (Barry et al., 2003).

EXERCISES

1. For this exercise, pick a location on campus that is roughly the size of your classroom. Go there and make observations for 20 to 30 minutes. Don't limit yourself to your sense of sight, but include sounds, smells, tastes and physical feelings (as appropriate). Try to be especially careful in the details that you record and then try to express them with concrete words and phrases. Your assignment is to write a description of this place that so clearly evokes its essence that anyone in the class would know what you are writing about. But you may not include in your description any proper name of a place, such as the name of a building or road.

2. As a young reporter, Gene Roberts was required to end the local column he wrote with a paragraph labeled "Today's Prettiest Sight." It was painful but invaluable training, Roberts later recalled (1996). For this assignment, take a walk around campus, and come back and write a paragraph that describes today's "somethingest" sight. It can be the prettiest, but it could also be the ugliest, weirdest, dumbest, etc. You job is to be vivid, graphic, descriptive.

3. Find a "third place," an informal gathering place somewhere on campus or in a nearby neighborhood, a place that you normally would not visit. Over the course of a week, spend at least 60 minutes there, on at least two different occasions. You should plan to go without having a notebook in hand so as to maintain a sense of informality and approachability. But as soon as you leave you

should memorialize, either in written notes or by recording your voice, everything that you have observed, sense details such as smells, sounds and sights as well as any conversations or interviews that you engaged in or overheard. Try to identify someone there who seems particularly articulate or knowledgeable, and get that person's name and contact information. Write up your notes into a brief report, contrasting the different timeframes when you visited.

4. This exercise is a variation of "Kim's game," the name of which is derived from the Rudyard Kipling novel *Kim,* and from the phrase "keep in memory." In Kipling's book, the hero, Kimball O'Hara, trains to be a spy by playing this game. The game has been adopted by the military for use in training snipers and sharpening their observational and memory skills. The instructor should take 10 or 15 items (such as pens, cups, ribbons), spread them on a table or large desk and cover them with a blanket or a sheet. The instructor removes the sheet and gives the class a certain amount of time to study the items but without writing anything down. The items are then covered back up, and the students attempt to make a list of all the items, describing their appearance (length, color, etc.), evaluating their condition (new, stained, dented, etc.) and identifying them by name. An acceptable set of answers would describe one item as a black, cylindrical object in good condition that is approximately 3 inches tall apparently made of ceramic with an open top and a handle while also identifying it as a coffee mug. If your classroom has a projector, this game can be played by showing slides either of actual landscape scenes or of a collection of objects. Variations can be introduced by changing the amount of time allowed for observation, introducing distractions or extending the time between observation and recording.

REFERENCES

Bailey, Carol A. *A Guide to Qualitative Field Research,* 2nd ed., Thousand Oaks, Calif.: Pine Forge Press, 2007.

Barry, Dan, David Barstow, Jonathan D. Glater, Adam Liptak, and Jacques Steinberg. "Correcting the Record; Times Reporter Who Resigned Leaves Long Trail of Deception," *The New York Times,* May 11, 2003, accessed December 8, 2013, at http://www.nytimes.com/2003/05/11/us/correcting-the-record-times-reporter-who-resigned-leaves-long-trail-of-deception.html?pagewanted=all&src=pm.

Booher, Harold R. *Handbook of Human Systems Integration,* Hoboken, N.J.: John Wiley, 2003, 705.

Brinkley, Douglas. *Cronkite,* New York: Harper Collins, 2012.

Burroughs, John. "The Art of Seeing Things," in *The Art of Seeing Things: Essays by John Burroughs,* edited by Charlotte Zoë Walker, Syracuse, N.Y.: Syracuse University Press, 2001.

Clark, Deena. "La Jolla, a Gem of the California Coast," *The National Geographic*, December 1952.

Conover, Ted. *Newjack: Guarding Sing Sing*, New York: Random House, 2000.

Critchfield, Richard. "The Village Voice of Richard Critchfield: Bringing the Third World to the Fourth Estate," *Washington Journalism Review*, October 1985.

Ferrante, Joan. *Sociology: A Global Perspective*, 8th ed., Stamford, Conn.: Wadsworth, 2012.

Filkins, Dexter. "In Falluja, Young Marines Saw the Savagery of an Urban War," *The New York Times*, November 21, 2004.

Harwood, Richard C. "Understanding the Community's Civic Life," *Nieman Reports*, Spring 2001, accessed December 8, 2013, at http://www.nieman.harvard.edu/reports/article/101735/Understanding-the-Communitys-Civic-Life.aspx.

Hemingway, Ernest. "Monologue to the Maestro: A High Seas Letter," Esquire, October 1935, 213–220.

Hull, Anne, and Dana Priest. "Creating an Investigative Narrative," *Nieman Reports*, Summer 2008, accessed December 8, 2013, at http://www.nieman.harvard.edu/reports/article/100033/Creating-an-Investigative-Narrative.aspx.

Jaggi, Maya. "Sight Unseen," *The Guardian*, August, 24, 2001, accessed December 5, 2013, at http://www.theguardian.com/books/2001/aug/25/biography.books.

Kroeger, Brooke. *Nellie Bly: Daredevil, Reporter, Feminist*, New York: Random House, 1994.

LeBlanc, Adrian Nicole. *Random Family: Love, Drugs, Trouble, and Coming of Age in the Bronx*, New York: Scribner, 2003.

Lisheron, Mark. "Lying to Get the Truth," *American Journalism Review*, October/November 2007, accessed December 8, 2013, at http://www.ajr.org/Article.asp?id=4403.

Long Island University. "Long Island University Announces Winners of 2004 George Polk Awards," February 21, 2005, accessed December 8, 2013, at http://www.liu.edu/About/News/Univ-Ctr-PR/Pre-2008/February/GP-Press-Release-Feb-2005.

Matthews, Matt M. *Operation AL FAJR: A Study in Army and Marine Corps Joint Operations*, Fort Leavenworth, Kan.: Combat Studies Institute Press, 2006.

Priest, Dana, and Anne Hull. "Soldiers Face Neglect, Frustration At Army's Top Medical Facility," *The Washington Post*, February 18, 2007, accessed December 5, 2013, at http://www.washingtonpost.com/wp-dyn/content/article/2007/02/17/AR2007021701172.html.

Roberts, Gene. "From Rural Ramblin' to a Bunker in Hue," *Columbia Journalism Review*, September/October 1996.

Robinson, Steve. "Pulitzers: Was the Mirage a Deception?" *Columbia Journalism Review*, July/August 1979, 7–8.

Silverstein, Ken. "Their Men in Washington," *Harper's Magazine*, July 2007, 53–61.

U.S. Army. *Field Manual No. 23–10 Sniper Training*, Washington: Department of the Army Headquarters, 1994.

Zinsser, William. *On Writing Well*, 3rd ed., New York: Harper & Row, 1985.

CHAPTER 5

Talking Your Way to the Story

The methodology described in this book—using documents, observation and talk as the basis for a news story—is hard to argue with as a matter of principle, but when events happen and deadlines loom, theory sometimes gives way to reality. Many a story has been reported and written without the support of documentary evidence. Just as document dives aren't always necessary, observation is often left out of the mix when reporters are putting a story together. In some situations journalists can do nearly all their reporting by working the phones or using electronic communication so that they have little to no need for going out and getting a firsthand look at their subject. But it is nearly impossible to conceive of a news account that does not in some way rely on talking to sources, whether for on the record quotes from officials or just to get directions to the scene of an accident. Thus of all the skills in the DOT methodology, talking is the one that reporters use the most.

Some journalists are born with the gift of gab, and chatting up everyone within earshot comes as naturally as breathing. But many journalists are at the opposite end of the shyness spectrum and would prefer to work from behind a protective shell. No matter what your personal proclivities are when it comes to interacting with news sources, you will benefit from thinking carefully about and learning the nuances of the process of purposeful talking, which is what interviewing comes down to.

As noted previously, this book prefers the term "talking" over the term "interviewing" because the former is at once more inclusive and less formal. Whichever term you prefer to use, the point is that reporters engage in this activity with a specific goal in mind, to gather information—to seek out answers that are needed to provide as complete and as accurate an account of a news event as possible. At the core of the interview is the asking and answering of questions, and for this reason it is useful to give some thought to the different ways it is possible to prompt someone to give you information. Consider the following alternatives:

- What's the best way to ask a question?
- Have you ever thought about the best way to ask a question?

- Help me understand what you think would be the best way to ask a question.

- If you need an answer in a hurry, what's the best way to ask a question?

- I have a funny story to tell about a question I once had to ask.

- Based on your experience of having questions posed to you, what's the best way to ask a question?

- It might be a good idea to take a moment to consider the best way to ask a question.

- Do you need to have a follow-up ready to make sure you get the best answer to your question?

- Isn't it true that the best way to ask a question is the way that gets you the best answer?

- Questions. The best way to ask them.

As this list demonstrates, there are many different ways to pose a question, and some of them aren't even questions. The truth is that there is no one right way to ask a question. Instead it is up to the reporter to size up the situation and to adopt the appropriate strategy, the one that is most likely to achieve the desired result. The idea of using different kinds of questions in different situations is a fairly common theme in reporting textbooks, and it is one we will return to. But there is a reason that this chapter is not called "questioning" or even "interviewing," namely that reporters should be always mindful that there are alternative ways, sometimes more effective ways, of getting information from human sources.

Richard Critchfield, the MacArthur Foundation fellow who was discussed in Chapter 4, spent much of his career working to bridge the gap between poor villagers in developing nations and the political and cultural elites living in the rich countries of the West. Over the years Critchfield refined the technique of what he called "village reporting," a form of immersion journalism that involved sharing the primitive living conditions and harsh working conditions of the people he was writing about. Eventually he came to the conclusion that as much as possible he would avoid interviews altogether.

The structured question-and-answer process, he felt, could mean "leading a subject, either consciously or unconsciously, along preconceived paths" and thus limiting the reporter's ability to gain a full understanding of the situation (Critchfield, 1978, 33–34). Critchfield's preferred approach was to rely on simple dialogue with his sources, whom he went to great lengths to put at ease. He wrote: "Early on I discovered the value of engaging in the same daily physical labor as the men I was writing about, perhaps because hard work was the basic fact in all their lives; after I spent many days with them helping them to herd sheep, spear octopus, harvest wheat or whatever they were doing, a barrier of reserve was overcome, and in time the principal characters began to take our mutual enterprise very seriously and developed what might be called a strong sense of integrity" (Critchfield, 1973, 4).

Critchfield, of course, had the luxury of time and the advantage of working with sources who had little in the way of worldly power or prestige that they needed to protect from the prying eyes of a journalist. Most reporters are rarely in this situation, and so they cannot wait for a free-form discussion to develop, although that doesn't mean they shouldn't be prepared to use Critchfield's conversational approach under the right circumstances.

Under other circumstances, reporters will likely need different strategies. But choosing the right interview strategy may not be as easy as it sounds, for two reasons. The first reason is the one demonstrated above—there are lots of different ways to ask a question. The second is that over the course of a single interview, and certainly over the course of a relationship with a source, different forms of questioning will lead to better, or worse, answers. The first thing a reporter needs to be aware of is the range of options that are available.

Unlike Critchfield, most reporters do not have the leeway to sit and talk with sources and let the conversation go where it may go. Instead they need to set clear goals for what they hope to get out of an interview. If it's a one-and-done session, the reporter needs to strategize about how to lead up to the key question and how to pose it in the way most likely to get a publishable response. In other situations, the reporter may want to hold off on asking the hardest questions until a mutual understanding has been established with a source. In any case, the reporter should have a road map for where the interview is going to go and to prepare a list of questions, or at least topic areas to cover.

Keep in mind the kinds of questions you can ask and how you can order them. Do use a mix of both open-ended questions and closed-ended questions, i.e., questions that require a yes or no response. It's a good idea to write your questions out in advance and try to think about how your source is likely to respond. Think of the interview occurring in a long arc, with an introductory phase, an information-intensive back-and-forth phase and, finally, a wrap-up phase, in which you try to gather up any loose ends while also laying the groundwork for future conversations. As you get more adept at this, and perhaps also develop more knowledge about your source and your subject matter, you may find it better to take a spontaneous approach without as much preparation. But until you get to a point where you have that much confidence in your ability to think on your feet and come away with needed information, it's probably impossible to over-prepare for an interview.

In *The Practice of Questioning*, J.T. Dillon examines eight "domains of questioning" (1990), which are specialized fields that have developed their own methodologies and protocols for making inquiries. His observations about journalistic questioning highlight one of the peculiarities about journalistic interviewing that can make it so often a frustrating, and even fruitless, experience. Dillon points out that both journalists and their sources are usually talking past each other, on the one hand, eliciting information on behalf of an audience that is not present and, on the other hand, addressing answers to that distant audience. Both sides are interested in the "quotable quote," the sound bite that will enliven a broadcast report or nestle as a little gem in the midst of a printed story, and the group that loses in this exchange is the news audience, since it most often gets shiny words rather than actual insight.

Sometimes reporters express frustration about the difficulty of getting sources, particularly famous ones, to move beyond their rehearsed messages. The clichés that tumble out of the mouths of athletes are a perfect case in point, extolling the virtue of team play, the importance of focus, the need to give 110 percent and so on without revealing any of the specific details that are the building blocks of good stories. Journalists who find themselves in such a situation would profit from reminding themselves that insipid answers often follow from insipid questions and that there are alternative strategies that can be taken from other fields that rely on interviews or similar exchanges for information.

Dillon's approach to questioning suggests how these alternatives might take shape. Instead of posing an open-ended question that allows the respondent to reply with nonanswers, journalists could imagine themselves as physicians working in a clinical setting and move crisply through a series of narrowly focused questions. Reporters could look to psychotherapists, who need to exert subtle control over therapeutic question-and-answer sessions and have a range of techniques that could be adopted. One of these is what Dillon calls "deliberate nonquestioning," which relies on silences, nonverbal sounds and declarative statements to draw out responses. Another tactic a reporter might consider would be to supply a range of answers along with the question, much the way social scientists do in using survey tools.

The news interview, whether in a high-profile setting such as a sports arena after a nationally televised game or in a darkened parking garage with a "secret" source like Deep Throat, is an integral part of contemporary reporting practice. But historians of journalism note that the news interview is a relatively recent innovation that came about in the 19th century. In the United States there is some debate about when the first interview was published; some scholars point to an interview with the abolitionist Gerrit Smith in the wake of John Brown's raid on Harper's Ferry, printed in the *New York Herald* in 1859, while others cite an interview with Mormon Church leader Brigham Young, which appeared that same year in the *New York Tribune*. But earlier examples have been identified, including an 1836 interview with the woman who ran a New York brothel, where a prostitute had been found murdered. This was conducted by James Gordon Bennett, the founding editor of the *Herald*, who is also credited with landing the first "exclusive" interview, with President Martin Van Buren (Nilsson, 1971).

Early newspaper interviews were often published in a question-and-answer format, borrowing in form from lurid trial transcripts, which were also the basis for much of the content that the penny press used to build readership. The newspaper interview often has much in common with the back-and-forth questioning that occurs in court, and reporters can borrow some of the techniques that trial lawyers use to elicit information from witnesses. For example, attorneys know the value of using open-ended questions, such as "What was the weather like that day?" to encourage a fuller explanation and mixing them up with close-ended questions, such as "Was it raining when you went out?" to pin down the facts. Journalists might also employ a tactic that lawyers use in the cross-examination phase of a trial, posing a question as a negative. This approach forces the source to rework the question mentally, possibly making it more difficult to come back with a stock answer.

But there are also important differences between court testimony and a journalistic interview. Lawyers have several advantages in posing their questions. In many cases the legal system can require witnesses to testify, and it can also impose sanctions if witnesses don't tell the truth. Journalists do not have these powers. They have to be able to persuade sources to talk to them, and reporters cannot take what they are told at face value. On the other hand, legal testimony is often taken in the context of a confrontation, and this is not always the case for journalistic interviews. Sometimes reporters get the chance to talk with sources, who may be artists or celebrities or sports stars or just ordinary people, in an informal, and frankly pleasurable, way.

In the realm of journalism there can be many different kinds of interviews. At one extreme is the open-ended backgrounder, where the only purpose is to gain some general information and perhaps to start a trusting relationship with a source, and at the other extreme is the "gotcha" interview, where the goal is to catch an official of a company or government agency in an embarrassing contradiction—if not an outright lie. Other interviews fall somewhere in between, maybe a set-piece "exclusive" with the author of a best-seller or the painful but necessary foray to get a "reaction" quote from the family of the victim of a car crash or industrial accident. In any case, a reporter should be clear about the purpose of the interview and the expected outcome so that the appropriate approach is taken.

THE INTERVIEW PROCESS

While no two interviews will be exactly alike, there is a standard process that reporters should follow in preparing for, carrying out and then following up on an interview. The process includes:

- Determining the scope of your sourcing.
- Identifying specific sources and figuring out how to contact them.
- Making contact and arranging for an interview.
- Preparing for a talk.
- Conducting the interview.
- Following up.

In determining the scope of your sourcing, you need to consider how many sources you need to contact and what kind. Going back to Bob Woodward, perhaps the most acclaimed reporter of modern times, we can see how he emphasizes the use of human sources and works his sources much harder than most. The key to success is "having many, many good sources—not one or 10 or 40 but hundreds," he says (Woodward, 1991).

In an ideal world talking to that many sources is a good idea, but under the time constraints that most reporters encounter, a much smaller number of sources will usually have to suffice. On a controversial story, and most worthwhile stories have some element of controversy, it's important to talk to sources with different points of view. Keep in mind that it isn't enough to get "both sides of the story," since a story may have three or four different sides. Experienced journalists avoid "one-source stories," but they also know that finding the right number of sources for a story is more than just math. Savvy reporters don't decide they have "enough" sources just because they have talked to three different people—but keep going until they have confidence in their grasp of the essential facts.

It's also important to try to use different kinds of sources, for example, both official and unofficial sources. Official sources are people who have a formal connection to a story, and they can be extremely useful because they are usually knowledgeable and are experienced in talking with reporters. But many of them are also good at staying "on message" and providing only limited information or information that is slanted toward a particular point of view. Unofficial sources, by contrast, may be in a position to speak more freely or may just have a different perspective. But because they are not used to dealing with the media, they may require more effort to locate and to coax into talking on the record. Getting both kinds of sources in a story will almost always make for a fuller account.

For example, a story about a proposed change in high school graduation requirements would surely include comments from educational experts, teachers and maybe even representatives from parent-teacher organizations. Although digging out other perspectives, perhaps from students or from local employers who have a stake in the education of future workers, would be much harder to do, it could be crucial in helping the community evaluate the proposal.

Sources can be categorized in other ways, in addition to the formal-informal system described above. For example, among formal sources many reporters use both senior officials as well as lower level officials whose job it is to deal with the press. The lower level officials are often gatekeepers, whose job duties include keeping reporters away from top executives. They can be frustrating to deal with, but for certain kinds of information, such as noncontroversial background material, they can be helpful. Senior sources are more knowledgeable, and under the right circumstances, they are actually more likely to be the source of leaks compared to lower level officials (Reich, 2009).

In thinking about sources for a particular story, it's also useful to consider the motivations and psychology of potential sources. James Reston, of *The New York Times,* had this advice for reporters who wanted to get to the bottom of a story: "Always look for the unhappy ones" (Halberstam, 1979, 222). By that he meant that people who were unhappy about an event or chain of events were more likely to provide critical insights than those who had a stake in protecting the status quo. Thus in the school curriculum example described above, students, who might be unhappy about tougher requirements, or potential employers, who might be unhappy about looser standards, would be good sources to approach because of the perspectives they would provide. Similarly, if the changes in the curriculum were the result of an internal debate, it would be very useful to know what those on the losing end of the argument might have to say about the potential pitfalls in the changes.

DETERMINING THE SCOPE OF YOUR SOURCING

Finding the names and contact information for many official sources is straightforward; most organizations have websites that include directories with names, titles and phone numbers (and even email addresses). But it's also good to get input from experts who do not have a direct connection to the story and can point out background issues or other considerations that those who are directly involved may not want to discuss. This is a place where skillful use of documents can help you locate good sources. Previously published news articles and reports can provide names, titles and affiliations of possible sources. Various online databases also provide links to potential specialists in various topic areas. Over the years such databases have been created and occasionally abandoned, or at least not kept up to date. Social media sites, such as Facebook and Twitter, are other useful tools for locating sources, especially unofficial ones. Whether dealing with official sources or unofficial ones, it's always a good idea to make some evaluation of the quality of the information that you are receiving and the credibility of the person you are talking with. It's also important to be careful about using friends or personal connections as sources. Sometimes they can provide good information, but they also may present ethical problems and conflicts of interest if, for example, they ask you to withhold certain details that might be important to include for the sake of reader understanding.

Once you have the name of someone you want to interview, the next step is to make contact. In some cases, particularly on deadline stories, you will have no choice but to pick up the phone or walk straight up to your source and start a conversation. But under other circumstances a more deliberate approach will be possible, one that will involve making a preliminary contact for the primary purpose of setting a time for an interview. Essentially you have three options for making this first contact: email, telephone or letter. Each one has its own advantages and disadvantages.

- Email is fast and direct, and it allows you to create a more or less permanent record. For younger and more technologically savvy sources, it may be the best way to communicate. But email has several serious drawbacks that should make you question whether it is the first tool that you want to use to set up (or conduct) an interview. First of all, emails can be ignored. Once you send an email out into the ether, you have no way of knowing whether it has arrived. You can attach a receipt requiring acknowledgment, but that is a mildly aggressive step that could frighten a source away. Keep in mind that while sending an email is easy and fast, the recipient of your email may be one of those people who is deluged with electronic messages and views email as an unpleasant chore. Also, it's harder to write out answers than to talk spontaneously, which may make some sources not want to communicate by email, particularly if the subject matter is complex and your knowledge about it is minimal. Other versions of electronic communication, such as Facebook messaging, are also possible and have many of the same drawbacks as email.

- The telephone is probably the most common way of arranging an interview. If you have someone's cell phone number and particularly if that person has voice mail, the telephone can be a great way to make contact with a source. But phones can also represent a barrier that you have to get through. For example, many official sources are likely to be protected by receptionists or private secretaries who screen their calls. A busy source may well use a gatekeeper to keep away unwanted annoyances, such as reporters. If you encounter this kind of situation, try to work around it. Perhaps you can catch your source at home. Another technique that has worked for a lot of reporters is to call a source at the office either before or after standard working hours. Many high-ranking sources answer their own phones when no one else is around.

- A letter may seem like a hopelessly old-fashioned way to set up an interview, particularly in today's lightning-fast media environment. But Steve Weinberg, a journalism professor and former executive director of the group called Investigative Reporters and Editors, says he uses this technique frequently if circumstances permit. Because they take time to write and are, frankly, old-fashioned, letters can be an effective way for a reporter to convey seriousness and sincerity, which are two of the most important characteristics to display if you are trying to get an interview with a source who doesn't know anything about you (Weinberg, 2002). If your first letter goes unanswered or if you want to make sure that the first one gets through, consider sending your request by a private delivery service, such as Federal Express.

No matter what strategy or technique you use, you may still find that a source won't return calls or respond to you at all. The main thing to keep in mind is that no one owes you an interview. That means you may have to work to earn one. Think back to the part of this chapter that discussed different domains of questioning. One of those domains is the job interview, and in many job interviews an interesting two-way dynamic takes place. A good job recruiter may be asking you questions to find out whether you would be a suitable worker, but at the same time the recruiter is trying to sell you on why you would want the job under the conditions that it is offered. That's what you have to do when approaching a potentially reluctant source: explain not only what you are looking for but also why it would be in the source's best interest to talk to you.

Too many inexperienced reporters jump to conclusions about why a source won't return a call. The most important sources you need are likely to be the busiest. You may not get a call back only because your source is busy with other things and not because the source won't help if it can be arranged. Be persistent. Don't stop trying to make contact. But also don't forget your obligation to explain why the source should help you.

A good salesperson knows that the most promising contact is one that is based on what is sometimes called a "referred lead," or more simply a referral. If you can contact a potential source by saying that you were referred by a third party who is known and trusted by that potential source, you may increase your chances of securing an interview. In the real world of reporting, no technique is foolproof, and this one does not always work. But, at least some of the time, it can be used to open some doors.

PREPARING FOR THE INTERVIEW

In almost all cases, the way to start getting ready for an interview is by using one or both of the other DOT tools. At the very least a reporter should check to see what has already been written on the topic or about the person who will be approached for an interview. A good reporter spends some time thinking about the interview, planning out questions and identifying any knowledge gaps that need to be filled. This will be easier to do if the reporter already has in mind the person who is going to be interviewed. Document review is even more critical when a story has been assigned without suggestions for sources. The main thing to keep in mind is that better questions will lead to better answers (and more usable quotes). The way to develop better questions is to gather as much information as possible on which to base your questions. If time permits, it's also a good idea to get out and look at what you are writing about. Your source will be impressed that you have taken the time to educate yourself and will appreciate the fact that you are not asking for information that you could have obtained on your own. On the other hand, there will be occasions when time does not permit, and you have to jump into an interview without preparation, such as a breaking news story involving an accident or a crime. In those cases, using the five W's of who-what-when-where-why is a good fallback position. They will at least provide you with a starting point.

As you develop your list of questions, you are trying to accomplish at least two things. First, you are trying to note the essential pieces of information you will need to take away from this interview. In addition, it is helpful to try to imagine how the interview will go, what questions, or kinds of questions, might get meaningful responses. As you do so, you should also strategize about the order in which you will introduce specific topics so that you don't tip your hand too soon or say something that your source may find off-putting. As the interview develops, you may find that it goes off in different directions than you expected, and you may find yourself abandoning your list of planned questions. That's ok, but that's another good reason to bring a written list of questions to an interview—you can refer back to them to make sure that you have covered all the necessary ground before the interview comes to an end.

How many questions should you prepare? You may think that 10 or 15 is enough, but the most accomplished journalists often cite a much higher number, like 50 or 75. You almost certainly won't have an opportunity to ask all of those questions, but if you want to be truly prepared for an interview, try to develop as many questions covering as many possible subjects as possible.

As you develop your list, you should prepare for the likelihood that your source will at some point become evasive and attempt to avoid giving detailed information. If this is information that you need for your story, you have to be prepared to respond to nonanswers. Three types of useful follow-ups are probing, specifying and interpreting questions. A probing question is some variation of "Can you tell more about that?" A specifying question steps up the intensity a notch by pressing for specifics: "What happened next?" or "What was her reaction when you told her?" Finally, an interpreting question is one in which you try to prompt a fuller response by offering a paraphrase: "Are you saying that . . . ?" In many case it will not be hard to anticipate the points at which a source may become reluctant to answer your questions fully, and you should try to be prepared to come back with a request for more information posed in a slightly different form (Kvale and Brinkmann, 2009).

Part of your preparation should be deciding whether to use a recorder or to take notes by hand. There are pros and cons to both approaches. Some sources may say a recorder makes them uncomfortable, since it eliminates deniability, but others may welcome your use of a recorder since it should lead to more accurate quotes. The main advantage of taking notes is that you can skip the time-consuming step of transcribing a recording, and, if you are on deadline, it may be your best option. But unless you know a system like Gregg shorthand, and few American journalists do, the practice of handwriting notes is likely to lead to gaps and inaccuracies.

Another reason to consider using a recorder, even though it is likely to be more time-consuming in the long run, is that the recorder will simplify an interview, which is a far more complex activity than you may realize. During an interview, you will be posing questions and processing the responses. Based on those responses you will also have to think up new questions to plug gaps or to pursue new avenues. It's a lot to do at once, particularly if you are also worried about getting exact quotes down. Another reason to use a recording device, particularly a digital recorder, is that you may want to post the interview on the Internet.

THE INTERVIEW

Once your interview has begun, the quality of your preparation will go a long way to determining your success. Sir David Frost (Figure 5.1), the late British newsman, was once asked to explain how he was able to get people to say things to him that they hadn't said to other interviewers. His response was immediate: "Simple point—you have to know what they've

FIGURE 5.1   *David Frost, the legendary British broadcast journalist, was known for his skill with interview subjects but said the key was the preparation that he did before he sat down to talk. Credit: Robert D. Ward/Office of the Secretary of Defense*

said before so that you can get something fresh." He then went on to explain that his extensive research allowed him to make the most of the fact that the interview process is dynamic and unpredictable, qualities that are at the heart of why interviews can be so exciting and valuable. "One vital thing about an interview is that you've got to be ready for anything to come up," he added (Frost, 2012).

The most productive interviews are two-way discussions that involve an exchange of information. On certain beats, such as political ones, reporters know that their ability to provide nonpublic information, even information that verges on gossip, to a source might be part of the expected transaction. Reporters who have information to share are often rewarded with additional information. Particularly at first, whether with a new source, on a new topic or in a new setting, it can be easy to be intimidated when talking to someone you don't know well. But try to keep in mind that you also have something to add, something that you can give to your source in exchange for the information that you are trying to obtain. For example, as a student interviewing the high-level university official or a local political official you may not feel confident, but your source can learn something from you as well (and the opportunity to get some student insight may have been part of the reason for agreeing to talk with you).

One all-too-common problem is having a source agree to talk who then doesn't seem willing to open up. If that happens, remember that the first step in getting people to talk to you is getting people to open their mouths. In other words, you should plan to spend the first part of your interview making small talk, exchanging pleasantries, showing that you are a fellow human being. There's no magic key that will unlock a person's mind and get the contents to come spilling out into your notebook, but you can't expect someone to tell you sensitive information right off the bat. Get your source talking about anything, get those jaws moving and then move on to the topic you need to explore.

Sometimes there are specific tools that you can use to promote a useful discussion. For example, relevant photographs or other kinds of documents might be enough to jog a source's memory. Veteran editor Bill Marimow is credited with developing a map technique, in which he asks a source to draw up a map of a particular incident (Zwerling, 2013). Sometimes this kind of visualization process may help a source recall specific details—and may also clarify for you exactly what the source is trying to convey.

On the other hand, you may encounter a situation in which your source won't stop talking but isn't giving you anything you can use. Many official sources, including corporate executives and government officials, have been exposed to "media training," in which they have learned that their goal in an interview is to "stay on message" and "play out the clock." No matter what your question, they will be trying to feed you sound bites of what they want to be quoted as saying, even if their answers don't relate to your questions. They will also try to deliver long, winding replies that fill up the time allotted to your interview. This can be hard to do, but sometimes you have to be willing to interrupt your source, talk over the speech you are hearing and force the interview back on track.

Start by being polite: "Excuse me, but can we go back to the question I asked?" This may or may not work. If you have some reason to believe in advance that your source is going to behave this way, you should come in with some pointed closed-end questions that require a yes or no answer. Another tactic would be to state a rephrasing of what your source has said in another context and then ask, "Is that right?" There is no tried-and-true way of dealing with this problem, and you should be prepared for resistance, perhaps outright hostility, as you try to pry something usable from your source.

In many cases, your source will be more knowledgeable than you, perhaps even an expert on the topic you are researching. But this is something you can turn to your advantage if you do your homework and use the DOT methodology appropriately. If you come prepared for an interview and ask good questions, your source is far more likely to open up to you. Many people who are experts in their field like to share their knowledge with others, particularly with interested others. Just be careful not to waste your source's time with questions that you could obtain the answers to on your own. If you expect your source to provide you with an elementary education on a topic, you also are cutting into the time allotted for your interview and reducing the chances that you get to ask a meaty question.

Among trial lawyers, there is a common saying that one should never ask a question of a witness unless one already knows what the answer is going to be. It's unrealistic to expect that you will be sufficiently prepared for every interview to that degree, but it's also good to try to put yourself in a position where you are not begging for information.

Another eventuality you must be prepared for is that your source agrees to talk—but then says the conversation must be "off the record." While this is hardly an optimal situation, sometimes it cannot be avoided. But first of all make sure you and your source are using the same terminology. There are degrees of anonymity that can be granted to sources, and you should push to use the least restrictive level. Not every journalist would necessarily agree with what the various terms associated with anonymity for sources mean, but here are some generally accepted guidelines.

- **Source.** Talking on a source basis means you can use the information, and even direct quotes, as long as the source is not identified by name. You and your source (and your editor) may also negotiate on the degree of identification that is provided, such as "a police department source" versus "a source close to the investigation" versus "a source who is knowledgeable about the investigation."

- **Background.** Talking on a background basis generally means you can use the information that is provided but without specific attribution. Since there is no attribution allowed, you should be careful about agreeing to this kind of interview, although there are times when it can be useful and even necessary.

- **Deep background.** Under this restriction, a reporter can use the information to do additional reporting, but the information itself is not for publication.

- **Off the record.** This is the most restrictive form of an interview, and it can mean that the information provided is not to go any further—not even as bait to lure another source into confirming its accuracy.

Even among professional journalists, the distinctions among these terms are not well understood or interpreted in the same way. A source may say that a conversation is "off the record" when the only thing the source is worried about is being quoted by name. You need to define your terms with your source so that you don't agree to a more restrictive set of conditions than you have to. A technique that a lot of reporters use is to allow a source to go off the record to provide a full explanation of an issue with the understanding that the source will subsequently go back on the record to provide usable material. This may not be an ideal strategy, and it can lead to a situation in which sources are bargaining for pre-approval of the quotes that can be used. But there are circumstances in which such an approach yields the maximum amount of information.

Always beware of becoming captive to your sources. While you definitely need their help, and may need some more than others, don't let your sources get into a position where they can dictate what you can report. A source who tries too hard to control you is a source to be very wary of. If a source speaks to you knowing that you are functioning as a journalist, do not feel obligated to agree to withhold information that has already been given to you. It is not uncommon for a source to ask that a statement that has just been given be kept off the record. A perfectly appropriate response is to say, "You knew I was talking to you as a reporter when you said those things, and as far as I am concerned we have been on the record up to this point. If you would like to go off the record from here on, we can do that."

There is always the possibility that as soon as you finish talking to a source you remember something that you forgot to ask. This happens. If you are on deadline and juggling multiple stories or story angles, it can be easy to end an interview without getting all the information you need. Sometimes you can call right back and clarify things, but sometimes—particularly if you are dealing with a busy source—you only have one shot to get every-thing and get it right. A partial solution to this problem is to develop a stock series of questions with which to wind up every talk. For example, you should double-check the spelling of your source's name and exact title. If your source prefers to be referred to by a nickname, get that as well. If it's relevant or if you need to use a courtesy title in your publication, make sure you get a female source's preference on Ms./Mrs./Miss.

Finally, you should always end your interview with a question about the question you didn't ask. You can try something like "Before we finish, is there anything else we should discuss?" or "If I were as smart as you are, what's the question I would have asked?" You may get nothing more than a chuckle, but you may also find your discussion going off in a whole new direction.

Ultimately the success of the interview will depend on your ability to exert control over the situation. Oriana Fallaci, the renowned Italian journal-ist and author of *Interview with History,* wrote about the difficulty in and the time required for obtaining an interview. She also stressed the importance of fighting for more time with her interview subjects, extending the conver-sation to make sure that she got answers to her questions. Fallaci's style of interviewing was extremely aggressive, even combative. When approaching world leaders, "I went with a thousand feelings of rage, a thousand questions that before assailing them were assailing me," she wrote (Fallaci, 1976, 9). If you have the temperament and presence to conduct yourself as she did, which sometimes involved dramatic physical gestures, her methods may work for you.

But most interviewers, even those known for asking tough questions, try to take a subtler approach. Mike Wallace, for example, talked about establishing a "chemistry of confidentiality," creating a sense of intimacy that allowed his sources to relax and open up. The key to this technique, he said, is in the preparation for the interview and the development of knowledgeable questions. As he put these questions to his interview subjects, "they begin to understand I know an awful lot about them" (Kelly, 2005).

THE FOLLOW-UP

Assuming you have asked all the questions you intended to ask, the first thing you need to do after an interview is preserve your record. If you have only taken notes, it's a good idea to go over them right away, allowing your short-term memory to fill in blanks (without making things up, of course) and writing over any scribbles that you might not be able to decipher at a later time. If you have recorded your interview with a digital device, it's easy to make a backup copy right away, perhaps by emailing or downloading the file.

It isn't necessary, or even appropriate, in every case, but there may be times when it makes sense to send a brief "thank you" note to a source.

A final word of warning about human sources is that you need to remember that it is very easy to be misled. Some sources may actively seek to mislead you, but you should also be careful about sources who accurately and honestly tell you something that may turn out to be wrong. You need to cross-check one source against another and against what you discover in documentary and observational research.

An interview is not a discrete event but rather part of a series of events. If things go well, these events will form the basis of what is perhaps a reporter's most important skill: source development. While you want an interview to be a success in itself and provide you the information you need for the story in front of you, in an ideal world your interview (and the subsequent published story) will help convince your source that you are a responsible journalist who can be trusted to report fairly and accurately. With this kind of reputation, you will be in a good position to get tips about stories to follow up on and, even better, leaks—the release, on an exclusive basis, of information that advances the public's understanding of an event or issue in a significant way.

Woodward, who has set the standard for exhaustive interviewing, says that to make sure of his information, he spends a lot of effort making sure of what he thinks he had learned in an interview. In some cases he will return to the same source "a dozen or two times" to nail down an important detail or to clarify a sequence of events (Woodward, 1991). While few journalists take the talk aspect of reporting to this extreme, Woodward's example provides an important lesson—the more you do this the better you will get at it.

Starting off, students and inexperienced reporters may find the task of extracting information from human sources extremely daunting, but, if they work at the task the way Woodward has, they may eventually arrive at a place where he is, where news sources believe that it is in their best interest to sit down and talk with him—and fear that they will pay a price if they do not.

In his memoir *All Too Human,* George Stephanopoulos, a onetime political operative who went on to a career in television journalism, talks about the way Woodward's reputation made it nearly impossible for even the most powerful people in Washington to resist talking to him. "His books invariably created embarrassing headlines for their subjects, but his sources were assumed to be the most important, connected, and knowledgeable people in Washington. I was wary of Woodward, but flattered and curious too" Stephanopoulos wrote (1999, 281).

He described the dilemma of getting an interview request from the *Post* reporter. "Do you cooperate and elaborate in return (you hope) for learning more and earning a better portrayal—for your boss and yourself?" The other alternative is try to stonewall and hope that everyone else refuses to cooperate. "If no one talks, there is no book," Stephanopoulos pointed out.

But given Woodward's reputation—for thoroughness, patience and truth seeking, this is not a realistic prospect. According to Stephanopoulos, "Someone—then everyone—always talks" (Stephanopoulos, 1999, 281).

EXERCISES

1. Review at least two recently published articles from a major newspaper, or its website, and make a list of all the sources who were quoted, either by name or on some source basis. Try to classify the sources as either official or nonofficial. For official sources, try to classify them as either senior executive or media specialist. Finally, try to classify them as to their state of mind—favoring the developments discussed in the story or opposed to them. In the final stage of your analysis, try to draw some conclusions about the relative strengths and weaknesses of the sourcing in the articles under review.

2. Select a topic that you might write a story about, such as a sports team, a campus organization or event, a local institution or community figure. Assuming you were to write a story on this topic, create a source map, identifying persons to interview, either by name or at least by position or status (if you cannot immediately name the sources you would approach). How many potential sources can you identify? What can you do to ensure that you have different kinds

of sources with different perspectives? For as many as possible, provide contact information, using directory sources, the Internet and social media.

3. The best interviewers are able to elicit information from sources that reveals something that is surprising or that the source might not necessarily want to reveal. This is a high art and is a formidable skill to develop. To get some practice in this area, pair off with a classmate and see if you can get that person to provide some mildly embarrassing information or perhaps just some little-known fact. As a first step, develop a list of questions, using both open-ended and closed forms. Imagine the interview as a kind of exchange, where you may get more information if you are willing to share some of your own. Try, based on Dillon's observation about trial attorneys, to ask a question in the negative, to move your source out of standard thought processes.

4. Conduct a critique of an interview conducted by a professional journalist and try to identify strengths and weaknesses of the interviewer's technique. Start by obtaining an interview transcript from a newspaper website or from a database like LexisNexis or by finding a video of an extended interview on an Internet service like You-Tube. Considering the types of questions defined by Kvale (probing, specifying, interpreting), try to identify which kinds of follow-up questions predominate and which kinds elicit the most substantive answers.

REFERENCES

Critchfield, Richard. *The Golden Bowl Be Broken: Peasant Life in Four Cultures,* Bloomington: Indiana University Press, 1973.

———. "Can Three Billion Peasants Be 'Covered'?," *Columbia Journalism Review,* January/February 1978.

Dillon, J.T. *The Practice of Questioning,* New York: Routledge, 1990.

Fallaci, Oriana. *Interview with History,* New York: Liveright, 1976.

Frost, David. "Video: Sir David Frost on the Art of Interviewing," British Film Institute, 10:12, November 27, 2012, accessed December 10, 2013, at http://explore.bfi.org.uk/51e9535cdad4f.

Halberstam, David. *The Powers That Be,* New York: Alfred A. Knopf, 1979.

Kelly, James. "10 Questions for Mike Wallace," *Time,* October 23, 2005, accessed December 10, 2013, at http://content.time.com/time/magazine/article/0,9171,1122034,00.html.

Kvale, Steinar, and Svend Brinkmann. *InterViews: Learning the Craft of Qualitative Research Interviewing,* Thousand Oaks, Calif.: Sage Publications, 2009.

Nilsson, Nils Gunnar. "The Origin of the Interview," *Journalism Quarterly* 48, December 1971, 707–13.

Reich, Zvi. *Sourcing the News: Key Issues in Journalism—an Innovative Study of the Israeli Press,* Cresskill, N.J.: Hampton Press, 2009.

Stephanopoulos, George. *All Too Human,* Boston: Little, Brown, 1999.

Weinberg, Steve. "Getting in the Door," in Brant Houston et al., eds., *The Investigative Reporter's Handbook: A Guide to Documents, Databases and Techniques,* Boston: Bedford/St. Martin's, 2002.

Woodward, Bob. Interview by Brian Lamb, *Booknotes,* June 23, 1991, accessed December 10, 2013, at http://www.booknotes.org/Watch/18547–1/Bob+Woodward.aspx.

Zwerling, Daniel. "Eliciting Vivid Stories," *IRE Journal,* winter 2013, 26.

PART TWO

From Principle to Practice

CHAPTER 6

Getting Started

Novice reporters may begin their careers with dreams of covering the White House or serving as a foreign correspondent in some exotic capital. But they are unlikely to start with such glamorous assignments. Instead they will most likely find themselves buried in routine, covering the kinds of day-in/ day-out stories that are at the core of the news: crime reports and obituaries and weather features. For some journalists, getting away from these kinds of topics as quickly as possible is an early goal, but other journalists develop an expertise in these areas and even build their reputations there. This chapter will show how to use the DOT methodology to get the most out of these kinds of stories—and maybe even to move on to more prestigious assignments.

THE POLICE BEAT

Traditionally, and for good reason, the police beat has been the starting point for many a journalism career. Police work encompasses everything from dramatic life-and-death stories to encounters with societal misfits and oddballs, but at the same time it is bound by specific routines that provide structure and ensure a steady supply of news. Whether it's known as crime reporting or simply as "cops" (as in, she's got "cops" this weekend), this is an area of journalism that inspires strong reactions, sometimes contradictory ones. News organizations are routinely criticized for putting too much emphasis on crime stories, particularly violent ones, but they also know that readers have a strong interest in public safety and that crime stories do attract an audience. Crime stories frequently focus on society's lower strata and often feature individuals with unattractive qualities who do foolish things— characteristics that some reporters find so repellent that they would rather cover almost anything else. But other reporters see these stories as a window on the human condition and make a career out of police reporting.

One of the most colorful figures in crime journalism is Edna Buchanan, a longtime writer for the *Miami Herald* who won a Pulitzer Prize in 1986 for "her versatile and consistently excellent police beat reporting" (Columbia,

1986) and has since become a novelist. In *The Corpse Had a Familiar Face: Covering Miami, America's Hottest Beat,* Buchanan said she knew of many reporters who had fled from cops coverage but couldn't understand why: "The police beat is about people and what makes them tick, what turns them into heroes or homicidal maniacs, what brings out the best in them, what drives them berserk. It has it all: greed, sex, violence, comedy, and tragedy." There was no better place in journalism to learn about the human race, she wrote (Buchanan, 1987, 271).

A case that she covered starting in late 1979 demonstrates both the powerful way in which people can react to a crime story as well as the importance of using documents, observation and talk to get the truth. In this case, unfortunately, getting to the truth did not mean getting to a happy ending. Her first story was an account of the death of Arthur Lee McDuffie, a 33-year-old, black insurance agent who was in many ways a solid citizen but who also was driving with a suspended license one evening when he caught the attention of police officers by pulling a wheelie on his motorcycle. A high-speed chase ensued, and some of the officers who arrived on the scene beat McDuffie to death. But that's not how they wrote up the incident. Instead the police report showed that McDuffie's death was the result of an accident that occurred after he lost control of his bike at 65 mph and apparently crashed into something—a curb, a streetlight, a restraining wall—that was hard enough to crack his skull.

The first lesson to be drawn from the McDuffie incident, then, is that a police report, like any other document, cannot be relied upon as an account of absolute truth. The second lesson, one that is true on many beats but is particularly true in police reporting, is the importance of cultivating and talking to knowledgeable persons. In this case Buchanan was alerted by a confidential source. Without having someone talk to her and tip her off, she would not have known to start looking into what had happened. After hearing from her source, Buchanan next made some calls, and then headed to police headquarters, where she listened to one documentary account, a tape of the chase, and read the accident report. The report raised questions in her mind because she recognized the names of some of the officers who took part in the incident, one of whom had a history of violent behavior and obvious antipathy toward blacks. The report also had other information—the name of the towing company that had taken away the wrecked motorcycle and the place where the accident had supposedly occurred. With that information, Buchanan then went to inspect the wreck and to take a look for herself at the place McDuffie's fatal accident had happened. What she found instead was evidence that something was amiss. For one thing, the bike didn't look like it had been in an accident so much as it looked like someone had attacked it— all of the glass and plastic, mirrors, light covers, gauges, had been smashed. More surprisingly, when she went to the supposed accident scene, she found that there was nothing that the motorcyclist could have run into—no curbs or streetlights or concrete walls.

The final piece of the story fell into place when Buchanan went to visit the McDuffie family, where she both talked to his survivors and gathered more documentary evidence, all of which added to her suspicions. She learned that McDuffie was a former Marine who had served in the military police and a community volunteer who was on his way up at the insurance company where he worked. Included in the documentary information that she took note of were numerous plaques on a living room wall attesting to the dead man's various achievements in sales.

Although Buchanan felt that her story was needlessly watered down, as an editor was unwilling to include some of her direct observations unless they could be attributed to someone else, it did the trick—prompting one of the police officers to go to his superiors and acknowledge that the accident story was a cover-up. Buchanan's use of all three methods of investigation—documents, observation and talk—was the key to getting the truth out of the shadows and into print. All three were needed, as the original police report was misleading, the quotes from the victim's family could have been easily dismissed and some of the observations were subject to alternative explanations. The McDuffie family later received a large monetary settlement in the case, but for the city of Miami the outcome of this case led to even greater tragedy. The officers who were initially implicated in McDuffie's death were acquitted by an all-white jury in a decision that set off several days of deadly rioting (Buchanan, 1987).

In recent years the nature of the police beat has changed dramatically, as Internet technology has intensified competition among traditional news organizations. Thanks to Web tools that include social media, organized groups of citizen journalists—or even just bystanders—are now in a position to post breaking news online from the scene of a crime or accident. Meanwhile some police departments have established websites to communicate crime news directly to citizens, and many have their own Twitter feeds. This heightened competition may have been one factor in recent examples of inaccurate coverage of breaking crime news, such as occurred with the December 2012 mass shooting at Sandy Hook Elementary in Newtown, Connecticut (Sullivan 2012), and in the aftermath of the 2013 bomb attack at the Boston Marathon (Rieder, 2013).

In today's environment journalists find themselves in a quandary, torn between staying on top of breaking news or trying to focus on larger trends. The bigger trend stories, often based on computerized analysis of crime statistics, can have a large impact in attracting readers and triggering reform efforts, but they often arise out of the nitty-gritty of daily coverage, which means that police reporters will be expected to do both—keep on top of breaking news while also keeping an eye out for investigative possibilities. In either case, reporters will need to familiarize themselves with certain kinds of documents while cultivating sources and also making time to get out on the street where the action is. Police departments often describe themselves as "quasi-military organizations," with individuals performing clearly defined duties within a strict chain of command. This arrangement presents both challenges and opportunities. On one hand, police departments typically generate vast amounts of information in written form, but, on the other hand, finding your way through all that material can be difficult. Reporters often have to rely on sources who can tip them to major crimes or arrests. But developing those sources can be a lengthy process, and negative stories about a police department can sour relationships.

Documents. Because police departments document nearly everything they do, police reporters need to understand what documents are available and how to get hold of them. While practices vary from state to state and city to city, the following description provides an overview of what reporters can expect to find. Historically, there have been two kinds of basic records that journalists rely on, but in the information age, there has been an explosion of other kinds of reports and databases. Let's start with the basics: the blotter and the incident report. To record its activities, a law enforcement agency typically maintains what is known as a police blotter but may also be called by different names, such as a day book or a run sheet. This document is commonly organized in chronological order and lists the activities of the department over the course of a day. While it may list all of the arrests, traffic stops and stranded cat calls that a police force responds to, it may be no more than a series of one-line summaries, showing the time, place and type of events. To find out what is really going on, a police reporter has to gain access to the underlying incident reports, which include names of victims and alleged perpetrators as well as a detailed narrative of what happened. Some departments may make these reports freely available, but others will require a specific request to see a specific report. In addition some departments may withhold parts of a report, or even the entire report, if the release of that information could affect an ongoing investigation.

Two other kinds of documents are also available to reporters and have proven to be extremely useful: recordings or transcripts of emergency calls to 911 and footage from dashboard-mounted cameras in squad cars. Police departments are unlikely to make these available on a routine basis, but they are considered public records that are subject to release under state laws. Such documentation has proven to be especially valuable in investigations of police misconduct.

Another way to use documents on this beat is to compare and contrast what you find in one set of records with what you find somewhere else. Following this approach several news organizations have shown that their local police agencies were misreporting crime statistics and creating a false sense of public safety. For example, *The Detroit News* compared reports from the medical examiner with those from the police and found that over the course of five years the Detroit Police Department misclassified obvious killings so as to lower the reported murder rate (LeDuff and Esparza, 2009). The *Dallas Morning News* took a slightly different approach, comparing police accounts of crimes with the way that they were being classified in reports to the FBI under the Uniform Crime Reporting Program. What the newspaper found was similar—a decline in reported crimes based on changes in reporting but not necessarily in criminal activity (Thompson and Eiserer, 2009). In Milwaukee, a review by the *Journal-Sentinel* using a similar comparison uncovered similar patterns of underreporting of serious crimes (Poston, 2012).

Observation. Police reporters may not get the chance to observe a crime in progress very often, but there are other ways that they can use this skill, sometimes after something happens and sometimes before. Visiting the "scene of the crime" whenever possible is a good idea, since it provides the opportunity both for firsthand inspection of the site and a chance for you to talk to police officers while they are still figuring out what happened—as long as you don't get in the way too much. Even long after a crime scene has been wrapped up, a reporter may find it useful to return, just to check to see how the official account of what happened squares with the physical geometry of the scene. Although based in fact, police reports often have serious shortcomings and are sometimes written with the intent to deceive, academic research has found (Fisher, 1993). Even if there is no intent to deceive, officers are often under severe disadvantages when writing reports, such as time pressures or the need to describe something that happened in the dark, which can lead to distortions.

Another form of observation that is critical on the police beat is done not with the eyes but with the ears. Most police agencies communicate by radio, and it is possible to monitor conversations using a scanner, although newer digital technology sometimes presents challenges. Most newsrooms have a scanner going at all times, and individual reporters may carry portable scanners, or download an app to their cell phone, to stay on top of what is happening. Keeping alert to scanner traffic can tip a reporter off to a major accident or other news event.

While police reporters need to be skeptical about what they hear, they also need to develop a level of trust with their law enforcement sources. One way of doing so is a form of observation: the ride-along. As part of their public outreach efforts, many police departments offer the chance for ordinary citizens to accompany officers on patrol, and it's a good idea for reporters to take advantage of such an opportunity. If a crime happens that requires a police response, you will be in a position to write a firsthand account. But even if the shift is quiet, the experience will allow you to observe police practices and develop a level of understanding that may come in handy at a later date.

Talk. Dealing with sources on the police beat means talking with a wide range of people—victims, criminals and alleged criminals, and law enforcement personnel. In many cases you will be dealing with people who are under stress, so you should be prepared to hear "no comment," or worse, with some frequency. But it's important to be persistent. People who have had a recent interaction with the police often have a need to express their feelings and opinions, whether their underlying emotion is grief, or anger or injustice (or embarrassment). Do not assume that people do not want to talk to you or will not talk to you, even if they are police officers who say they are under strict orders not to talk to the press. Many investigations of police wrongdoing have been prompted by internal whistleblowers who are willing to take a risk because of their own sense of right and wrong. Often the key to get such sources to talk to you is being available. Another important key is demonstrating, through your reporting, a sense of fairness and a commitment to thoroughness and accuracy.

THE WEATHER

Traditionally, weather stories have been regularly recurring accounts of regularly occurring events: the first snow, the hottest day of the year, the fall foliage forecast, the April showers and the May flowers. But in recent years, with heightened fears of climate instability, the weather stories that have gotten the most attention are not about routine events but about extreme ones: hurricanes, blizzards, high winds and flooding. In either case, however, reporters use similar tools and techniques to produce their accounts. Reporting and writing a routine weather story can be good practice for the day when a weather disaster hits.

It may seem like a pretty big leap from a routine weather story to covering a major natural disaster. But by reading some prize-winning coverage, you can see how documents, observation and talk come together to produce powerful journalism. You can also see how learning your way around this beat, before disaster strikes, can ensure that you are following the advice of emergency response experts: Be prepared.

During the afternoon and evening of April 27, 2011, a supercell thunderstorm set off a tornado that travelled for more than 80 miles across Alabama with maximum winds of 190 mph, according to the National Weather Service. At times the tornado was a mile and a half wide, and by the time it was gone roughly 1,500 people were injured and 65 were dead. One of the cities it passed through was Tuscaloosa, the home of the University of Alabama. Adding to the inherent challenges in covering such a large news event was the fact that power outages forced the local paper, the *Tuscaloosa News*, to shift its printing to another publishing facility 50 miles away. The Pulitzer judges cited the paper's use of "social media as well as traditional reporting to provide real-time updates, help locate missing people and produce in-depth print accounts" (Columbia, 2012). The examples that were included by the *News* in its Pulitzer entry provide strong evidence that social media and other technological tools are not so much replacements for traditional reporting methods as they are ways to make the most of those methods.

As with nearly all weather stories, observation is a key part of reporting on a tornado. The accounts in the *News* included descriptions like this:

> Few, if any, houses and buildings remained standing.
>
> Trees and power lines were strewn everywhere. Cars were flipped over, stair-wells were twisted and people were trapped in their homes, calling to first responders for help.
>
> People sifted through the remains of their homes looking for anything they could salvage. (*Tuscaloosa News*, 2011a)

To convey the impact of a major weather event, the story has to be told in terms of specific visual details. Reporters need to get out on the street to gather this kind of information (see Figure 6.1).

The quotes above were published the day after the storm, April 28. But, thanks to Twitter, the paper had already been distributing its observations

FIGURE 6.1 *In the aftermath of severe weather events, like the 2011 tornado that ripped through Tuscaloosa, Alabama, reporters are called upon to describe scenes of devastation. Credit: Jeffrey Henon/U.S. Army Corps of Engineers*

about the damage caused by the tornado. At 5:46 the previous evening reporter Aaron Suttles had tweeted:

> Out surveying damage. It's bad, folks. Tuscaloosa around 15th street and McFarland is gone. Total destruction. CVS gone. 15th wiped out.

At 6: 15 p.m. he added:

> It's much worse than I could ever explain. Trying to tweet pics but towers are down. Hokkaido is gone. Just gone like it never existed.

And then at 6:24, he pushed out this message:

> I don't mean to overstate, but it looks like bombs went off. Nothing left standing. Complete rubble. Cars upside down and caved in. (Suttles, 2011)

Suttles was not the only *News* reporter who was out making observations. One noted the smell of natural gas hanging in the air, presumably from broken mains. Jamon Smith tweeted:

> I'm watching firemen try to dig a girl out of the rubble of my apartments right now. (April 27, 2011)

Talking to human sources is critical in developing a natural disaster story (as it is with routine weather stories). The actual words of people who have experienced a weather event add drama and urgency to a reporter's descriptive prose. The first-day accounts included quotes like these: "It was huge and all you could see was black and it was just spitting trees and things everywhere," and "This is like a nightmare, I just want to wake up" (*Tuscaloosa News*). Reporters also gathered anecdotes to include in their accounts. In one particularly hard-hit neighborhood, Rosedale Court, a distraught family described how four relatives were outside when the tornado came. All were able to get inside, except a 15-year-old nephew. "We told him to come in, but the wind blew the door shut and that was the last time we saw him," one survivor recounted (Smith, April 29, 2011).

Documents form the backbone of many weather stories, as reporters use statistical data to provide context for recent or current conditions. One of the innovations that the *News* used in its tornado coverage was an online, interactive document that it created to help members of the community as well as distant friends and relatives locate missing persons. This tool, based on the Google Docs application, allowed people to post the name, last known location and other potential clues about people who were missing. People who were thought to be missing but had only left town or lost telephone connections were able to use the tool to update their contact information. The list had close to 400 names within 24 hours and ultimately close to 1,600. The paper took the online information and published it in print with free copies going to shelters and emergency locations (*Tuscaloosa News*, 2011b).

When weather conditions become extreme, they often spark investigative follow-up reporting based on documents. For example, Jeremy Finley of
WSMV-TV in Nashville, Tennessee, was intrigued to hear that victims of the
May 2010 floods in that city had thought they were safe from rising waters
based on what they had heard from National Weather Service forecasts, only
to find themselves and their property suddenly inundated. Such comments
led him to request internal documents, including reports and email communications from the weather service and the Army Corps of Engineers. Based
on this documentation, he was able to report that decisions were made to
dump vast amounts of flood water from behind a threatened dam and that
these decisions were not made public in time for residents to react because
of bureaucratic issues, bad data and poor communication. Finley's reporting
led to a congressional hearing as well as internal reforms at the weather service and the Corps (Finley, 2010).

Because of the intensity of the debate over what is often called "global
warming" but might be better characterized as "climate change," you can
expect that even a routine story about a local weather event may be challenged either from the perspective of environmental advocates, for glossing
over long-term threats to the planet, or from that of skeptics, who accuse
you of raising a false alarm or suggesting a false connection between a local
phenomenon and broader ones. The DOT methodology can help in these
circumstances by promoting thorough and balanced coverage and by demonstrating the systematic effort you have made to produce a truthful article.
Connecting the DOT is a more subtle approach to reporting that can be particularly useful when subtle distinctions need to be made, both to increase
understanding by readers and to protect the credibility of journalists.

Careful journalists acknowledge that weather is not climate—no single
local event can definitively be tied to larger global trends. On the other hand,
climate is created from the accumulation of many individual weather events—
stormy periods and still ones, dry spells and wet ones. Thus writing about
climate and weather are connected, and weather news helps shape public
opinion about climate change. News coverage often focuses on the politics of
climate change, including arguments about the causes and the potential solu-
tions, but the focus on conflicting policy positions tends to obscure the degree
to which many people agree on what is happening to the climate.

A Gallup poll released in April 2013, for example, showed that only
15 percent of American adults believe that global warming will never happen and that 54 percent believe that the effects have already begun to be felt
(Saad, 2013). Warnings about a warming planet are often seen as emanat-
ing from a liberal concentration of university- and government-sponsored
scientists who put too much emphasis on theoretical models, but this view
is misleading. Military leaders in the United States, who can scarcely be
described as left-leaning or unpragmatic, have identified global warning as

a top national security threat. "The ice is melting and sea is getting higher," Admiral Samuel J. Locklear III told *The Boston Globe.* "If it goes bad, you could have hundreds of thousands or millions of people displaced and then security will start to crumble pretty quickly" (Bender, 2013).

In the face of such strongly held views, it is somewhat surprising that climate change remains such a contested area. Part of the reason is the standard approach to news gathering, which relies on an effort to balance competing perspectives. This approach may make sense in certain contexts, but it raises the possibility of creating what's been called a false equivalence or a false balance if a position held by a minority of experts in a given field is given equal weight with the dominant or consensus view. Rather than providing competing arguments and leaving it at that, a reporter using the approach outlined in this book would attempt to go further and provide some evaluation of the relative strength of those competing arguments. In the case of climate change, one way to do that is to investigate the amount of peer-reviewed scientific research on a given side of an issue as well as the scientific credentials of those who are advancing one or another argument.

Even the most ardent advocates of the need to take action to limit human influences on global warming will acknowledge that there is a great deal of uncertainty when it comes to climate science, just as there is a great deal of uncertainty in predicting the weather. This kind of uncertainty may make some journalists uncomfortable, since there is a natural tendency to try to tie up news stories into neat packages for easy understanding. But failing to include an acknowledgment of uncertainty in almost any scientific story is misleading. In 2012 the American Meteorological Society presented an award for distinguished journalism to the author of an article who detailed the gaps in current climate science, not because the article debunked global warming but because it demonstrated the complexity of the topic and the areas where more research is needed (Curry, 2012). Unfortunately, one of the areas in which climate science is currently the weakest is in predicting regional or local effects from global changes, which means that a reporter covering a local weather event will need to be careful in how the story is put into context. (See Chapter 8 for a discussion of some of the nuances of science reporting generally.)

Here are some tips for using the DOT methodology in covering the weather:

Documents. When you set out to do a weather story, either a routine one or one based on an extreme event, one of the first places to start is online, with the National Climatic Data Center. There you will find historical information and up-to-the-minute data from land, marine, radar, satellite and balloon observations covering temperature, precipitation, humidity, wind and lightning. Information is available on national, international and regional levels and is broken down by industrial sector, so that you can research weather effects on, for example, agriculture, insurance, tourism or transportation. Because this site is so extensive, a reporter should try to spend some time gaining familiarity with it rather than just trying to use it on deadline. Other data sources are also available online, including local information from the National Weather Service, searchable by city or ZIP code.

Another important kind of documentary source on this topic is scientific research, much of which is government funded and available online. Some science journals, however, can be expensive to access and difficult to locate. One possible aid is an online site called the Journalist's Resource, which is based at Harvard University's Shorenstein Center on Media, Politics and Public Policy. It provides summaries of and, in some cases, links to scholarly research in a variety of areas, including climate change, and can be accessed at http://journalistsresource.org/.

Observation. What a meteorologist calls observations, journalists would call measurements, things like the speed of the wind, the amount of precipitation, the humidity, the temperature. These are, of course, important in a weather story, but reporters will usually want to record the effects, and aftereffects, of these indicators: trees down, or roads closed, or shivering (or sweating) local residents. These weather observations are generally not difficult to make—if a weather event is important enough to make the news, there is usually nothing subtle about it. But some of the general guidelines about observations are good to keep in mind, especially about location. You may have to go to more than one place to record the best available observations to include in an article.

Talk. In stories about the weather, talking to sources may be some of the easiest, or some of the hardest, interviews that you ever do. A story about a pleasant stretch of days or the end of a difficult period like a drought will often bring you in contact with people who are feeling good about their circumstances and happy to talk. On the other hand, a story based on an extreme weather event could bring you in contact with people who have gone through every kind of trauma, from physical injury, to loss of loved ones, to involuntary homelessness.

Dan Grech is a media innovation fellow at Florida International University who has worked as a correspondent at "Marketplace," the *Miami Herald* and "Nightly Business Report." As a radio correspondent, he covered the aftermath of Hurricane Katrina and developed this list of tips for interviewing victims of traumatic events:

- Disaster victimization is about a loss of control. In your interview, try to give a measure of control back to your subject. It can be subtle gestures, such as allowing the person to pick which chair he or she sits in.

- The good news is that people are very resilient. It's not easy to retraumatize someone with the questions you ask.

- You don't have to shy away from conflict or distress in your interview. It may very well be an upsetting interview. Just give your subject permission at the beginning to end the interview at any time.

- Be most cautious when asking about the particular moment that caused the trauma. You may trigger a flashback, in which the person relives the traumatic experience, with the same vividness as the original experience, the same terror and panic.

- When you're talking about the traumatic moment, don't ask, "What did you do?" Instead ask, "What happened to you?" This is a technique to handle the common response of survivor's guilt, the feeling that the victim should have done more to prevent the disaster. Most people don't feel heroic after a disaster. They feel ashamed that they didn't do more.

- Use active-listening techniques, such as reflecting and rephrasing what you're hearing, rather than analyzing or judging. Often active listening is all you need to do to successfully interview a trauma victim. It's upsetting to feel like no one is able to help you. It's more upsetting to feel that no one is listening and no one cares.

- When someone expresses "suicidal ideation"—when he or she talks about wanting to commit suicide—the red flag is when someone has a specific plan and timeline for how he or she plans to do it. This is often cause for a therapist to hospitalize a person. But just talking about wanting to be dead . . . isn't a plan to commit suicide. (Grech, 2011)

OBITUARIES

Traditionally, the obituary page has been the place for very young journalists at the beginning of their careers or very old ones at the end of theirs. What could be worse than being stuck writing about dead people? But a truism that obituary writers learn early on is that they are not writing about death—but rather about life, even if it is a life that has just ended. Obituaries are not the same as news stories about a murder or a fatal car accident. They are separate accounts, detailing the deceased ups and downs, triumphs and disappointments. It is this shift in focus, away from the end of a life to the fullness of that life, that accounts for the fact that many accomplished journalists have found an unexpected amount of fulfillment on the obit desk.

Obituary writers find that they are performing an important public service, and that their articles—rather than ending up on the bottom of a bird cage or in a stack of recyclables—are clipped and preserved as precious family mementos. Obituaries are more than the "first rough draft of history"; in many cases they are history, as they become important source materials for researchers trying to understand particular moments of the past (Nigro, 2011).

Jim Nicholson, a onetime investigative reporter for *The Philadelphia Inquirer* who ultimately spent almost 20 years on that paper's "death beat," found the experience to be transformative, removing the cynicism that had built up in him and replacing it with a more positive view of humankind. He discovered that instead of taking information, often from reluctant sources, he was giving, starting with the giving of recognition to the deceased but then going much further. "I gave the dead person's family my sympathy and then a tangible remembrance for generations unborn," he wrote. "My words gave readers thousands of moments to remember of little lives well lived. Perhaps I even gave them the secrets of how to live one well" (Nicholson, 2006, 86–88).

Obituaries are often written according to a formula, but they leave much room for originality. Part of the formula calls for certain facts to be included: name, age, occupation, military service, professional affiliations, memberships, survivors, burial arrangements and the dates of birth and death. Causes of death, particularly for well-known figures, are typically called for, but obfuscation is sometimes employed in the case of suicide, with phrases like "died unexpectedly" used to avoid going into details. Cancer was once considered such a dread disease that it was omitted as a cause of death and replaced with a term like "after a long illness." Changing public opinion has an effect on obituaries in other ways, as gay relationships as well as tangled family structures from divorces and remarriages are more likely to be included in obituaries than they were even in the recent past.

Many obituaries start by identifying the deceased and bringing into focus some distinctive detail about the person's life. They often end with a kicker anecdote that summarizes or brings into relief a key quality of that person's character. To get that kind of information requires careful and thorough reporting, and the DOT methodology can help guide your efforts. Although many obituaries are written with nothing more than old story clippings and perhaps some outline data from a funeral home, a fully engaging obituary will include much more.

Documents. If your subject was a newsmaker, then the first place to start will be your publication's library of previously published articles. But many fascinating obituaries get written about people who did not make it into the headlines. To get their stories you will need to be more creative with the kinds of documents that you use. Older people who have children or grandchildren may have been the subject of an oral history project, which is a popular assignment for students in high school or junior high school. Another kind of document to consult is the family scrapbook, which in the digital age may take the form of Facebook pages or Instagram posts. Another source for documentation is not any kind of publication but something that may be made out of wood or metal, including plaques, awards or commendations that may be hanging on a wall or perhaps stored in a box.

Observation. If someone is dead, you might think that it would be impossible to include observations about how that person walked or talked in your obituary. With the increasing prevalence of video, that is certainly not true (although a video might be considered more a form of documentation than observation). Observation can also come into play when writing what's called an advance obituary. Major newspapers have long maintained stocks of these prewritten stories just to be ready in case someone of historical significance died without warning. This has led to some awkward moments. At *The New York Times,* for example, obituaries of Bob Hope, Elizabeth Taylor and George McGovern all carried bylines of writers who were already dead (Jaffe, 2012). These obituaries were often based on face-to-face interviews with the subjects, sometimes long before their deaths. In recent years the *Times* has used technology to take the idea of advance obituaries one step further and video-recorded interviews and commentary with people who wanted to have "the last word," a phrase that the paper adopted for this feature.

Talk. Great obituaries depend on great interviews. Depending on the circumstances, it can be very easy or very difficult to get the survivors to talk. A master at eliciting quotes from people, even when they are under great duress, is the radio journalist David Isay, who has produced roughly 70 sound documentaries and since 2003 has headed an ambitious oral history project called StoryCorps, which has recorded more than 30,000 interviews and contributes a weekly segment to National Public Radio's *Morning Edition.* Isay believes one of the great gifts that one human being can give to another is listening and that with a little training and support anyone can become a great listener (2007). In 2008 the StoryCorps began promoting a "National Day of Listening" on the day after Thanksgiving. To assist in the process of encouraging deep conversations, the organization came up with a list of "great questions" and posted them on the Internet. The questions are worth studying for any journalist who is trying to prepare for a difficult interview situation because of the way that they are framed and the way that they mix direct and indirect forms of question, while easing the way for an interviewee to open up.

One section of the list has to do with remembering someone who has died, and it is there that great ideas for obituary questions can be found (StoryCorps, 2013). The questions include:

- What is your most vivid memory of _____?
- Are you comfortable/can you talk about _____'s death? How did _____ die?
- Can you talk about the biggest obstacles _____ overcame in life?
- Did you have any favorite jokes _____ used to tell?
- Is there something about _____ that you think no one else knows?

EXERCISES

1. Make arrangements to inspect the police blotter with a local law enforcement agency and to review a handful of incident reports from a given day. If you are in a place that has overlapping jurisdictions of campus, city and county police agencies, complete this exercise with at least two agencies and compare their policies and procedures for releasing basic information.

2. Arrange for a ride-along with a local police officer. Use this as an opportunity to practice observations (looking both at what goes on inside the squad car and what can be seen happening on the outside) and to practice talking to a source. Try to learn background information about police policies and routines and also see if you can get the officer to describe specific incidents that did or did not make the news.

3. Visit the scene of a crime with a crime report in hand and test it for accuracy. Check the description of the written report against the physical layout that you observe. What were the officer's lines of sight? Were there any obstructions or missing or misplaced structures?

4. How would you cover a major weather event in your community? Pick something that is likely to occur, such as a flood or a blizzard or an extended drought and draw up a reporting plan.

5. Write an obituary for a friend, family member or acquaintance (perhaps a professor?) who is still alive. Make sure that you list the key pieces of information for an obituary, and use the obituary formula lead:

NAME, some colorful, descriptive phrase about the person, died TIME ELEMENT, (usually CAUSE or perhaps PLACE or perhaps HOW). S/HE was AGE.

Consult the StoryCorps question generator (http://storycorps.org/great-questions/question-generator/) to help you formulate your questions.

REFERENCES

Bender, Bryan. "Chief of U.S. Pacific Forces Calls Climate Biggest Worry," *Boston Globe*, March 9, 2013, accessed December 12, 2013, at http://www.bostonglobe.com/news/nation/2013/03/09/admiral-samuel-locklear-commander-pacific-forces-warns-that-climate-change-top-threat/BHdPVCLrWEMxRe9IXJZcHL/story.html.

Buchanan, Edna. *The Corpse Had a Familiar Face: Covering Miami, America's Hottest Beat,* New York: Random House, 1987.

Columbia University. "1986 Winners and Finalists," *The Pulitzer Prizes,* Pulitzer.org, accessed December 11, 2013, at http://www.pulitzer.org/awards/1986.

———. "The 2012 Pulitzer Prize Winners: Breaking News Reporting," April 16, 2012, accessed December 12, 2013, at http://www.pulitzer.org/citation/2012-Breaking-News-Reporting.

Curry, Judith. "The Real Holes in Climate Science," *Climate Etc.,* January 3, 2012, accessed December 12, 2013, at http://judithcurry.com/2012/01/03/the-real-holes-in-climate-science.

Finley, Jeremy. "Official Entry Form 2010 IRE Awards," Investigative Reporters and Editors, December 30, 2010, accessed (with password) December 12, 2013, at http://ire.org/resource-center/stories/24908/.

Fisher, Stanley Z. "Just the Facts, Ma'am: Lying and the Omission of Exculpatory Evidence in Police Reports," *New England Law Review* 28:1, Fall 1993, 1.

Grech, Dan. "Covering Trauma, Surviving Trauma and Gaining New Insight into How To Handle It," *SEJournal* October 15, 2011, accessed December 12, 2013, at http://www.sej.org/publications/sejournal/covering-trauma-surviving-trauma-and-gaining-new-insight.

Isay, Dave. *Listening Is an Act of Love: A Celebration of American Life from the StoryCorps Project,* New York: Penguin Press, 2007.

Jaffe, Harry. "David Rosenbaum's Byline Appears in the 'Times' 6 Years After His Death," Capitol Comment Blog, *The Washingtonian,* October 22, 2012, accessed December 12, 2013, at http://www.washingtonian.com/blogs/capitalcomment/media/david-rosenbaums-byline-appears-in-the-times-6-years-after-his-death.php?utm_source=feedburner&utm_medium=feed&utm_campaign=Feed%3A+washingtonian%2FCapitalCommentBlog+%28Capital+Comment+Blog%29.

LeDuff, Charlie, and Santiago Esparza. "Detroit Police Routinely Underreport Homicides," *The Detroit News,* June 18, 2009, accessed December 12, 2013, at http://www.detroitnews.com/article/20090618/METRO/906180406.

Nicholson, Jim. "The Making of an Obituary Writer—And a Man," *Nieman Reports,* Fall 2006.

Nigro, Carmen. "The Great Obituary Hunt: A Genealogy Research Guide," New York Public Library Blog, November 9, 2011, accessed December 12, 2013, at http://www.nypl.org/blog/2011/11/09/great-obituary-hunt-genealogy-research-guide.

Poston, Ben. "Hundreds of Assault Cases Misreported by Milwaukee Police Department," *Milwaukee Journal Sentinel,* May 22, 2012, accessed December 12, 2013, at http://www.jsonline.com/watchdog/watchdogreports/hundreds-of-assault-cases-misreported-by-milwaukee-police-department-v44ce4p-152862135.html.

Rieder, Rem. "On Boston bombing, media are wrong—again," *USA Today,* April 19, 2013, accessed December 12, 2013, at http://www.usatoday.com/story/money/columnist/rieder/2013/04/18/media-boston-fiasco/2093493/.

Saad, Lydia. "Americans' Concerns About Global Warming on the Rise," Gallup, Inc., April 8, 2013, accessed December 12, 2013, at http://www.gallup.com/poll/161645/americans-concerns-global-warming-rise.aspx.

Smith, Jamon. Twitter post, April 27, 2011, in Columbia, 2012 (Works), accessed December 12, 2013, at http://www.pulitzer.org/files/2012/breaking_news_reporting/08tuscaloosa.pdf.

———. "Authorities Restrict Access to Rosedale Court," *The Tuscaloosa News,* April 29, 2011, in Columbia, 2012 (Works), accessed December 12, 2013, at http://www.pulitzer.org/files/2012/breaking_news_reporting/05tuscaloosa.pdf.

StoryCorps, "Great Questions List," www.storycorps.org, 2013, at http://storycorps.org/record-your-story/great-questions/list/#remembering%20a%20loved%20one.

Sullivan, Margaret. "Errors in Newtown Shootings Coverage Reflect Growing Pressures," *The New York Times,* December 17, 2012, accessed December 12, 2013, at http://publiceditor.blogs.nytimes.com/2012/12/17/errors-in-newtown-shootings-coverage-reflect-growing-pressures/?_r=0.

Suttles, Aaron. Twitter posts, April 27, 2011, in Columbia, 2012 (Works), accessed December 12, 2013, at http://www.pulitzer.org/files/2012/breaking_news_reporting/08tuscaloosa.pdf.

Thompson, Steve, and Tanya Eiserer. "Experts: Dallas Undercount of Assaults Builds 'Artificial Image,'" *Dallas Morning News,* December 15, 2009, accessed December 12, 2013, at http://www.dallasnews.com/news/community-news/dallas/headlines/20091214-Experts-Dallas-undercount-of-assaults-6330.ece.

Tuscaloosa News, "Survivors Crawl from the Rubble," April 28, 2011a, 1A.

———. "People Locator," April 28, 2011b, in Columbia, 2012 (Works), accessed December 12, 2013, at http://www.pulitzer.org/files/2012/breaking_news_reporting/07tuscaloosa.pdf.

CHAPTER 7

The Journalistic Core

This chapter addresses three beats that are central to a newspaper's role in promoting accountability in government: city hall, the statehouse and local courts. Many routine governmental actions are boring, and there's little to be done about that. But it's also the case that controversy, and wrongdoing, can often be found beneath, or behind, routine and well-established practices. This chapter begins with an overview of the history and current state of government reporting, sometimes called public affairs reporting. It then examines the ways that major stories have been developed in this area. The focus is on local government, but the same principles can be seen at work on the national level. Because government actions nearly always generate records, a key area of emphasis is documents. But personal observation and talking with officials and citizens also come into play.

News organizations in the 21st century publish stories on many topics, and journalists could find themselves covering anything from extreme sports to eyeglass fashion and from videogames to vacation hotspots. But articles on these kinds of subjects, even if reflecting solid journalistic technique and attracting avid readers, are not the kind of reports that motivated the framers of the Constitution to include extensive protection for the news media in that document, prohibiting Congress from taking action to interfere with the freedom of the press. The special standing of journalism in the United States as a constitutionally protected activity is based on the idea that vigorous, independent reporting is needed as a check on government and to help promote a free society. For this reason, the core of journalistic activity is reporting on government actions and decisions.

Just as government is divided into three branches, the core journalism beats are those that focus on the executive, legislative and judicial arms of government. This chapter examines these branches at the state and local level, although the same concepts and methodologies apply for the federal government. For local news organizations, the three key areas of attention are known as city hall, the statehouse and courts. The first two of these span both legislative and executive activities, at the city and state level, respectively. Unlike the federal government, local and state governments are more compact and interconnected, and local reporters may be expected to cover both of these branches. Customs vary from jurisdiction to jurisdiction, with some executives holding a dominant position while legislative power may be more significant in others. Reporters divide their attention depending on individual circumstances and the relative power of either branch, although in general executives, such as mayors, city managers and county administrators, tend to get more attention at the city or county level. Each state also has its own system of courts, the organization of which varies by jurisdiction. Some states have local courts established at the county level, while others have courts—often with limited functions—at the municipal level.

As a report from the Federal Communications Commission noted, the starting point for most discussions of the relationship between government and the press in the United States, and the most famous quote on the topic, comes from Thomas Jefferson: "Were it left to me to decide whether we should have a government without newspapers, or newspapers without a government, I should not hesitate a moment to prefer the latter" (Waldman, 2011, 8). In this case, however, Jefferson was not arguing for an aggressive press focused on government accountability. Instead he was emphasizing the flip side of the equation, namely the role of the press in creating an informed citizenry by providing information related to policy and public affairs. Jefferson believed that Shays' Rebellion, a relatively short-lived but violent episode in the years after the American Revolution, could have been headed off if its supporters had better information (Waldman, 2011).

In today's hyper-partisan environment, in which many press reports of whichever party is in power seem to be critical, it's easy to forget that public affairs reporting is not necessarily adversarial. Very often government officials turn to the press as a way of explaining emerging policies and initiatives, and political scientists have come to view the press as holding a key, if sometimes ill-defined, role in governance (Cook, 1998). A report from the Knight Commission on the Information Needs of Communities in a Democracy described journalists as intermediaries in the realm of public affairs. The commission said:

> Access to news and information is critical to democracy. Journalists serve as watchdogs over public officials and institutions, as well as over the private and corporate sector. They provide information for citizens to run their lives, their communities and their country. News organizations also foster civic understanding, engagement and cohesion. (Knight Commission, 2009, 3)

In the Internet era most government entities have some form of Web presence and make certain kinds of information available online. In theory this information is available to any citizen who wants to take the time to acquire it. But such citizens face two problems. The first is the matter of time, since there can often be an almost overwhelming amount of information available on a government site. The second is a matter of context, since government information is often presented in a way that can obscure its significance because it is not presented as a part of, or perhaps a deviation from, a larger pattern. Reporters help to solve these problems for citizens through their deep knowledge of government and their ability to make connections between seemingly discrete pieces of news.

In recent years, however, the number of journalists working in the area of local public affairs reporting has dropped precipitously. The FCC report included these datapoints (Waldman, 2011):

- A study by Pew Research Center's Project for Excellence in Journalism found that in one major city the leading newspaper published in 2009 a third few stories than it did a decade earlier and 73 percent fewer compared to 1991. The paper, *The Baltimore Sun,* covered one major story, on state budget cuts, with only one seventh as many articles as it did in 1991, when a similar round of belt-tightening occurred.

- The *American Journalism Review* reported that in one five-year stretch, 2003 to 2008, the number of statehouse reporters across the country fell by a third with much steeper declines in some individual states.

- From 2003 to 2010 an organization of journalists who specialize in depth reporting, Investigative Reporters and Editors, lost about a quarter of its members.

- Over a longer period of time, 1984 to 2010, the number of entries in the Pulitzer Prize public service category fell 43 percent.

The effects of these declines are measurable. One study, published as a working paper by the National Bureau of Economic Research (NBER), showed that elected officials with less press coverage work less hard for their constituents and are more likely to vote on purely partisan lines (Snyder and Strömberg, 2008). Another NBER study concluded that when news coverage declines fewer candidates stand for office and voter turnout falls (Schulhofer-Wohl and Garrido, 2009). David Simon, a onetime newspaper reporter who went on to write books and television scripts and is perhaps best known as the creator of *The Wire,* was even more direct in his assessment of the situation: "You know, the next 10 or 15 years in this country are going to be a halcyon era for state and local political corruption," he testified at a 2009 hearing in the U.S. Senate. "It is going to be one of the great times to be a corrupt politician, all right?" (Simon, 2009).

Simon's view is certainly one way of looking at the situation. But another is that the recent decline in local news coverage, which shows no sign of recovering anytime soon, has also created a great opportunity for enterprising reporters, whether working for an established news organization, contributing to an alternative news site or operating as freelancers. There are a lot of great stories that are going uncovered, and they are just waiting for someone to find them. Reporters who know where to find the documents and make the observations and how to talk to sources are likely to be well rewarded for their efforts.

CITY HALL

City hall is both a physical and a metaphorical construct. In most places, city hall (or the town hall or the county administration building) holds the offices of key officials, provides meeting space for decision-making bodies and houses many of the records related to the community. It is also the center of local bureaucratic power whose decisions and policies hold great sway. As the old saying goes, "you can't fight city hall," meaning that it is impossible to go against the insiders who set the rules. But it is precisely because of this extensive, and often inflexible, control over a broad range of activities that city hall is such an important focus for reporting.

At city hall decisions are made, and sometimes reconsidered, on matters that affect citizens' homes and cars and pocketbooks. For example, city hall sets the rules, and sometimes the prices, on garbage removal. Do you want to put an addition on your house or put up a fence around your yard? Chances are you will need a permit from city hall. The treatment and testing of the water that comes out of your tap is overseen from city hall. At city hall someone, or perhaps a larger group, will decide where to restrict parking and how stringently to enforce the regulations. How about local speed traps? Decisions about where and when to set them up are also made at city hall. Should a developer get the chance to tear down a handsome old building and replace it with some drab design? City hall is where the dispute will be decided. How much money does the community need to raise from residents through property taxes, and how should that money be spent? Those budget decisions, again, belong to city hall. The local library, parks and pools, sewers, buses, streetlights and fire trucks all come under the control of city hall.

Reporters who work the city hall beat are likely to have their hands full covering routine stories as well as the predictable debates over fees and taxes and spending that come up on an annual cycle. But by carving out some time to look more closely at specific matters, journalists can often discover that there are important stories to be found underneath seemingly routine or longstanding practices. For example, one thing that citizens often discover they can't fight city hall over is a traffic ticket, but two reporters at *The Baltimore Sun* uncovered systematic flaws in the city's automated speed camera program, which is used to issue citations for driving faster than the posted limit (Calvert and Broadwater, 2012).

When the *Sun* story appeared, in November 2012, the city's speed camera operation had grown to be one of the largest in the country with an annual take approaching $20 million. But the *Sun*'s review revealed that thousands of tickets had been withdrawn and that cases were being routinely thrown out of court because of obvious flaws in the camera system and the evidence it was producing. Although officials initially defended the camera system, a few months later they decided to replace all of the cameras that had been installed around the city.

Because "city hall" is such a broad term, covering both executive and legislative functions, it's important for reporters to start by studying an organizational chart, which can be used as a road map to sources, records and stories. Local governments are typically headed by an administrator in charge of operations, who may be an elected mayor (or county executive) or who may be an appointed official, with a title like "city manager." Typically, this administrator will in turn supervise the major operating departments of the municipality, including the units that collect the trash, run the parks, pay the bills, collect the taxes, operate the buses and repair the streets. The fire and police chiefs typically report to the mayor on paper, but they often operate autonomously.

The activities listed above are all executive functions, meaning they involve carrying out policies or decisions that are made in a legislative context. The legislative responsibilities of local government belong to an elected body, which may be known as a city council or by other names, such as board of supervisors or board of aldermen. In larger cities these councils may form into subcommittees to handle specific topics, as one would find in the U.S. Congress. But in most local governments, the city council or board operates as a single unit. It is not uncommon, however, to find a whole series of satellite bodies that provide input to the city council and that may even be required to make preliminary recommendations on specific topics. These bodies, which are typically made up of citizens who have been appointed to their roles, are set up to consider such things as zoning and land use decisions and fee structures and policies for local parks. They may also provide oversight for public safety operations, such as police, fire and ambulance services. One of the reasons that reporters want to keep an eye on these bodies, even if they have only an advisory role, is that issues and controversies will often surface there first, before moving on to consideration by the city council or county board.

There is a natural rhythm to covering city hall, because city halls tend to operate on a cyclical basis. The most important of the annual cycles is tied to the adoption of budgets for long-term "capital" projects and for shorter-term operational spending. A spending budget is typically adopted once a year, usually as part of the same process that sets tax rates and fees for various city services. The budget proposal is put together by the executive staff and then presented to the legislative body for review. Budget decisions are arguably the most important ones that city councils make, but they aren't the only ones. City councils have an ongoing meeting schedule throughout the year. Depending on the size of the community, such meetings may occur once a week, every other week or once a month.

Documents. Local governments develop their own, idiosyncratic ways of doing things, and it isn't always easy to see what they are up to. But they also generate pages and pages of documents that can provide great insights into your local government and your local community. Some of the documents are easily accessible—as some communities even put them in the local library—while others will require a formal request. But in either case, you are likely to find that a good way to start covering city hall is to start asking for records and reports. Here are some possibilities.

Compensation, including overtime. Salaries of government officials are public records, and citizens have a right to know how much officials are making and whether salaries are in line with those of other local employers. Some departments, particularly the police, often generate large amounts of overtime, which may be a sign of inefficiency or abuse.

Complaints and settlements. City workers, including police officers, regularly spark criticism from citizens, who may lodge relatively minor complaints of rudeness to more serious charges of incompetence or even illegal behavior. You can ask to look at these records, which would also encompass cases of careless driving by city workers that led to accidents or injuries.

Land use and planning documents. Local governments rely extensively on their ability to levy taxes on real estate, and the value of that real estate is determined to a large degree by how it's used: for homes, industries, businesses or some nonprofit activity, like a nursing home or a university. Learning how your local government designates different areas for different kinds of activity, now and in the future, can alert you to significant trends and acquaint you with key behind-the-scenes players, since influential property owners and developers often wield significant power in local decisions.

Observation. There is no substitute for showing up at public sessions of local boards and councils. This may not always be convenient from a scheduling standpoint, and often these sessions, which are usually bound by a set of parliamentary rules of order, can drag on. But going to meetings, seeing and being seen, is an important way to identify potential sources and to learn about issues while they may still be in preliminary stages of development. Reporters cannot rely on published agendas to tell them what a city council or subcommittee is deciding because the language used in meeting agendas can be vague and general, obscuring what is actually under consideration.

Just keeping your eyes open in your community can also be a great way to get stories. A number of news organizations around the country have conducted investigations into traffic cameras, and one thing that spurred their interest was simply seeing that more and more were being installed. The NBC affiliate in Hartford, Connecticut, sent a camera crew to city hall to investigate reports of leaking water and general disrepair. That might have been a story in itself, but once they got there the crew spotted boxes and boxes of city records, including personal and financial information relating to individual citizens, in unsecured rooms. The story that aired, and that led the city to clean up its act, focused on the potential invasion of privacy that the city was inviting by leaving documents lying around (Kuriakose, 2012).

Talk. After you get a city/county staff directory, which should be one of the first documents you obtain, you can start identifying the official sources you will need to develop. In general, you will find that elected officials, who need to go in front of the voters on a regular basis, are more likely to take your phone calls and talk with you than appointed officials. At the same time, at the city level elected officials are very often part-timers, who do not have the time to immerse themselves in the details of the issues they decide. As a result, the city staff, made up of full-time employees, often has deeper knowledge, which they can use to influence the outcome of council deliberations. While in some government organizations the directors of individual units or offices may insist that they are the only ones who can talk to the press, it is often people lower down in the ranks who do the work and know the details. You should try to get to know them as well.

Try to avoid getting caught up too much in insider stories that only matter to people who work in city hall. One way to do this is to make sure that you are talking to individual citizens as much as possible. In many communities, there are people or groups with a particular interest in good government and a practice of attending meetings and following the minutia of government business. Examples may include retirees who are looking for something to do or volunteer organizations like the League of Women Voters. They can be extremely useful resources, especially in providing historical context, and you should seek them out. You may also notice that there are individuals or groups that follow particular issues. While they may not attend every council meeting, they can be good sources in their particular areas of interest.

STATEHOUSE

Like city hall, the statehouse is a real place as well as a term that is used as shorthand to describe a beat, in this case the one that takes in the entirety of a state's government, encompassing both executive and legislative functions. In the early years of the 21st century, a paradoxical development has occurred—state governments have become more significant as sources of news while established news organizations have reduced their staffing resources, which means that a great deal of news is going uncovered.

State governments typically engage in a broader range of activities than do local governments, with units involved in environmental protection, higher education, facilities for the elderly and the mentally ill, rail and water transportation, tourism promotion, financial regulation and emergency response management as well as the basic health, police and infrastructure functions that local governments have. State governments even have military responsibilities through their local National Guards. In many cases it falls to the states to carry out national policies established in Congress, but individual states have leeway in how they implement some programs and have developed very different approaches in certain areas.

Statehouse reporting is different from local government reporting for a couple of structural reasons. First of all, most states, all except Nebraska, have a lower and upper house that make up their legislatures. This adds to the complexity of the legislative process, and from a reporter's perspective, provides more entry points into stories as well as the potential for more sources to talk to and controversies to write about. Unlike city councils, which function year-round, and Congress, which functions year-round except for certain extended breaks, many state legislative bodies are in session for only part of the year. In those states a certain part of the year, from six weeks to three months in length, is filled with activity as bills are introduced, reviewed and voted either up or down.

Although states have individual wrinkles and idiosyncrasies, they also have certain things in common, particularly with neighboring states. As a result, statehouse reporting is not merely about looking at policies or decisions in isolation. For example, there are good stories to be found by comparing your state's policies and recent performance in a particular area, such as economic development or environmental enforcement, with those of nearby states. Individual states are sometimes used as test beds for policy innovations that are later adopted on a national scale, or, as is the case with national health care reform, states can choose to opt out of certain parts of the program or implement them in different ways.

Another reason why the statehouse is worth keeping a close eye on is that in recent years a statehouse has been the launching pad for national political careers of both Republican and Democratic presidents, including Jimmy Carter, Ronald Reagan, Bill Clinton and George W. Bush. In many local governments, candidates run for office on a nonpartisan basis, but state governments are fully politicized, creating another category of coverage as political parties maneuver for advantage and individual legislators decide whether to cross party lines on particular votes. National interest groups have realized that one way around the gridlock in Washington is to push for changes at the state level, a recognition that has brought more money and lobbying activity to the state level. Running for state office is expensive, and candidates are required to fill reports on donations and expenses of their campaigns, reports that can often yield stories about the dynamics of policy-making in the state capital.

Although the intensity of coverage in this area has dropped in recent years, you may find some new forms of competition in your state capital as nonprofit news organizations have stepped in to fill the void. Some of these are made up of journalists who operate with the independence and disinterest that are traditionally seen as the hallmarks of credible news coverage. Others, however, are funded by organizations with clear policy objectives and are perhaps more similar to the partisan newspapers of the 19th century. In any case, there is little question that the volume of state reporting has declined and that there are stories going uncovered.

A good example of how the DOT tools can be used at the state level can be found in a series of broadcasts aired by Indianapolis station WTHR from March through November 2010. The series was called "Reality check: Where are the jobs?" (WTHR, 2010) and examined claims by the Indiana Economic Development Corp. (IEDC) that it had created 100,000 jobs and attracted billions of dollars of investments to the state. As it turned out, however, many of those jobs, up to 40 percent of them, never materialized. To make matters worse, the station's investigative team found the agency was taking credit for creating jobs at facilities that were never built or never used. In some cases companies that had received tax credits to hire workers were actually laying off workers.

The story got started, as these kinds of stories often do, with a document. In this case it was a press release from the IEDC claiming to have created 85,000 new jobs over four years—even while the state's unemployment rate continued to climb to record levels. When the journalists couldn't get detailed information about these supposed jobs, they launched their investigation. Eventually they would file more than 100 public records requests and base their story on thousands of pages of documents, including IEDC annual reports, commitment letters, incentive agreements and tax abatement contracts.

Observation helped provide some of the most dramatic information that the journalists uncovered. They traveled more than 8,000 miles around the state to see for themselves, and their viewers, what had become of the promised job sites. What they found, instead, included empty fields and padlocked factories that were being described to state taxpayers as business locations.

This kind of investigation does not get done without the contributions of many human sources. In its description of the project that was submitted as part of the annual awards competition of Investigative Reporters and Editors, the station noted that "WTHR interviewed current and former employees at IEDC; local economic development managers around the state; executives, HR staff, and current and former workers at companies listed as 'economic successes'; economists and business analysts working for private firms and Indiana universities; economic development leaders from other states; and Indiana's governor" (Segall, 2010). But at the core of the story were the individual workers who were affected, such as Gary Kirk, a 30-year employee at a company called Columbus Components, where he was laid off a few months after the state announced an expansion that was supposed to mean 125 new jobs. The state called the company a success story, but Kirk didn't see it that way. He told the TV station, "For a lot of people, they worked there all their life, then there was no more job there, so I don't know how they can consider that a success story" (WTHR).

Documents. State governments are sprawling entities that produce a vast range of public documents, everything from agency annual reports to weekly newsletters, blog posts and databases of inspections and enforcement actions. They also generate an enormous amount of internal records, which are not routinely made public but are typically subject to formal records requests according to individual state law. This category includes contract information with companies that do business with a state, calendars and emails of officials, and complaints filed by consumers against businesses and professionals who are licensed by the state.

In addition to state-specific information, reporters can turn to information sources that can help them spot national or regional trends that may turn into stories in their states. An excellent example of this is the Stateline news service operated by the Pew Charitable Trusts, which generates its own original reporting as well as tracks reporting by other news organizations. Search tools allow for finding stories either by individual state or by topic. Other national organizations that can provide useful background information include associations of various kinds of state officials, including governors (National Governors Association), legislators (National Conference of State Legislators) and commissioners of insurance, one of the few major industries that is regulated at the state level (National Association of Insurance Commissioners).

Observation. As WTHR's missing jobs investigation demonstrates, there is no substitute for getting out in the field to check official statements against reality. But state coverage does pose major challenges in doing so simply because of the geographic expanse of so many states. A further complicating factor is that some state capitols are in locations that are remote from major population centers, a factor that academic researchers recently linked to higher levels of corruption (Campante and Do, 2013). Reporters covering state government need to take steps to deal with this situation. One is simply to make time to get out and see how state policy decisions and budgets are having an effect around the state. The other is to use technological tools as much as possible. For example, many states have started cable channels to provide coverage of legislative activity, which can allow reporters to keep

FIGURE 7.1   *Reporter Lucy Morgan. Credit: State Archives of Florida, Florida Memory,* *http://floridamemory.com/items/show/13931*

tabs even if they are not physically present. Lucy Morgan (see Figure 7.1), who was recognized as one of the best statehouse reporters in the country during her long career with what is now called the *Tampa Bay Times,* once had to rely on television coverage of the Florida legislature after breaking an ankle in a fall and finding herself confined to a hospital bed. It was from this vantage point that she noticed a legislator withdrawing a controversial bill, an observation that she passed on to another reporter who turned it into a scoop for their paper (*Columbia Journalism Review,* 2000).

Talk. As with any beat, developing sources for statehouse coverage is an ongoing process that entails finding knowledgeable, reliable informants at many levels and in many different places. Ordinary citizens, experienced lobbyists, mid-level bureaucrats—all of them can provide useful perspectives and need to be cultivated. Students are sometimes surprised to learn that busy state officials will take time out to talk with them and walk them through complicated issues. It's important not to be intimidated by titles or to get put off if phone calls or emails do not draw an immediate response. State government does have its rhythms, and sometimes sources are overwhelmed at a given moment with specific tasks. That doesn't mean officials won't be available to talk at a later date.

James B. Stewart, the Pulitzer Prize winner and best-selling author, warns that a too common problem among reporters, particularly novice ones, is a belief that sources won't want to talk to them. But his experience shows that it's often more surprising what sources will say than what they won't say. "I believe that nothing is so important in my own efforts to get people to reveal information than a willingness to listen without judging," he says. He has come to the conclusion that many people are starved for the attention of a good listener, and, "as a result, are lonely. They are waiting for you to call" (Stewart, 1998, 89). George Skelton, a political columnist for the *Los Angeles Times,* believes that a lot of his success in getting sources to talk to him is based on his approach to his sources, which includes a measure of sympathy for elected officials. "I basically have respect for politicians," he said. "It's not that I'm not skeptical, but instead of trying to trick them into giving a good quote, I try to let them talk and find out what they are really thinking" (*Columbia Journalism Review,* 2000, 50).

COURTHOUSE

Covering the courthouse is often a matter of paradox. From time to time, there will be the "trial of the century" kind of case, a celebrity murder or the prosecution of a massive drug ring. But that's not the true nature of legal reporting, which mostly consists of routine coverage, dozens and dozens of cases every day involving nothing more unusual than a divorce or a charge of driving while intoxicated. Then there's the matter of openness. In many ways what happens in a court case is transparent—documents are filed in the clerk's office and are available for inspection while arguments are heard and testimony is taken in open court. At the same time, however, there is much maneuvering that reporters don't have access to, in the judge's offices or sometimes at the front of the courtroom, in what are called "bench conferences" where the lawyers and judges talk in whispers to decide procedural matters. Court reporting is its own journalistic specialty that requires learning a vocabulary and a set of rules to understand what is going on. For good reason, major news organizations have reporters who are assigned to this area full time. But reporters on almost any beat may find themselves taking a trip to the courthouse, which is the place where many disputes in society are settled, matters involving such disparate topics as sports contracts, educational issues, social policy, medical malpractice and consumer marketing.

Because the volume of cases moving through the court system is so great, it should not be surprising that many newsworthy cases get overlooked. In a college town, for example, it might not be hard to find cases in which a star athlete is getting special treatment on criminal charges or in which a controversial professor is forced to make amends for shoplifting. Perhaps the local university has become a frequent plaintiff, suing former students for unpaid tuition bills. Once found, such cases are usually easy to report because of the way courts operate. The substance of cases is reduced to writing in documents that are filed in the clerk's office with the key points emphasized. In addition, court filings include names and contact information for the attorneys involved, which makes it easy to track down knowledgeable sources.

The courthouse is a good place to find stories about the local community, but journalists should not overlook reporting on the legal system itself. To a certain degree it is a world of its own, sometimes run for the convenience of the well-connected. In some places a lack of adequate oversight has allowed for irregularities to become commonplace, even to the point of outright corruption. In 1994, for example, the *Providence Journal-Bulletin* won a Pulitzer for investigative reporting based on its examination of questionable spending and cronyism in the Rhode Island Supreme Court (Columbia), articles that led to the resignation and conviction of the chief justice in that state (Formanek, 1993). In 2006 *The Seattle Times* published a series of articles demonstrating that local judges were regularly sealing records that should have been public. This may seem like just a minor inconvenience, but the paper argued that this information needed to be public because the "sealed records hold secrets of potential dangers in our medicine cabinets and refrigerators; of molesters in our day-care centers, schools and churches; of unethical lawyers, negligent doctors, dangerous dentists; of missteps by local and state agencies; of misconduct by publicly traded companies into which people sink their savings" (Armstrong, Mayo, and Miletich, 2006). It cost the paper more than $200,000 in legal bills to get court records unsealed (Armstrong, 2013).

There is often an uneasy relationship between journalists and lawyers, who come to depend on each other while also distrusting each other. Lawyers sometimes find that they can gain advantage in the courtroom, or at least inflict damage on the clients on the other side, by leaking information to the press or pointing out unflattering information that appears in court files. Reporters know that lawyers, even the ones who don't venture onto the ethically dubious territory of leaking nonpublic information, can be very helpful in explaining technical details of a case or the nuances of legal issues that are under review. While many journalists see the First Amendment as an absolute endorsement of the "people's right to know," there is another Constitutional amendment, the Sixth, that guarantees a fair trial before an impartial jury. Particularly in high profile cases that draw extensive coverage, these two competing impulses, one that argues for wide dissemination of information and the other for a controlled process of inquiry, come into conflict.

Documents. The starting point for courts coverage is the "docket sheet," which is a listing of all the actions that have been taken in a case. The docket is kept in the office of the clerk of the court. In some places you may need to go to the clerk's office to see it, but sometimes you can view it online. The docket sheet functions as a table of contents, or road map, of a case, listing in chronological order things like the original pleading, counter-claims, evidence in the form of depositions (witness testimony recorded under oath) or written answers to questions (called interrogatories), motions and orders issued by the judge. The docket will also list the names of the parties involved, including attorneys and the judge to whom the case has been assigned. With some exceptions, such as for cases involving juveniles, items that are listed on the docket are available for public inspection.

Court documents are considered to be "privileged," meaning that the information found there cannot be used as the basis of a successful defamation claim. As a practical matter, this means journalists can use these documents as the basis for reporting without having to verify their accuracy or veracity independently.

In some cases documents can provide the background details necessary to tell a current story. Because filings are often made in advance of an actual trial, they can be used as a way to preview future developments. For example, in May 2013 *The New York Times* reported on the case of a wealthy heiress who spent the last two decades of her life living in a hospital, where, according to her relatives, she had been tricked into making millions of dollars of donations. While this story is newsworthy in itself, it is also an illustration of an added advantage of court documents, the way that they can illuminate a larger issue. As the paper wrote, "The case is scheduled for trial in September, but until then, the documents provide a rare look at the inner workings of a nonprofit hospital's fund-raising operation" (Hartocollis, 2013). In other words, the documents not only tell the story of this particular case, but also provide some insights into operations that are conducted on a broader scale.

Court documents can also be used to learn about topics that are incidental, or even largely unrelated, to the dispute at hand. Divorce lawyers, for example, may attempt to gain leverage for their clients by including in the court record documents detailing the assets or the business dealings of the soon-to-be ex-spouse. Such records can easily be more noteworthy than the divorce itself. Court records can also be used to research political candidates or other newsmakers since they will reveal such things as traffic violations or involvement in previous litigation.

Other kinds of documentary research also come into play in legal coverage. For example, biographical and educational information about judges and lawyers might be helpful in providing a clearer picture to readers about the dynamics of a particular case. Some of this may be available through a simple Web search, but there is also a firm, Martindale-Hubbell, that maintains a detailed database about lawyers that can be accessed over the Internet (http://www.martindale.com/).

The trial court is the place where judicial decisions are first made, but cases can continue on appeal to other levels. Rulings in appeals cases are available through subscription databases, such as LexisNexis, and in many states can also be found on government websites.

Observation. In covering the courts, an obvious place to make observations is within the context of a trial, where judges, lawyers, plaintiffs, defendants, witnesses and courtroom visitors may influence the outcome of a case through their deportment and behavior. Veteran court reporters, however, are aware that the courtroom is sometimes like a theatrical stage, and so statements and actions that occur in court cannot always be taken at face value. What appears to be harsh questioning of a lawyer by a judge, for example, may not indicate actual hostility but rather an effort to get the lawyer to make a stronger argument.

In some instances a judge will decide that the jury needs to inspect something, perhaps a wrecked car, that is crucial to the case and take the proceedings outside of the courtroom. But even if this does not happen, reporters should not be shy about making direct observations on their own about places or people who figure in a case.

Talk. Lawyers and judges are often sensitive to the perception that cases are being tried in the media as opposed to in the courtroom, and they often go to some length to discourage reporters from asking questions, even imposing in some cases gag orders, which prevent parties to a case from talking to the press (or at least from being quoted by name in the press). But leaks are not at all uncommon in court cases, and in some states judges must run for office and so may feel inclined to maintain cordial relationships with reporters. It never hurts to ask to speak to a judge or a lawyer, although you shouldn't be surprised to have your request brushed off.

Plaintiffs, defendants, witnesses and jurors are all potentially useful sources, but court cases always involve some degree of conflict and tensions can run high among those involved. In some cases, the identities of jurors are placed under seal, and limitations have been imposed on how aggressively journalists can seek information from a juror, even after a trial has concluded. The Reporters Committee for Freedom of the Press has developed a guide to these and related issues, which is available through its website (http://www.rcfp.org/).

Reporters should not be put off by the trappings and rituals of the legal system to the extent that they do not raise legitimate questions. While getting parties to a case to talk can be difficult, there are also circumstances under which certain parties will be willing, and even eager, to talk to reporters. In civil cases that have dragged on for a long time, parties, and their lawyers, may decide that talking to the press is to their advantage. Jurors in long-running, high profile cases may find it cathartic to talk about their experiences or may feel a need to justify or explain their decisions. You'll never find out if you don't ask.

EXERCISES

1. Cover a meeting of your local city council or board of supervisors. Begin with documents, by obtaining a copy of the agenda for the meeting. In addition to the summary agenda, you should be sure to get whatever material is distributed to individual members of the council (or board). Whereas the agenda listings will give you some indication of the topic to be discussed, the backup material is usually much more detailed and often contains key details that may or may not be discussed at the meeting. When you go to the meeting, spend some time observing the key players, which will include both the elected members as well as the staffers. Finally, take advantage of the fact that you will have access to elected officials, who may not always be good at returning phone calls. After the meeting or during breaks, you should be able to approach them, introduce yourself and ask questions.

2. Pick a state agency that has operations in your community and start to research it using documents, observation and talk. For documents, start with the agency's website and see if it reports statistics that might be checked for trends. Also, look to see if it publishes an annual report summarizing recent accomplishments. Next, look to see if there are any reports from your state's legislative audit bureau that raise questions and suggest potential problem areas. Next, plan a visit to its offices. As a public agency, it should be ready to deal with walk-in members of the public, although if it's a prison or a hospital, there may be restrictions. Finally, identify some potential sources, perhaps the head of the local office or the official press contact. Develop a list of three to five story ideas based on this preliminary research.

3. For this assignment you will pick a current (with the latest development no more than 30 days ago) court case that was filed in the local courthouse. If your state has an online database of court filings, start there. Otherwise you may have to make a trip to the clerk's office to review recent filings. Once you have identified a case that looks interesting, obtain at least one page of documents from the case from the clerk's office. Write a one-paragraph summary of the case.

4. To see how documents are handled in different court systems, go online and create an account with PACER, the federal system that provides Public Access to Court Electronic Records. Find a case that

looks interesting and download the docket sheet and perhaps the original pleading. (As long as you do not ask for an excessive number of pages of documents, you will not be billed. Check the website for the current billing policy.) Write a one-paragraph summary of what you have found.

REFERENCES

Armstrong, Ken. "Let the Readers Know: How Journalists and the Public Can Work Together," *Nieman Reports,* Spring 2013, accessed December 14, 2013, at http://nieman.harvard.edu/reportsitem.aspx?id=102913.

Armstrong, Ken, Justin Mayo, and Steven Miletich. "The Cases Your Judges Are Hiding From You," *The Seattle Times,* March 5, 2006, accessed December 14, 2013, at http://seattletimes.com/html/localnews/2002845009_seal05m.html.

Calvert, Scott, and Luke Broadwater. "City's Lucrative Speed Camera Program Dogged by Problems," *The Baltimore Sun,* November 18, 2012, A1.

Campante, Filipe R., and Quoc-Anh Do. "Isolated Capital Cities, Accountability and Corruption: Evidence from US States," National Bureau of Economic Research Working Paper 19027, May 2013, accessed December 14, 2013, at http://www.nber.org/papers/w19027.

Columbia Journalism Review. "Sages of the Statehouse," July/August 2000.

Columbia University, "Investigative Reporting," *The Pulitzer Prizes,* accessed December 14, 2013, at http://www.pulitzer.org/bycat/Investigative-Reporting.

Cook, Timothy E. *Governing with the News: The News Media as a Political Institution,* Chicago: University of Chicago Press, 1998.

Formanek, Jr., Ray. "Former RI Chief Justice Convicted on Misdemeanor Ethics Counts," The Associated Press, November 29, 1993, accessed December 14, 2013, at http://www.apnewsarchive.com/1993/Former-RI-Chief-Justice-Convicted-On-Misdemeanor-Ethics-Counts/id-c0dad4ddcdbb94bd93d58197d3e918fd.

Hartocollis, Anemona. "Hospital Caring for an Heiress Pressed Her to Give Lavishly," *The New York Times,* May 29, 2013, accessed December 14, 2013, at http://www.nytimes.com/2013/05/30/nyregion/hospital-caring-for-an-heiress-pressed-her-to-give-lavishly.html?pagewanted=all&_r=0.

Knight Commission on Information Needs of Communities in a Democracy. *Informing Communities: Sustaining Democracy in the Digital Age,* Washington: The Aspen Institute, 2009.

Kuriakose, Sabina. "City Hall Documents Out in the Open," *NBC Connecticut,* August 14, 2012, accessed December 14, 2013, at http://www.nbcconnecticut.com/investigations/City-Hall-Document-166066356.html.

Schulhofer-Wohl, Sam, and Miguel Garrido. *Do Newspapers Matter? Short-run and Long-run Evidence from the Closure of The Cincinnati Post,* National Bureau of Economic Research Working Paper 14817, March 2009, accessed December 13, 2013, at http://www.nber.org/papers/w14817.pdf.

Segall, Bob. "Official Entry Form 2010 IRE Awards," *Investigative Reporters & Editors,* December 30, 2010, accessed (with password) December 14, 2013, at http://ire.org/resource-center/stories/24901/.

Simon, David. Quoted in "The Future of Journalism," U.S. Senate Subcommittee on Communications, Technology and the Internet, May 6, 2009, accessed December 13, 2013, at http://www.gpo.gov/fdsys/pkg/CHRG-111shrg52162/html/CHRG-111shrg52162.htm.

Snyder, James M. Jr., and David Strömberg. *Press Coverage and Political Accountability,* National Bureau of Economic Research Working Paper 19378, March 2008, accessed December 14, 2013, at http://www.nber.org/papers/w13878.pdf.

Stewart, James B. *Follow the Story: How To Write Successful Nonfiction*, New York: Touchstone, 1998.

Waldman, Steven. *The Information Needs of Communities: The Changing Media Landscape in a Broadband Age*, Washington: Federal Communications Commission, 2011, accessed December 14, 2013, at http://www.fcc.gov/infoneedsreport.

WTHR Indianapolis. "Reality Check: Indiana Job Numbers Don't Add Up," WTHR.com, March 1, 2010, accessed December 14, 2013, at http://www.wthr.com/story/12066021/reality-check-indiana-job-numbers-dont-add-up.

CHAPTER 8

Specialized Topics

Picking up where the last chapter left off, this one starts by focusing on the elected officials who are responsible for overseeing government and on the political process that puts them in office and allows them to maintain and exercise power. From there it shows how the DOT methodology can apply in a variety of other specialized topic areas (science/medicine, money/business, education, sports, arts/entertainment, travel/leisure, religion) and describes some of the pitfalls and opportunities that appear in each area.

Newspapers and other news organizations are hierarchical, with a clearly defined set of priorities and career stations. At the top of the beat structure of almost any news outlet is politics, especially national politics. The political beat has an extremely high profile and is extremely competitive, and for those reasons it is usually the domain of experienced reporters who have proven their ability to stay on top of fast moving events and even to move stories ahead with exclusive information and insights. The irony of this situation, however, is that news audiences don't share journalists' enthusiasm for political news. In a 2012 survey, "politics/Washington news" came in seventh among reader interests, behind weather, crime, community, sports, health and local government. Only 17 percent of those surveyed said they followed national political news "very closely" (Pew Research Center for the People and the Press, 2012, 31).

It's impossible to know, of course, how much the lack of interest in political news can be traced to the characteristics of the political process itself and how much is the fault of the way that process is covered. Political news often concerns complicated, contentious issues that do not lend themselves to colorful or entertaining kinds of coverage. Many people may find the controversies themselves tiresome or difficult to think about. In that light, the fact that readers don't want to read about the intricacies of a new budget bill or the demographic analysis that lies behind some candidate's new campaign strategy may not be all that surprising. But press critics point to certain qualities of political coverage that they say discourage the average citizen from wanting to follow along.

Thanks first to cable news and then to the expansion of online news, the volume of political coverage has grown dramatically as the pace at which it is delivered has also increased. Practically speaking, however, the only way to fill this expanded news hole is with a certain kind of story, often based on a misstep or a misstatement by a political figure caught in an unguarded moment, that is easy to report and easy for news audiences to grasp. Perhaps the classic example of this kind of political reporting is the story of John McCain's inability, during the 2008 presidential campaign, to recall exactly how many homes he and his wife owned (Martin and Allen, 2008). The story was first reported by *Politico,* the online news site, and was quickly spread by other political journalists and by his opponent, Barack Obama. But even journalists who picked up on this "scooplet" later questioned the lasting value of this kind of reporting (Sherman, 2009).

In this context of high-speed hypercompetition, it might seem like the idea of working through documents, observation and talk would be a hopelessly outmoded approach because of the time required to go through those steps. But another way of looking at the situation is to recognize that the public has a great interest in news that makes sense of a confusing world full of quick hits of pieces of unrelated information. This book emphasizes the importance of making connections and testing to see if patterns exist that may not be easily recognized, which is precisely the idea behind a "conceptual scoop" (Clark, 2004). This kind of story, introduced in Chapter 2, is a powerful way to make your reporting stand out when you find yourself in the continuous news cycle of a beat like politics. Conceptual scoops come from news that is fully visible and available to other reporters; the difference is in the way that this information is organized by pointing out an underlying pattern. Charlie Savage, then a reporter for *The Boston Globe,* won the Pulitzer Prize for National Reporting in 2007 based on his coverage of the way that President George W. Bush used a device called a signing statement, in which he signaled that he did not feel bound by all of the provisions of a bill that he was signing into law. The Pulitzer committee described Savage's article as containing "revelations" (Columbia, 2007). But Savage had a slightly different take. As he told *The Harvard Crimson,* the pattern he found "was hiding in plain sight, but no one was talking about it" (Daly, 2007).

One way to think about the political beat is to divide it into two areas— personalities and policies. In each of these areas, the first focusing on individuals who are elected to office and the second on what policies they pursue in office, begin your reporting with documents, studying information that comes from politicians, from their opponents and from third party analysts. Next turn to observation. One of the great weaknesses in political reporting is a lack of direct observation. It is fairly easy, for example, on an issue like immigration to gather statements or even conduct interviews with political leaders to get their views. Understanding the impact of these positions on immigrants, however, means going out and observing the lives of immigrants. It will be a time-consuming process, but it is the best way to make sure that your reporting is more than just a megaphone for advocates on either side of the issue. Once you have armed yourself with information from documents and from observing the actual lives of immigrants, you will be in a much better position to conduct meaningful interviews with the politicians who are involved in the matter.

While politics is a field that is crowded with journalists, it is also a field with many gaps in coverage. One place where this is certainly true is right where you are—in one of the 435 congressional districts in the United States. Unlike national political figures such as the president, the average member of the House of Representatives gets relatively little coverage outside of election campaigns. Those who serve in leadership positions such as the speaker of the House will draw more attention for what they do in the Capitol as opposed to what they do for their districts. A major issue that limits congressional coverage is what scholars call "congruence" (Bawn et al., 2012), the degree to which a representative's district overlaps with a defined media market. In many cases, one of two situations occurs. In a large metropolitan area, a congressional district will fall within a given media market, but other districts will also be within that market, limiting the amount of attention for one representative. In less populous areas, a district will cut across multiple media markets, which also limits the amount of attention that news outlets will give to that representative.

See the Exercises for a step-by-step plan for using the DOT methodology to learn more about political coverage by expanding your knowledge of your local member of Congress.

SCIENCE

Although we live in a highly advanced technological society, many people have surprisingly little knowledge or interest in science news, generally speaking. (Exceptions include health news and environmental issues to some extent.) Yet scientific advances affect our economy and even our understanding of human behaviors (see Figure 8.1). A decade ago most national newspapers had separate science reporting staffs, but this coverage has been a victim of budget cuts. Nonetheless, science news could be a promising career opportunity because a good number of specialty magazines cover science. (Some pay very well.)

The first challenge of science reporting is also the most obvious—most journalists lack the academic training that would prepare them to understand the technical details of scientific advancement, so they are at a serious disadvantage when trying to translate this kind of information into a form that is accessible to the average reader. In this regard, there is no substitute for a major investment of time in learning the material. It is also an occasion

FIGURE 8.1   *Visiting scientists in their labs is a good way to gain deeper insight into their work. Credit: National Cancer Institute*

to implement the DOT approach, recognizing the importance of using all three methods to research a science-related topic.

The starting point for most science stories will be documents, most likely in the form of a report published by a major research organization or an article published in a peer-reviewed journal. Peer review is at the heart of scientific developments, as researchers submit their work for analysis and criticism by others knowledgeable about their area. Research that passes this test is then published in a scholarly journal. There are many journals, covering many different specialties and subspecialties, but some of them are far more selective than others. Articles published in the most prestigious journals, such as *Science* or *Nature,* are often viewed as more significant and newsworthy than those published in more obscure venues. But the less well-known journals can also provide useful starting points for inquiry, especially if they have articles that have been overlooked.

Observation in scientific reporting can present challenges that cannot be completely overcome. Some science is done in inaccessible locations, such as at the bottom of the ocean, or on such a scale, involving very small particles of matter, that a reporter is unlikely to be able to witness directly. But even if direct observation of an experiment is not practical, it is possible to meet with scientists face to face, a situation that may yield useful insights about the way a particular question is being researched and is also likely to result in an opportunity to talk through the topic at hand.

One very good reason for meeting with scientists in their own laboratories is to try to bridge the gulf that exists between scientists and reporters. Common criticisms of science journalism are that it is exaggerated, out of context or just plain inaccurate. But a 2011 study by Brechman, Lee and Capella, published in the *Journal of Communication,* suggests that at least some of these problems can be reduced when reporters spend more time talking with a broader range of sources, not just the scientists who have published experimental results but other specialists in the field.

Scientific topics are complex, but there are other factors that science journalists need to be prepared to deal with. As noted in Chapter 6, on controversial topics journalists are sometimes drawn into providing "false balance" or "false equivalency" when they include competing explanations for some phenomenon, such as climate change or the side effects of vaccinations. While it is generally good practice to include both sides of the story, sometimes the weight of scientific evidence tilts so strongly in one direction that giving equal prominence to opposing viewpoints is misleading (Dixon and Clarke, 2013). Journalists must also be aware of ethical conflicts that can arise in the course of scientific inquiry, and there have been cases of falsified data or improper financial arrangements that could call into question the results of a study (Wahlberg, 2013).

But perhaps the biggest challenge for the scientific journalist is the nature of scientific knowledge itself. Most, if not all, scientists would agree that the knowledge derived through lab testing, observation, computer modeling and other accepted methods is provisional, the best understanding at the moment but not necessarily the final word. While it is tempting to present new scientific findings as fact, they are more rightly viewed as simply the latest step in an ongoing process of discovery. In other words, there is a degree of uncertainty associated with scientific results, an uncertainty that can be challenging to deal with but cannot be ignored (Friedman, Dunwoody, and Rogers, 1999). In many cases scientific results are couched in statistical probabilities (Cohn, 1997), a way of expressing uncertainty that scientific journalists need to understand well enough so that they can explain the underlying conditions, including contingencies, to a lay audience without oversimplification.

MONEY/BUSINESS

Once the backwater of most newsrooms, the business news desk has assumed an increasingly important role over the last several decades as interest in issues related to money and finance has soared. Another factor behind the growth of this area of coverage is the recognition that in a market-based economy like that of the United States almost every story is potentially a business story, or at least has an angle related to business. Consider the range of stories recognized for excellence in a recent annual competition. The Society of American Business Editors and Writers (2012) cited reports on the demise of the company behind Twinkies, the foreclosure crisis, the iPhone, fatalities on cell phone towers, the subprime mortgage market, global trafficking in body parts, questionable use of aid funds after a natural disaster, data mining, funeral costs, the paper industry, employment practices at banks and healthcare.

Since almost everything having to do with this beat is measured—stock prices, unemployment, consumer prices—documents are a frequent starting point for stories and projects related to money and business. Many of these documents are available from the federal government, either from agencies that generate information, such as the Bureau of Labor Statistics, or agencies that collect information, such as the Securities and Exchange Commission. Important business-related documents are also available from state governments, which register corporations and other business entities, and from local governments, which typically maintain property tax and other real estate records.

Observations are sometimes difficult to make on this beat, as stories may take you to private property, where companies can legally restrict your access. It is sometimes possible to accompany government officials who can demand access to otherwise restricted areas. Going undercover is another option, although this approach can raise legal and ethical issues if deception is involved. Reporters have found success, however, by using their real names and applying for jobs where they were able to witness problematic working conditions. In 2001, for example, Barbara Ehrenreich published *Nickel and Dimed: On (Not) Getting By in America,* a book recounting her efforts to survive on the wages from a series of menial jobs in various cities across the nation. In applying for jobs, she omitted the fact that she had a doctorate and described herself "as a divorced homemaker reentering the workforce after many years," which she said was "true as far as it goes" (5). More recently, a reporter for *Mother Jones* magazine got herself hired at a large warehouse for a company that provides free shipping for the online retail industry. Her article, "I Was a Warehouse Wage Slave," was an effort to show readers how the low prices they enjoy on Internet purchases are based on working conditions that few consumers would be willing to endure (McClelland, 2012).

Interviewing skills are critical on this beat, because it encompasses every facet and level of society. Reporters may find themselves talking to anyone from an unskilled, entry-level worker all the way up to the chief executive officer of a major corporation. It is also an area that requires the mastery of specialized vocabulary for technical and financial matters. A reporter who goes to interview a chief financial officer without sufficient preparation may get an earful of answers that won't do much good if they can't be deciphered. To avoid missing a critical comment, or misinterpreting one, reporters may have to learn some basic business jargon as part of their interview preparation.

EDUCATION

In November 2012 a reporting team for the *Chicago Tribune* capped off a 10-year investigative effort by publishing a shocking package of articles showing the extent to which truancy was crippling the educational prospects of public school students in that city. The team's key finding was that thousands of students were missing as much as a month of school per year, and within a matter of days government leaders were at work on finding ways to address the problem. The investigative package, called "An Empty-Desk Epidemic" (Jackson, Marx, and Richards, 2012), won the Fred M. Hechinger Grand Prize for Distinguished Education Reporting (Education Writers Association, 2013).

One judge praised the package for its use of multimedia and narrative techniques but also pointed out that the journalists developed their account using "ingenuity and old-fashioned shoe-leather reporting" (Education Writers Association, 2013). The story of how the articles came together is an outstanding example of the way that documents, observation and talk can be used to uncover hidden problems and bring them the attention they need. Two of the reporters, David Jackson and Gary Marx, explained how the story came to be, at the Education Writers Association annual meeting in May 2013 (Jackson and Marx, 2013).

Jackson began his talk by describing how he makes a practice, when visiting a new place, of trying to meet with judges from the local juvenile justice system. Juveniles are usually protected by privacy laws when they have run-ins with the law, but the judges can talk generally about the trends they are seeing. Those trends may be happening out of public view, but because they are affecting young people, there is a good chance they hold the seeds for larger problems down the road.

When Jackson visited Nashville, Tennessee, in the late 1990s a judge told him that many of the young people who came through her court had started getting into trouble after dropping out of school at a very young age. This talk with the juvenile court judge got the reporter thinking about how he could investigate and document the issue back in Chicago. He filed a public records request to obtain data from the Chicago Public School system. But even after taking pains to avoid asking for specific information that would raise privacy concerns, he was turned down. His newspaper then began a four-year legal battle to obtain the data but lost its case before the Illinois Supreme Court.

Although this fight was lost, along the way Jackson learned that educational researchers were able to get their hands on the data he was seeking. Ingeniously, he decided to apply for a fellowship at Harvard University's Nieman Foundation. Using Harvard as a base and working with scholars there, Jackson went back to the school system and asked for the truancy data. The analysis he did, with the help of Harvard researchers, was shocking to him, and, not surprisingly, the school system would not allow him to publish it. But now with the data in front of him, he was able to go back and file even more narrowly focused records requests, which were granted.

There is still a long way to go between having compelling data and having compelling journalism. Jackson's colleague, Gary Marx, explained how they used direct observation and further interviewing to put their story together. "You have a data spine but how do you bring it to life?" Marx asked (Jackson and Marx, 2013). The key was getting people to tell their stories. So the two spent months going to schools on the West Side of Chicago meeting with principals and trying to earn their trust. From there they worked to meet families and persuade them to tell their stories. According to Marx, the most important step was "building trust, transparency, letting people know what you're working on and finding people who want to cooperate and tell your story, the story you think is important."

The *Tribune* reporters focused on a particular kind of data, truancy, but anyone who covers education will tell you that school systems collect data across a vast array of information categories. Public databases that are available online and don't have to be pursued through freedom of information requests can be the starting point for many stories, comparing individual schools or school systems as well as education outcomes by race and other demographics. But the example that Jackson and Marx provided—of taking a tip from an interview, looking for documents to analyze the idea further and then using direct observation and more interviewing to flesh out a story—is one that can be followed to good effect on the education beat.

SPORTS

Sports is a key ingredient in daily news coverage, and most news organizations devote significant resources to this topic, with regular reports on athletes at a range of levels, typically with the most emphasis on high school, college and professional teams. Unlike other kinds of news, sports "news" often isn't really news. A funny thing about sports stories is that many people who are drawn to read them already know a good deal about what happened. For example, many millions of football fans will read the coverage of the Super Bowl the day after having watched the game on television.

As a result, sports reporting, like entertainment reporting generally, has two dimensions. Part of your challenge is to recreate the moment—through careful observation of detail and creative use of language. The other part is to bring some added dimension to your account that makes reading it worth the time and trouble of the reader. After all, most readers will already know the basic outline of your story.

Another reason why sports journalists need to find a way to go beyond the basics is that their core function, turning the facts and figures of a game or other event into a story, has been reduced into a formula by a company called Narrative Science. Narrative Science, which got its start as part of a research project at Northwestern University's Medill School of Journalism, has developed a computer formula, known as an algorithm, to take the statistics that are generated from a sporting event and turn them into a narrative, a story about the game. While the resulting stories may not compare with the very best accounts that could be produced by a human journalist, most people who have read them say that they are quite satisfactory (Paskin, 2010). It should also be noted that journalists generally need to take note of this trend as Narrative Science has turned its attention to other fields, like finance and education, that generate large data sets and has successfully produced reports for a variety of news organizations, including Forbes (Groenfeldt, 2013) and ProPublica (Klein, 2013).

In some ways this development can be a positive one. If a computer program can allow reporters to skip over the most tedious parts of their jobs (and eventually almost all news beats can get bogged down in routine), then reporters can focus their attention on finding that extra dimension that will attract readers and hold their attention. How to add the extra dimension? There are different strategies depending on what you are covering and how knowledgeable you are. But at the heart of this process is, as always, the skillful use of documents, observation and talk.

As previous examples have indicated, of the three essential skills involved in reporting the one that is most often overlooked on most beats is observation. Far too many stories get reported without journalists getting out on the street to see what is actually going on. The one exception to this general rule is sports. In sports coverage, because so much of it is based on live events and competitions, reporters spend a great deal of their time observing—watching athletes, coaches and fans as they take part in the spectacle that most major events have become.

Talking is another obvious key to successful sports writing, especially for those reporters who are not satisfied with canned clichés and have the skill to get athletes to open up and tell their stories. Consider, for example, the challenges that Barry Bearak of *The New York Times* faced as he prepared to write a profile of Quanitta Underwood, the Olympic boxer who had been sexually abused by her father. As she developed her boxing career, she also posted on the Web biographical information that included hints about her past. When Bearak asked for more details, she said she would provide them, but as the reporter later wrote, "the agreeing proved far easier than the telling." As the boxer recalled, "This is like totally X-rated stuff." Three long interviews were required to get the information the reporter needed (Bearak, 2012).

It's instructive to note that this story began with documents, the Web pages where Underwood alluded to her past, before moving on to observation and talk. Documents are the key foundation of a credible news report, and sports writers use certain kinds of documents all the time: rosters, score sheets, media guides with player bios. But there have been occasions when sports writers, captivated by the story before them, have failed to do the appropriate amount of documentary research.

Take the case of Manti Te'o. He was the Notre Dame football player whose tragic story made him first an inspirational hero and then a bit of a national laughingstock. The heroics came as he responded to the news that two of the people he was closest to, his girlfriend and his maternal grandmother, had died within the space of six hours. A few days later he went out and led the Fighting Irish to a 20–3 victory over Michigan State in what his coach called a "signature win."

As the Associated Press reported, "And Te'o was the signature player. The senior linebacker had 12 tackles, one for a loss, and broke up two passes, playing just a few days after the deaths of his girlfriend, who had a long battle with leukemia, and his grandmother" (Lage, 2012). The story that the AP told was one that other media outlets had also related. But sports fans soon came to learn that the football player had likely been the victim of hoax, a hoax that was unintentionally propelled by sports journalists who had gotten their story by watching and by talking and by skipping over the all-important step of looking for documentary support for what they had seen and been told.

It was true that Te'o's grandmother had died, but the girlfriend was the creation of a man who later said he was in love with Te'o. The news organization that broke the story of the hoax was an online sports site called *Deadspin*. On Jan. 16, 2013, its story described the lack of documentation for the supposed death of the supposed girlfriend: no death records from the Social Security Administration, no obituary in a widely used online news database, no story in her school newspaper and no record from that school of a student by that name (Burke and Dickey, 2013). *Deadspin* went several steps further, using social media accounts to track down the person whose photo had been used, without her knowledge, on television and elsewhere as the representation of the fake girlfriend (Reimold, 2013). As is so often the case, documents were the key to the story, and the *Deadspin* journalists were smart to look for them in traditional ways, by checking news accounts and databases, and in innovative ways, by mining Twitter.

ARTS/ENTERTAINMENT

According to one count, the number of full-time art critics at American newspapers and magazines had fallen to fewer than 10 as of mid-2013 (Regatao, 2013). A similar declining trend has also been noted for movie critics (Cheshire, 2012). These statistics may suggest that there isn't much demand for this kind of reporting or many prospects for jobs. But a more expansive view of the field, taking into account online websites as well as newer forms of artistic expression such as videogames, would lead to a different conclusion (see box below for a list of web resources for specialized journalism). In fact there are many opportunities for journalists who are interested in the field of arts and entertainment coverage.

Web Resources for Specialized Journalism

If you are interested in pursuing a career in a specialized area of journalism, you can find some excellent resources on the Web. On many of these beats, the reporters and editors who have developed expertise in a particular topic area have formed nonprofit organizations that provide training and other resources. By visiting the sites on this list, which is intended to be representative rather than exhaustive, you will find reporting tips, examples of high quality work and relevant industry news.

Name/URL	Self-description
Arts/Culture	
Music Critics Association of North America http://www.mcana.org/	MCANA is the only North American association devoted solely to professional classical music critics.
National Society of Film Critics http://www. nationalsocietyoffilmcritics.com/	The purpose of the NSFC is to promote the mutual interests of film criticism and filmmaking.
Education	
Education Writers Association http://www.ewa.org/	The EWA is dedicated to improving the quality and quantity of education coverage to create a better-informed society.
Money/Business	
Alliance of Area Business Publications http://www.bizpubs.org/	The AABP represents 70 regional and local business publications in the United States, Canada, Australia and Puerto Rico.
Society of American Business Editors and Writers http://sabew.org/	SABEW's mission is to encourage comprehensive reporting of economic events without fear or favoritism and to upgrade skills and knowledge through continuous educational efforts.

Science/Medicine

Association of Health Care Journalists http://www.healthjournalism.org/	The AHCJ is an independent, nonprofit organization dedicated to advancing public understanding of health care issues.
National Association of Science Writers http://www.nasw.org/	The NASW was formally incorporated in 1955 with a charter to "foster the dissemination of accurate information regarding science through all media normally devoted to informing the public."
Society of Environmental Journalists http://www.sej.org/	The SEJ is the only North American membership association of professional journalists dedicated to more and better coverage of environment-related issues.
World Federation of Science Journalists http://www.wfsj.org/	The WFSJ is a not-for-profit, nongovernmental organization, representing science journalists' associations globally.

Sports

Associated Press Sports Editors http://apsportseditors.org/	The purposes of APSE are to improve professional standards of member organizations, to discuss and attempt to resolve issues faced by the same, and to recognize professional excellence among the membership.
Association for Women in Sports Media http://awsmonline.org/	The AWSM is an international organization whose male and female membership supports the advancement and growth of women— both student and professional—in sports media.

Travel/Leisure

Association of Food Journalists http://www.afjonline.com/	The AFJ offers networking and education for professional food journalists. It also promotes high ethical standards in food writing, editing and restaurant criticism.
Society of American Travel Writers http://www.satw.org/	The SATW's mission is to promote responsible journalism, provide professional development for its members and encourage the conservation and preservation of travel resources worldwide.

Religion

Religion Newswriters Association http://www.religionlink.com/	The RNA is the world's only association for journalists who cover religion.

It is true, however, that art is viewed by many in American society as a secondary activity, more of a luxury than a necessity. This attitude tends to diminish the significance that is attached to art and culture, and it is one that journalists working in this area, or hoping to work in this area, should be prepared to encounter. They may find useful counterarguments by listening to artists talk about their work and the way that it intertwines with their lives.

Stew, a rock-and-roll musician whose given name is Mark Stewart and who is probably best-known for his Tony award-winning play *Passing Strange,* is adamant that art is an integral part of human existence and not the exclusive province of a select group of people known as artists. "Art is what we do, not something we go see," he told a campus audience in October 2013. "Creativity is not the exclusive realm of the artist." In this view, art takes many forms and comprises all of the different kinds of actions that humans undertake when they feel the need to cope with their environment. These actions range from the stammering excuse a driver makes to a police officer after being caught in a speed trap to the way a grandmother arranges photographs and knick-knacks on a shelf. "The act of creation is this idea that something is missing," Stew said. "We need to see a reflection of ourselves because something is missing," he added. "Your grandmother is a stone-cold installation artist" (Stew, 2013). An approach to arts, and arts reporting, that is based on the idea that art belongs to everyone rather than just to an educated, cultivated elite, is also a smart way to build reader interest in this topic.

Like sports, arts reporting relies heavily on observation, and the journalists covering this beat will be judged in part by their perceptive abilities and their ability to translate those perceptions into a news account or a piece of criticism. Practice is probably the best way to improve your observational skill on such assignments. But another way to make the most of your observational opportunities is through preparation, especially through documentary research on your subject. This kind of documentary research need not be confined to text documents but should include sound recordings, videos and images.

In addition to covering specific events on this beat, reporters should be attuned to the major institutional players, whether they be corporate owners of music and film properties or not-for-profit organizations that operate museums or performance spaces. The role of government funding in arts and culture is another area that deserves close journalistic scrutiny.

TRAVEL/LEISURE

Americans spend an enormous amount of time and money on leisure activities, ranging from backyard activities like gardening to exotic, and potentially dangerous, trips to remote destinations. Their desire to learn more deeply about their areas of interest, and about new ones, is an opportunity for journalists working in a range of formats, from weekly news columns to full-length books.

The documents-observation-talk methodology is particularly well suited for journalism on these topics because many readers are often highly knowledgeable and are looking for deep information that extends and enriches their experiences. Some of these topics also have a political dimension, such as food writing that also explores the agricultural subsidies affecting the kinds of ingredients that go into our meals. It is only by using a comprehensive approach to reporting that journalists can hope to delve into this kind of subject matter in a way that is satisfying for readers.

Michael Pollan's *The Omnivore's Dilemma: A Natural History of Four Meals*, which received a James Beard Award and was named by *The New York Times* as one of the most influential books of the year, is a good example of how a skillful reporter can take a seemingly simple question and use it as a springboard for a deep and thought-provoking investigation (Pollan, 2006). In this case, Pollan started with the question most people ask themselves every day, "What should I eat?" (17). This question in turn led him to two deeper questions—about the makeup of the food that was available to him and about where it came from. Pollan ended up focusing on four different meals, tracing the foods back to their sources and examining the tradeoffs involved in producing them.

RELIGION

There was a time when religion coverage at many news organizations consisted of little more than notices about church social events and fundraisers with an occasional feature about specific practices or perhaps an announcement of a change in personnel at a well-known institution. Religious holidays prompted the predictable coverage of services and sermons, but for the most part religious news was kept in the background. In 1966 *Time* magazine published its notorious "Is God Dead?" cover, perhaps marking the point at which the role of religion in American culture and society was seen to be at its lowest point. Whether God is dead or not, there is not much argument today about the significance of religion in contemporary issues that reverberate both nationally and internationally, from debates over abortion and gay rights to the ongoing conflicts in the Middle East.

At the same time, news organizations devote relatively little attention to religion. "In a country that is highly religious, the subject is not a major focus of the news," the Pew Research Center said in a report published in 2012. When religion does make its way into the headlines, Pew found, the coverage is often driven by a major event, such as the visit of an international religious leader or a public protest, such as a burning of a holy book like the Quran (Pew, 2012). As a result, many religious topics remain under the radar—and available for exploration by enterprising journalists.

The Religion Newswriters Association has published a guide to getting started on the beat that emphasizes the importance of using documentary resources to learn about the topic. Even journalists who hold religious beliefs and belong to religious organizations will likely need to educate themselves about some aspects of the field, including other faith traditions. Observation is also a critical step, as religion reporters need to visit churches, temples, mosques and other places of religious gathering to gain a deeper understanding of religion issues and pick up story ideas. "There is no substitute for visiting churches, mosques, synagogues or temples for worship and other gatherings," the RNA says. "The sights, sounds, rituals, textures, mood and conversations will tell you more than any book ever can" (Connolly, 2006, 78).

The talking part of covering religion should be wide ranging, the RNA recommends. While clergy members may be the most visible and most articulate people in a congregation, their views may not necessarily reflect the views of those in the pews. Scholars who study religion are also good sources who can provide balance or competing analysis of news and events. But as the RNA points out, religion can be a sensitive subject, and it may be important to phrase your questions in a way that allows your sources to open up about their beliefs rather than making them feel that they have to minimize or defend the role of faith in their lives. Asking generally about values and beliefs, for example, might be better than quizzing sources about the specific tenets of their religion.

EXERCISES

1. **Covering your Congressperson.** Chances are the person who represents you in the House of Representatives doesn't get much attention in the local media, at least not on issues that have a specific effect on the district where you live. Almost certainly there is a good story to be found by digging deeper. Here is an outline of how you can "connect the DOT" to find a newsworthy item or two.

   Documents: Start by checking the "clips," recent accounts from the news. Has your representative been in the headlines lately? Have there been editorials praising or criticizing your representative's actions? Your next step should be your representative's website to make sure you understand policy positions, legislative proposals and voting patterns.

   After you have obtained this kind of general background information on your representative, consult the specialized websites that have been established with more specific information. These include:

   - My Congressional District. This site, operated by the U.S. Census Bureau, will give you authoritative statistics on five key areas about your district. You can use these statistics to see how your part of the country compares with national averages. This might give you some insight into what your representative's priorities are.

- Sunlight Foundation.

- OpenSecrets.

- http://www.opencongress.org/

Observation: Based on this documentary analysis, take a trip around your campus and your neighborhood. Can you see any ways that your congressional representative's positions affect you? There is probably a story there whether the answer is "yes" or "no."

Talk: Start by talking to a neutral observer, perhaps a political science professor at your school. Other people you will want to talk to include political supporters and opponents, members of your representative's local and Washington office staffs and, of course, your representative.

2. **Science.** In this assignment, you will cover and localize some recent scientific development, with "recent" being defined as something that has come to light this year. Don't worry—there are lots and lots of scientific discoveries to pick from.

   Your starting point will be http://www.eurekalert.org/. This is a website operated by the American Association for the Advancement of Science that collects press announcements about newly published research. Most scientific breakthroughs come to light by way of peer-reviewed publication.

   Spend some time looking through the different papers that are referenced there. You will see that they come from many different specialties and cover all kinds of things, including sex, drugs and rock 'n' roll. (The paper will be the D in DOT.) Once you have selected the paper to write about, you will localize and humanize the story. You will localize the story by finding some expert on campus or in the local community and interview that person about the topic.

   You will humanize the story by interviewing someone to get some "street" reaction to the development. These last two steps should provide you with the O and T for your article.

3. **Education.** All of us know from experience that a major part of the educational system is the report card. Increasingly parents, taxpayers and political leaders have insisted that schools and school systems

(and universities) subject themselves to grading and produce regular report cards.

At least once a year a school system will have new set of grades. These indicators may vary from state to state, but they will likely include:

- Results of standardized tests.

- Demographic data.

- Teacher licensing.

- Costs.

- Student discipline.

Try to find this kind of information for your middle school or high school, and look for items that suggests news, inconsistencies or patterns that appear unusual. Next draw up a reporting plan. What other documents would help you flesh out your story? What are some observations that you could make or visual details that you could include in your story? Finally, put together a source list. Who are people whom you might interview for background information? Who are people whose comments you would need so that you could explain the inconsistencies that you have spotted.

REFERENCES

Bawn, Kathleen, Martin Cohen, David Karol, Seth Masket, Hans Noel, and John Zaller. "A Theory of Political Parties: Groups, Policy Demands and Nominations in American Politics," *Perspectives on Politics* 10, No. 3, September 2012, 571–597.

Bearak, Barry. "The Living Nightmare," *The New York Times,* February 11, 2012, accessed December 16, 2013, at http://www.nytimes.com/2012/02/12/sports/quanitta-underwood-a-contender-for-olympic-gold-and-a-survivor.html?_r=0.

Brechman, Jean M., Chul-joo Lee and Joseph N. Cappella. "Distorting Genetic Research About Cancer: From Bench Science to Press Release to Published News," *Journal of Communication* 61, No. 3, June 2011, 496–613.

Burke, Timothy, and Jack Dickey. "Manti Te'o's Dead Girlfriend, the Most Heartbreaking and Inspirational Story of the College Football Season, Is A Hoax," *Deadspin,* January 16, 2013, accessed December 16, 2013, at http://deadspin.com/manti-teos-dead-girlfriend-the-most-heartbreaking-an-5976517.

Cheshire, Godfrey. "If Critics Go, Culture Will Suffer," *The New York Times,* October 8, 2012, accessed December 16, 2013, at http://www.nytimes.com/roomfordebate/2012/10/07/do-we-need-professional-critics/if-critics-go-culture-will-suffer.

Clark, Roy Peter. "The Conceptual Scoop," Poynter.org, September 1, 2004, updated April 21, 2012, accessed December 16, 2013, at http://www.poynter.org/uncategorized/25137/the-conceptual-scoop/.

Cohn, Victor. "Coping with Statistics," in Deborah Blum and Mary Knudson, eds., *A Field Guide for Science Writers*, New York: Oxford University Press, 1997, 102–109.

Columbia University. "The 2007 Pulitzer Prize Winners National Reporting," *The Pulitzer Prizes*, accessed December 16, 2013, at http://www.pulitzer.org/citation/2007-National-Reporting.

Connolly, Diane. *Reporting on Religion: A Primer on Journalism's Best Beat*, Westerville, Ohio: Religion Newswriters Association, 2006.

Daly, Gabriel J. "Savage '98 Wins Pulitzer Prize," *The Harvard Crimson*, April 19, 2007, accessed December 16, 2013, at http://www.thecrimson.com/article/2007/4/19/savage-98-wins-pulitzer-prize-a/.

Dixon, Graham, and Christopher E. Clarke. "The Effect of Falsely Balanced Reporting of the Autism-Vaccine Controversy on Vaccine Safety Perceptions and Behavioral Intentions," *Health Education Research* 28, No. 2, April 2013, 352–359.

Education Writers Association. "Fred M. Hechinger Grand Prize," ewa.org, May 10, 2013, accessed December 16, 2013, at http://www.ewa.org/site/PageServer?pagename=contest_grandprize.

Ehrenreich, Barbara. *Nickel and Dimed: On (Not) Getting By in America*, New York: Henry Holt, 2001.

Friedman, Sharon M., Sharon Dunwoody, and Carol L. Rogers, eds. *Communicating Uncertainty: Media Coverage of New and Controversial Science*, Mahwah, N.J.: Lawrence Erlbaum Associates, 1999.

Groenfeldt, Tom. "Lots Of Data, One Analyst, Many Reports—Narrative Science," Forbes.com, September 5, 2013, accessed December 16, 2013, at http://www.forbes.com/sites/tomgroenfeldt/2013/09/05/lots-of-data-one-analyst-many-reports-narrative-science/.

Jackson, David, and Gary Marx. "How I Did the Story: An Empty-Desk Epidemic," presentation to the 66th National Seminar of the Education Writers Association, May 4, 2013, 7:15. Posted June 12, 2013, at http://vimeo.com/68270210.

Jackson, David, Gary Marx and Alex Richards. "An Empty-Desk Epidemic," *Chicago Tribune*, November 11, 2012, accessed December 16, 2013, at http://media.apps.chicagotribune.com/truancy/index.html.

Klein, Scott. "How To Edit 52,000 Stories at Once," *ProPublica*, January 24, 2013, accessed December 16, 2013, at http://www.propublica.org/nerds/item/how-to-edit-52000-stories-at-once.

Lage, Larry. "No. 20 Notre Dame beats No. 10 Michigan State 20–3," *The Big Story*, September 16, 2012, accessed May 6, 2014, at http://bigstory.ap.org/article/no-20-notre-dame-beats-no-10-michigan-state-20-3.

Martin, Jonathan, and Mike Allen. "McCain Unsure How Many Houses He Owns," *Politico*, August 21, 2008, accessed December 16, 2013, at http://www.politico.com/news/stories/0808/12685.html.

McClelland, Mac. "I Was a Warehouse Wage Slave," *Mother Jones*, March/April 2012, accessed December 16, 2013, at http://www.motherjones.com/politics/2012/02/mac-mcclelland-free-online-shipping-warehouses-labor.

Paskin, Janet. "The Future of Journalism?" *Columbia Journalism Review*, October 27, 2010, accessed December 16, 2013, at http://www.cjr.org/behind_the_news/the_future_of_journalism.php?page=all.

Pew Research Center. "Religion in the News: Islam and Politics Dominate Religion Coverage in 2011," Pew Research Religion & Public Life Project, February 23, 2012, accessed December 16, 2013, at http://www.pewforum.org/2012/02/23/religion-in-the-news-islam-and-politics-dominate-religion-coverage-in-2011/.

Pew Research Center for the People and the Press. *In Changing News Landscape, Even Television Is Vulnerable: Trends in News Consumption: 1991–2012*, Washington: Author 2012.

Pollan, Michael. *The Omnivore's Dilemma: A Natural History of Four Meals,* New York: Penguin Press, 2006.

Regatao, Gisele. "Art Talk: Why Art Critics Matter," WYNC News, May 9, 2013, accessed December 16, 2013, at http://www.wnyc.org/story/292175-art-talk-why-art-critics-matter/.

Reimold, Daniel. "5 Reporting Tips from the College Student Who Helped Break Deadspin's Manti Te'o Story," Poynter.org, January 22, 2013, accessed December 16, 2013, at http://www.poynter.org/how-tos/newsgathering-storytelling/201290/5-reporting-tips-from-the-college-student-who-helped-break-deadspins-manti-teo-story/.

Sherman, Gabriel. "The Scoop Factory," *The New Republic,* March 4, 2009, accessed December 16, 2013, at http://www.newrepublic.com/article/the-scoop-factory.

Society of American Business Editors and Writers. "Best in Business Contest Results, 2012 Contest Year," sabew.org, undated, accessed December 16, 2013, at http://sabew.org/2013/02/2012-best-in-business-competition-winners/.

Stew. "Art: Luxury or Necessity," lecture, University of Wisconsin Oshkosh, Oshkosh, WI, October 17, 2013.

Time. "Is God Dead?" cover, April 8, 1966.

Wahlberg, David. "UW Spine Surgeon's Career, Life Marked by Controversy, Tragedy," *Wisconsin State Journal,* June 2, 2013, accessed December 16, 2013, at http://host.madison.com/news/local/health_med_fit/uw-spine-surgeon-s-career-life-marked-by-controversy-tragedy/article_a213b34b-0461-5e42-a8c0-1ec647ea7e2f.html.

CHAPTER 9

Specialized Forms

There are certain kinds of stories a reporter might be asked to write no matter what the beat: a personality profile, a "curtain-raiser" or preview story, a trend story, a chronology. In addition digital publishing platforms have given rise to the creation or adaptation of forms that can work particularly well on the Internet, such as listicles, fact-checkers and social media curations. This chapter will go into greater detail about how to use DOT in these situations. Accompanying the discussion of each specialized form is a guide to getting started on that kind of assignment.

THE PROFILE

The personality profile is often associated with feature sections and feature news, but it is a staple across all news beats. Profiles are often used to introduce individuals who have taken on new roles or have arrived at some new level of prominence because of an unexpected turn of events. In politics, newly announced candidates can expect this kind of spotlight treatment, just as in sports newly drafted players and newly hired coaches and managers are likely to be profiled. Profiles are especially common in arts and culture reporting, especially when someone has reached a new level or achievement or is, perhaps, attempting a comeback. The profile of a highly successful business or organizational leader has become an increasingly common type of journalism in recent years.

From the reporter's perspective, the profile presents a range of challenges and opportunities. The challenges include the possibility that a profile subject may not cooperate—or may even intervene to make sure that other sources do not cooperate. But the biggest problem is simply the difficulty of getting a full and accurate picture of another human being, who like all of us has a mix of positive and negative characteristics, friends and enemies, successes and failures, blemishes and attractive qualities. People who are the subjects of profiles are often at the pinnacle (or perhaps the low point) of their lives and careers, and there is always the danger of falling into hero worship or becoming overly sympathetic toward the person you are writing about.

Despite these concerns, there are many good reasons why a reporter would want to attempt a profile. Reporting a profile is an opportunity to develop close relationships with the profile subject and other contacts. The subject of an honest and accurate profile, even—or perhaps especially—one that presents a balanced, nuanced "warts and all" picture—is likely to respect the reporter who produces it and may be in a position to provide insights and exclusive information on future occasions. In addition profile subjects are almost always the subject of much fascination and speculation. They are interesting people, and getting to know them well enough to write authoritatively about them can be an enjoyable and gratifying experience in itself. Finally, writing a profile can be an intensely engaging intellectual exercise that leaves the reporter with a sense of the satisfaction that comes from solving a puzzle or decoding a secret phrase.

Profiles most often provide background information on a person who is already well known, but they can also be vehicles for breaking news. *The New York Times* counts as one of its "most famous" stories a 1965 article that profiled the head of New York state's Ku Klux Klan—and revealed that this man, Daniel Burros, was Jewish (Fox, 2013). The article was written by a legendary stylist named McCandlish Phillips and began with a tip—that was then confirmed through documentary research and by talking with the Grand Dragon's neighbors and acquaintances. The documents that were used to prove the man's Jewish identity and trace his racist evolution included the kinds of paper records one would expect to use—from schools, employers, the U.S. military—as well as some that might not be so obvious. For example, Phillips noted that he had found an inscribed memorial stone at a synagogue that carried the name of Burros' grandfather.

As with most profile assignments, the finished piece hinged upon a face-to-face meeting with the subject, in which both observations and quotations could be collected. In this case Burros said he would not engage in a formal interview but agreed to talk to Phillips and answer a few questions, which was all that the reporter needed. Based on that direct encounter, he was able to include this sentence: "'We must make the world safe for blond-haired, blue-eyed children,' the blond-haired, blue-eyed extremist declares" (Phillips, 1965, A1). Two paragraphs later, Phillips drops his bombshell about Burros's Jewish lineage and upbringing, a revelation that initially prompted Burros to threaten to kill the reporter and was likely a major factor in the man's suicide (Fox, 2013).

While talking to and spending some time with a profile subject may seem like necessary ingredients for this kind of article, there are some extraordinary examples of very successful profiles that were written without any cooperation at all. One of the best known of these is a profile that Mark Bowden wrote of the Iraqi dictator Saddam Hussein for *The Atlantic Monthly* (2002). As Bowden later recounted, he tried to get an interview but did not expect to have his request granted, especially since this was the period between 9/11 and the 2003 invasion of Iraq. His next step, naturally, was to review the available documents on Hussein. He quickly discovered that they were numerous but in many cases clearly biased, either for or against, and sometimes just repeated previously published rumors that could not be substantiated. In the end, he relied most heavily on interviews to gather the information he needed. The most valuable sources were the ones who knew Hussein well enough not only to describe the atrocities he committed but also to respect the personal characteristics that allowed his rise to power (Stossel, 2002).

Even though Bowden was unable to make his own firsthand observations about the dictator, he recognized the power of these details and based on his reporting was able to introduce the article by describing the conditions under which Hussein lived and by giving a sense of his physical presence. The reporter's goal, he said in a later interview with an *Atlantic Online* editor, was to reveal something about Hussein's human character (Stossel, 2002). What emerged was a contradiction, something that was not supposed to be, namely that this seemingly all-powerful national leader was actually living a fairly precarious life, isolated and in constant fear of assassination.

The key to a successful profile is finding that kind of central detail that summarizes or defines the profile subject. It is often a paradox or a contradiction, as these two examples show, that serves to clarify and bring to the surface an otherwise overlooked or unknown quality or experience. There is no magic formula for finding that kind of central detail, and it may come from luck or happenstance or even a throwaway question that elicits a surprising response. The author James McBride has recounted a failing interview he was conducting with Richard Pryor that was saved when the reporter happened to remark upon the comedian's outdoor aquarium. The aquarium was stocked with catfish, an apparently odd choice. But as Pryor explained, the species reminded of him of his childhood, including the fish that he caught with his grandfather, who ran a brothel where Pryor spent some of his early years. In that detail was revealed a source of the formative experiences that would later fuel Pryor's biting humor (Scanlan, 2003).

A successful profile can be developed using the DOT suite of information-gathering tools.

Documents. Use these to gather information about the person's background (birth, upbringing, education, occupation). Primary documents are the gold standard, but you may have to settle for secondary documents, such as newspaper clippings, in which you should verify what you find there through other means. Written accounts may also help you develop a news peg as well as providing anecdotes and information about incidents involving the subject.

Observation. Including visual details about the profile subjects is critical to bringing them to life on the page. Take note of a subject's physical appearance (height, weight, hair color, eye color, manner of dress), demeanor (tone and pitch of voice, posture, mannerisms) and possessions (house/neighborhood, car, clothes, books, pets, office furniture).

Talk. Be sure to include quotes by the individual relevant to his or her newsworthiness. You will also need comments of those who know the subject.

One last thing to keep in mind is that in a generally negative profile, it's good practice to include something positive and likewise, in a generally positive profile, something negative. This kind of balance will add to your credibility.

PREVIEW

Although we usually think of news reports as looking backward at events that happened in the recent past, there are many occasions when journalists try to look forward at events that have not yet happened to help readers prepare for what they might soon see or hear. Preview stories, sometimes called "curtain-raisers," are written in advance of major events, such as a big game or public address, and in anticipation of a new season, of politics or of fashion or of crops. In certain respects these kinds of stories are highly artificial—as they are making "news" of something that hasn't even happened—but they can be useful tools both for readers and reporters as they navigate their way through complicated topics or merely try to identify significant individuals or issues in the midst of an overloaded information environment.

Preview stories can be a particularly useful way for reporters to get ahead of their competition or at the very least establish themselves as interested observers who should be kept in the loop as a story or controversy develops. The first step in writing a preview is to identify when there is an opportunity to do one. This requires the ability to disengage briefly from the ongoing flow of news and to look "over the horizon" at stories that are likely to dominate the headlines or at least be ongoing concerns for readers in the coming weeks or months. Some of the opportunities are fairly obvious, such as the beginning of a new school year, legislative session, hunting season or campaign cycle. In other cases a preview looks at something that is not a part of a regular cycle, such as zoning changes that could usher in new real estate developments or the opening of a new terminal at an airport that may change existing travel patterns.

The starting point for a preview story could be reading a document, making an observation or talking to a source. (Sometimes the starting point is a slow news day, when a reporter needs to focus time and attention on something that could turn into a story.) Official calendars from public agencies like school districts or nonprofit organizations like art museums can be extremely valuable documents when looking for a preview opportunity. The best reporters spend a portion of their time in undirected reading and can find ideas in overlooked or underreported details. Similarly, conversations with sources, over lunch or a cup of coffee, can tip you off to something that is coming together behind the scenes and has not yet been brought to public attention. Walking or driving around can also lead to preview stories. For example, some communities require notices of zoning changes to be posted at the actual site of the land in question.

Although a preview story looks around the curve to see what is coming down the road, it is necessarily based on what has come before. The reporter is not free to indulge in ungrounded speculation but rather needs to develop an article using the familiar tools of documents, observation and talk. Journalists also need to be careful not to get too far ahead of the story. Writing about the U.S. Census count five or six years before it is going to be taken will likely be ignored, whereas a story closer to the count—or the release of the data—will attract greater interest.

GETTING STARTED ON A PREVIEW

Since writing a preview draws on the same skills and techniques you would use on other story assignments, the big challenge in this area is finding something to preview in a way that will actually break news. Use documents, observation and talk to get started. Let's assume you want to write a preview about something that is happening on your campus.

> **Documents.** Review your school's calendars, often found on the university website, to identify key dates, commemorative events, speakers or similar items. Also, look back at policy announcements from the administration or from governance groups like the faculty senate or student government. Do any of those include dates or deadlines that are worth further study?
>
> **Observation.** Take a walk around campus. Are there construction projects underway that will be finished at some future date? Are there promotional posters for upcoming events sponsored by groups that don't often get much attention?
>
> **Talk.** Identify at least three leaders, for example, from your student government group, the residence hall boards or the sponsor of campus entertainment activities. Ask them to meet with you to talk about issues, events or ideas they expect to be involved with in the coming semester.

TRENDS

Great journalism helps to make sense of the world around us, allowing us to see beyond seemingly random and unrelated happenings to discern a pattern. That kind of reporting also helps us prepare for the future by identifying ideas and opportunities while they are still in their early stages so that we can take advantage of them—or at least be sure not to be disadvantaged by them. These desires to find order and to be prepared for what comes next help to explain why the trend story is such a popular form. Trend stories are everywhere—from the most obvious areas like fashion and music to arcane areas of technology and finance. Because they put the reporter and the reader out in front of forces that are just starting to have an effect, trend stories can be a lot of fun to work with. These kinds of stories can make readers feel more fully informed and give the reporter a sense of having made a deep discovery, which means that writing or reading a successful trend story can be exceedingly satisfying.

But a trend story is always a risky proposition as the reporter is making a singular judgment call that may not bear up to close scrutiny, or the simple passage of time. The joke in many newsrooms is that three occurrences of anything signify a "trend," an excuse to put together a story that purports to identify and explain some phenomenon that for some reason no one else has noticed. Media critic Jack Shafer has written on numerous occasions about what he calls the "bogus trend story," and it's worth bearing his observations in mind before you go too far out on a limb (2010b). His major complaint is that bogus trend stories are unverifiable, relying on anecdotal evidence and often omitting statistical evidence or ignoring the mathematical logic that would undermine the idea that a trend is happening at all.

A story that appeared in *The New York Times* in 2010, for example, reported that many criminals apprehended in that city were wearing Yankees baseball caps, more than 100 over the previous decade (Fernandez, 2010). Shafer's retort relied on simple math to point out that over that time period there were at least 1 million criminal complaints filed with the police, suggesting that the real surprise would be if 100 or more people involved in criminal acts over the decade had not been wearing apparel from a favorite local team (2010a).

While Shafer's criticisms are fair, trend stories are still worth doing, especially if you approach them in a systematic way to avoid making easily refuted assertions. A trend story develops in two stages: First, you need to identify what you think is a trend, and then you need to do the careful work to verify the existence of that trend, knowing that you may just have to move on if the evidence you are looking for does not exist.

SPOTTING THE TREND

Documents. Some kinds of documents are better than others when spotting trends. Published reports and articles may contain the seeds of ideas that you can extend, but more likely they will be looking retrospectively rather than prospectively. On the other hand, they may contain overlooked references or, in the case of reports, overlooked sets of raw data. Such data, describing perhaps the growth in popularity in certain majors or the locations of crime stops on campus, could be the starting point for a trend investigation.

Observations. Getting out and looking at people and situations can be an excellent starting point for a trend story. Are students wearing a certain kind of outfit this semester? Have they moved on from one popular electronic accessory to another? Are certain kinds of music getting played more frequently in a given residence hall?

Talk. Both random conversations and directed ones can be useful for spotting trends. Listen to how your friends talk—is there a new catchphrase that has been creeping into their speech? Where did it come from? What might it signify? You might also try to find people whose job it is to work with individuals in some helping capacity, such as tutors or counselors or even store clerks, and find out whether they have seen some incipient pattern of behavior.

VERIFYING THE TREND

Documents. In making sure the trend you think you see will stand up to wider scrutiny, documents will be your best form of evidence. The problem is that newsworthy trends are typically those that have not yet been documented. But that doesn't meant there isn't some kind of confirming data that you can find. If you are unable to find such confirming documents, at the very least you should disclose that lack—and you may want to think carefully about going forward with an article. Many of the bogus trends that Shafer has attacked over the years are ones that explicitly noted that supporting data or documentation was unavailable, which won't be a very good excuse if your trend does not bear up over time.

Observation. Many trend stories are based on anecdotes collected through direct observation. This is a two-edged sword. As noted in Chapter 4, first-person views seem like they should be highly believable but they can be fatally biased. If your trend story is based largely on observation, you should look for counter-examples as well, which may help you arrive at a more nuanced, and more defensible, assertion of a trend.

Talk. Find sources who are in a position to question the trend you are looking at. Sometimes, particularly on a feature story, sources may decide they are helping you by giving you a supporting quote. That may help you get your story into print, but if your source's quote proves to be wrong, it will be your story that gets criticized.

CHRONOLOGY

The chronology, known in journalism slang as a "tick-tock," is a moment-by-moment reconstruction of events. It is deployed across a range of situations, everything from last-minute budget negotiations in Washington to a military action in a remote part of the world. The form is sometimes criticized because of the way it can be used by inside sources to frame the public's understanding of an event and to cast political leaders in an unduly positive light. This result is achieved when tidbits and details are slipped to reporters who are looking to flesh out their accounts with previously undisclosed information (Allen and Burns, 2009). As the chronology is essentially a sequential listing of events, it is susceptible to this kind of manipulation because it does not encourage, and may not even allow for, nuanced exception-taking and background explanation (Garber, 2008).

But this criticism also reflects the power of the form, which is attractive both to readers and to reporters because of the way it helps make sense of the jumble in which breaking news often arrives. If it is done properly, it can also set the stage for further investigation, by creating a baseline against which subsequent statements and interpretations can be judged.

Using documents, observation and talk in a systematic and comprehensive way can help a reporter avoid the pitfalls that accompany the chronology form while also contributing to a more satisfactory execution of this kind of assignment.

Documents. Tick-tocks are often written in the immediate aftermath of a dramatic event or decision and so do not always lend themselves to documentary research. But there are occasions, such as the reconstruction of a major crime or other high-profile police incidents, when documents do exist, although a reporter may have to wait some time to obtain them. A push for documents is also a good way to minimize the kind of insider manipulation that can occur with a chronology. Rather than take a source's word for how a political leader handled a moment of crisis, a careful reporter should ask for some kind of corroborating documentation, which could be just an email note, before accepting as fact a firsthand account, even if it is offered on an exclusive basis.

Observation. Taking the time to visit the scene of an incident to gather firsthand detail and to gauge the credibility of a source's account is a smart move. Is it really believable that a certain private conversation occurred in a certain place out of earshot of all other participants and possible witnesses? Retracing the steps of your sources or inspecting the locations described in documents may help you pinpoint discrepancies that need to be examined more closely. This can be a time-consuming process, but skipping this step can make it harder for a reporter to develop an authoritative account that stands the test of time.

Talk. Many chronologies are developed by talking to participants or witnesses, and such conversations can yield many rich details and quotes, although sometimes they are offered on a source basis. For chronologies, especially when written under tight deadline, reporters are often forced to rely very heavily on interviews, which can be difficult if not impossible to corroborate. At the very least reporters need to acknowledge the difficulty of verifying statements and should seek out competing perspectives from others who have inside knowledge.

LISTICLE

The word "listicle" comes from combining the words "list" and "article." It is a form of journalism that uses a numbered list as the organizing device for information that could have been presented in one or more traditional news articles. In some ways the listicle is the ideal way for dealing with the flood of information that can be found on the Internet. The listicle allows for a quick summary and review of the major points in a complicated issue in a format that lends itself to redistribution across the Web in the process known as "going viral." That is, a listicle can easily be shared through social media, linked to or even incorporated in a website or blog.

A well-reported listicle can be a useful tool for helping readers work through complex topics or for subverting the conventional wisdom about a person, organization or controversy. But listicles have been frequently applied to trivial matters or in a jocular way. As a result, listicles are frequently derided as nonserious and inconsequential (Cashmore, 2013).

One website that has made extensive use of listicles is BuzzFeed, which was established with the express purpose of taking advantage of the social qualities of the Web (see Figure 9.1). There one can find listicles applied in a range of circumstances, from government coverage to lifestyle news, and sometimes combining the two, as in "9 Political Views We Can Deduce from Your Drinking Habits" (Mikkelineni, 2013). BuzzFeed also demonstrated that the listicle approach can be applied to a form that can be stultifyingly boring, the opinion column, when it published a listicle by a U.S. Senator urging Congress to take action on student loan rates (Blumenthal, 2013).

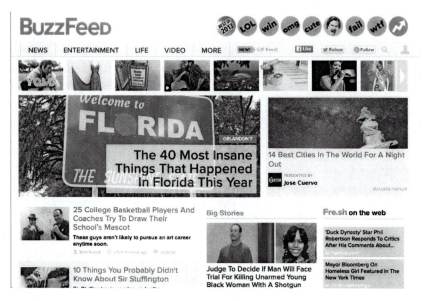

FIGURE 9.1   *Websites like BuzzFeed make frequent use of listicles, which can be an entertaining way to help news consumers deal with information overload.*

While it might be tempting to dismiss BuzzFeed and its extensive use of listicles as lightweight distractions from the important business of news, the site's executives say that their strategy is to connect with younger news audiences by relating to their interests and media consumption habits. "You have to write and produce news for the social Web," said Jon Steinberg, BuzzFeed's chief executive officer. "It has to be novel, important and have this social imperative behind it" (Dredge, 2013).

Steinberg said his site has a stronger focus on hard news than some journalists may realize because its stories are reported and produced with the express purpose of being retransmitted across the Internet. "The most important thing you can do is to think to yourself 'why would somebody share this content?'" The key, he argues, is "high quality" (Dredge, 2013).

The popularity and ubiquity of listicles has grown with the spread of social media, but the underlying concept is not new and in fact has been the mainstay of the magazine industry for decades. That's because magazine editors discovered long ago that cover lines that included numbers (such as "Top 10 investments in today's financial markets" or "15 ways to lose pounds and keep them off") were surefire ways to boost newsstand sales and readership.

Some listicles are straightforward, presenting a ranking of items based on objective or easily verifiable factors. Examples of this approach would include a listing of airlines by the percentage of on-time flights or of cities ranked by population. But many listicles rely on irony or humor. The off-beat nature of such listicles may also have its roots in traditional media, in particular the popular Top 10 lists that late-night host David Letterman turned into a running gag on his show and later published in book form (Letterman and O'Donnell, 1995).

Without a doubt listicles can be trivial, but they are unlikely to get shared very much through social media if they are insubstantial. Some traditional news organizations have recognized the value of the listicle as a way of attracting the attention of readers and then helping them come to a deeper understanding of an issue. *The Washington Post,* for example, has published an extensive series of listicles that begin with the phrase "five myths about." Topics have ranged from Jesus Christ (Aslan, 2013) to the millennial generation (Glassman, 2013).

The typical listicle includes three parts: a title, a short introduction explaining the issue at hand and then the itemized list. The title, which is critical both in identifying the topic and in conveying the tone of the listicle, also has three parts: a number, a connecting device and then a reference to the subject matter.

The number in the title corresponds to the number of individual facts or observations included in the listicle. In some cases the number is determined by the nature or extent of the underlying story, but more often a number is chosen by the author of the listicle to make a particular point. For example a round number like 10 can be used to convey a certain authority while a larger number, like 25, can be used to convey thoroughness. The use of certain odd numbers, such as 17, might serve to suggest that the author is trying to present a deliberately skewed view. A very low number, such as three or five, can be used to suggest urgency or simplicity.

The connecting phrase links the number to the topic of the listicle and can range in tone from objective to outrageous. In many cases the connecting phrase depends on the superlative form of an adjective, such as "least expensive" or "highest paying." Since the purpose of the listicle is to provoke discussion and sharing, the connecting phrase almost always carries with it a sense of revelation: "10 most surprising things you didn't know about . . ." or "the three things we learned from last night's . . .," where the event last night might be a political debate, a critical sporting event or an awards ceremony. This sense of discovery can also be created by referencing concepts that are often private, such as secrets or advice, or exotic, like a particular kind of cultural experience, such as food or music.

Writing a listicle begins with selecting a topic. Topics that make good listicles are usually based on recent news developments or timely controversies, although it is also possible to draw on certain subjects that seem to be of perennial interest—such as sex, diet and weight loss, and financial matters—or rankings of things such as schools, places to live or forms of entertainment. As BuzzFeed's Steinberg pointed out, the important thing is to think in terms of something that is likely to prompt a reader to want to share the resulting list.

> **Documents.** After you have selected your topic, you need to begin researching it, always with an eye for uncovering, so that you can highlight, overlooked facts or perspectives. Listicles are most often derivative, that is, based on some previously reported event, which means documentary analysis is the most frequently used of the three research methods available to journalists. As you sort through different news articles, blog posts, tweets and videos on your topic, you should take a connoisseur's approach, selecting out the most intriguing, insightful, inspiring, inventive or intellectually stimulating points that you can find.

> **Observation.** It is also possible to assemble a listicle based on what you have seen. Listicles are often published after celebrities make their way down the red carpet at some highly public event. Another major listicle type consists of visual forms of information, charts or other data displays that can be organized to explore a topic or make a point.

> **Talk.** A traditional way of publishing an interview is in a question-and-answer format, but a listicle is an alternative that should be considered. A listicle can be an excellent way to draw out the main points of an interview so that you can easily summarize for your readers the most significant, or startling, comments.

A successful listicle is one that gets widely shared and commented on. To achieve that status it has to provide something new. Usually this something new is not completely new information, but rather a creative approach to existing information that is often developed either by grouping information in a new way or by subverting the conventional way of looking at well-known information.

Listicles can be published in print format, and, as Letterman has demonstrated, they can be a mainstay of broadcast television. But in some ways the greatest potential for a listicle can be achieved on the Web, and for this reason it makes sense to produce listicles with the Web in mind, taking advantage of Web capabilities that don't exist in legacy media. In practice, this means your listicle should include links to your original sources of information. This technique makes it easier for the news audience to check further and to gauge your credibility and powers of interpretation.

A second way to make use of the Web is to illustrate your listicle with appropriate images or graphics and then to convert your material into an interactive slideshow. The slideshow format can be an inviting way for Web users to control their consumption of information, including going back and forth through the listicle to make comparisons and check assumptions. A variety of low-cost tools and services are available for creating online slideshows.

FACT-CHECKER

Although checking facts has long been an essential part of being a journalist and although fact-checking can occur in print, the information explosion on the Internet has helped to popularize and enhance this form of reporting in recent years. With so many competing claims made on so many issues, readers need a way to sort out fact from fiction. By using hyperlinks that connect to primary sources and adding supplemental information, journalists can help to shoot down outright lies while also providing greater context for statements that may have some element of truth but also obscure or distort important aspects of a situation.

Perhaps the best known fact-checking website is PolitiFact, which was started by the *Tampa Bay Times* in 2007 and now consists of a network of news organizations. It received the Pulitzer Prize for national reporting in 2009 (Adair, 2009). But there are several other sites that perform similar work, including factcheck.org, The Fact Checker page at *The Washington Post* and snopes.com, which specializes in researching online rumors.

Some of these sites have been criticized for failing to stick to the facts. As it turns out, many of the claims that the sites evaluate for truthfulness are not so much statements of fact but rather rhetorical flourishes. For example, PolitiFact declared that the "Lie of the Year" for 2011 was a Democratic claim that many Republicans had voted to end Medicare. The problem is that while a vote on that particular wording did not occur, Republicans did push for major changes in Medicare that would turn it into a different kind of program. So had the Democrats told a monstrous lie? Or was it that they had engaged in some misleading labeling of a set of facts that are not really in dispute (Folkenflik, 2011)?

Despite this ambiguity about what the sites are actually evaluating, there is some evidence that the existence of fact-checking sites can make politicians at least more careful about some of the things they say (Nyhan and Reifler, 2013). The exercise of fact-checking is also a way to get reporters to examine more carefully some of the shorthand formulations that are so widely used and to acknowledge the need for more nuanced descriptions and explanations.

As the first step in a fact-checking exercise, it is a good idea to decide on the rubric you will use to evaluate your findings. PolitiFact, for example, rates statements based on six different levels of truthfulness: True, Mostly True, Half-True, Mostly False, False and Pants on Fire! Snopes.com uses a traffic light approach, using green, red and yellow to signal whether a rumor is true, false or somewhere in between (Mikkelson and Mikkelson, 2013). *The Washington Post* gives out "Pinochios" based on how much a lie it perceives a statement to be (Kessler, 2013).

The next step is to pick out a person and a policy statement to evaluate. Potential evaluation targets could be elected officials who represent your area at the state or federal level, or perhaps a high-ranking official on campus. If you go with an elected official, you might try to find a statement related to higher education and see how much factual support there is. For example, your local congressman, no matter what his or her political affiliation, has almost certainly expressed strong support for higher education, reducing its costs and increasing its accessibility. You could find a statement to that effect and use it as your starting point for fact-checking.

> **Documents.** Many fact-checks rely most heavily on documents because of their authoritativeness. This is a good place to start. If your congressman, for example, has made a statement about support for higher education, look for two things: legislation introduced (or cosponsored) and votes cast. Check out the congressperson's website, and also go to the Congressional website known as Thomas, which is operated by the Library of Congress.

> **Observation.** Few fact-checkers find a need to make direct observations. It's true that most fact-checks relate to statements that can be confirmed or denied without making a visual inspection. But there is still value to seeing what there is to see. For example, if you are fact-checking a statement of support for higher education, the question is what should be the actual manifestation of that support. Is it higher enrollment? Enrollment of nontraditional students? New facilities? Although these may not be perfect measures, there is value in trying to include a visual dimension to your fact-check to help move the discussion from the abstract to the concrete.

> **Talk.** Clearly, the person you are fact-checking is someone to go back to for comment and possibly clarification. You should also interview disinterested parties who are knowledgeable about the subject. It's also a good idea to talk to average readers or citizens. One of the criticisms of the fact-checker genre is that it is too much of an insider's game, focusing on gradations of meaning that may not matter outside selected circles of interest. By talking to individuals who are directly affected by an issue and not necessarily part of the policy debate, you may get valuable insights.

SOCIAL MEDIA CURATIONS

When news occurs in your community, you can expect that social media platforms will light up with tweets, posts, still images and videos. The direct participation of citizens in the coverage of an event is a two-way opportunity for journalists, who can aggregate these disparate reports into an account and also use them as a way to identify and connect with potential sources for follow-up stories.

Various digital platforms, such as Storify or Paper.li, make it easy to search social media for content and then with no more than a mouse swipe assemble different elements into a story. The resulting stories often stand out for their immediacy and a kind of comprehensiveness that would be difficult for individual reporters to attain. But such accounts are also based on self-selected observers, who may also be participants, and as a result they can contain significant biases and omissions.

Journalists who wish to engage in this kind of social media reporting should supplement the social media elements with documents, observation and talk to ensure that the finished product is as close to an accurate reflection of events as possible.

Documents. The social media elements that are assembled into a story are essentially documents, and so a social media curation by definition is document-derived. But these social media documents are often produced in the heat of the moment in response to some spontaneous event, and their reliability necessarily is in question. Journalists should seek out other forms of documents to provide appropriate context.

Observation. Some forms of social media, such as photos and videos, provide news audiences with the opportunity to see a news event unfolding firsthand. It may be impossible to supplement such visual journalism with your own inputs. But it is important to realize that the images and raw footage you find on social media may or may not be accurate reflections of events on the ground. While this kind of material should be incorporated into your account, you may also want to include caveats to the audience about any difficulties there are in verifying its content or assessing its reliability.

Talk. As powerful as social media content can be, journalists should never forget that it is unprocessed and in many ways a form of digital gossip. But social media participants are public and identifiable. Don't simply accept the posts that are made to social media platforms, but use them as invitations for further discussions and information-gathering. It is also important to talk to sources off of social media platforms to obtain necessary context.

EXERCISES

1. Following the steps outlined above, identify some ideas for possible trend stories.

2. Think about some people on campus or in the local community who might be worth profiling. Develop a research plan, including a listing of potential sources to interview.

3. Following the steps outlined above, create a listicle. Find a slideshow-creation tool on the Web, and use it to publish your listicle in that format on a personal or class blog.

REFERENCES

Adair, Bill. "PolitiFact Wins Pulitzer," Politifact.com, April 20, 2009, accessed December 18, 2013, at http://www.politifact.com/truth-o-meter/article/2009/apr/20/politifact-wins-pulitzer/.

Allen, Mike, and Alexander Burns, "The Art of the Tick-Tock," *Politico*, December 6, 2009, accessed December 18, 2013, at http://www.politico.com/news/stories/1209/30248.html.

Aslan, Reza. "Five Myths About Jesus," *The Washington Post*, September 26, 2013, accessed December 18, 2013, at http://articles.washingtonpost.com/2013–09–26/opinions/42421357_1_nazareth-david-s-jesus-s.

Bowden, Mark. "Tales of the Tyrant," *Atlantic Monthly*, May 2002, 35–53.

Blumenthal, Richard. "11 Reasons Why Congress Needs To Fix Student Loan Rates Now," *Buzzfeed*, July 11, 2013, accessed December 18, 2013, at http://www.buzzfeed.com/senatorblumenthal/11-reasons-why-congress-needs-to-fix-student-loan-c703.

Cashmore, Pete. "11 Reasons Why We Should Still Love Listicles," *The Guardian Short Cuts Blog*, September 1, 2013, accessed December 18, 2013, at http://www.theguardian.com/media/shortcuts/2013/sep/01/11-reasons-why-still-love-listicles.

Dredge, Stuart. "BuzzFeed president: 'We feel strongly that traditional media have given up on young people,'" *The Guardian*, October 9, 2013, accessed December 18, 2013, at http://www.theguardian.com/media/2013/oct/09/buzzfeed-facebook-al-jazeera-social-news.

Fernandez, Manny. "Crime Blotter Has a Regular: Yankees Caps," *The New York Times*, September 15, 2010, accessed December 18, 2013, at http://www.nytimes.com/2010/09/16/nyregion/16caps.html?_r=0.

Folkenflik, David. "With 'Lie of the Year' Controversy, Fact Checking Comes Under Scrutiny," npr.org, December 22, 2011, accessed December 18, 2013, at http://www.npr.org/blogs/itsallpolitics/2011/12/22/144136535/with-lie-of-the-year-controversy-fact-checking-comes-under-scrutiny.

Fox, Margalit. "McCandlish Phillips, Who Exposed a Jewish Klansman, Is Dead at 85," *The New York Times*, April 9, 2013, accessed December 18, 2013, at http://www.nytimes.com/2013/04/10/business/media/mccandlish-phillips-times-reporter-dies-at-85.html.

Garber, Megan. "A Time for Tick-Tock," *Columbia Journalism Review*, September 26, 2008, accessed December 18, 2013, at http://www.cjr.org/the_kicker/a_time_for_ticktock.php.

Glassman, Mark. "Five Myths About Millennials," *The Washington Post*, August 20, 2013, accessed December 18, 2013, at http://articles.washingtonpost.com/2013–08–30/opinions/41600377_1_millennials-jeffrey-jensen-arnett-generation-y.

Kessler, Glenn. "About the Fact-Checker," *The Washington Post*, undated, accessed December 18, 2013, at http://www.washingtonpost.com/blogs/fact-checker/about-the-fact-checker/#pinocchio.

Letterman, David, and Steve O'Donnell. *David Letterman's Book of Top Ten Lists and Zesty Lo-cal Chicken Recipe*s, New York: Bantam Books, 1995.

Mikkelineni, Arun. "9 Political Views We Can Deduce from Your Drinking Habits," *Buzzfeed*, September 16, 2013, accessed December 13, 2013, at http://www.buzzfeed.com/arunmikkilineni/9-political-views-we-can-deduce-from-your-drinking-habits.

Mikkelson, Barbara, and David P. Mikkelson. "Ratings," snopes.com, undated, accessed December 18, 2013, at http://www.snopes.com/info/ratings.asp.

Nyhan, Brendan, and Jason Reifler. "The Effects of Fact-Checking Threat: Results from a Field Experiment in the States," New America Foundation, October

2013, accessed December 18, 2013, at http://www.newamerica.net/sites/newamerica.net/files/policydocs/nyhan-reifler-report-naf.pdf.

Phillips, McCandlish. "State Klan Leader Hides Secret of Jewish Origin," *The New York Times*, October 31, 1965.

Scanlan, Chip. "Finding the 'Black Pearl' with James McBride," Poynter.org, February 20, 2003/updated March 2, 2011, accessed December 18, 2013, at http://www.poynter.org/how-tos/newsgathering-storytelling/chip-on-your-shoulder/7080/finding-the-black-pearl-with-james-mcbride/.

Shafer, Jack. "A Midsummer's Stew of Bogus Trends," *Slate*, July 19, 2010a, accessed December 18, 2013, at http://www.slate.com/articles/news_and_politics/press_box/2010/07/a_midsummers_stew_of_bogus_trends.html.

———."Bogus Trend of the Day: NYC Criminals Wear Yankee Caps," *Slate*, September 16, 2010b, accessed December 18, 2013, at http://www.slate.com/articles/news_and_politics/press_box/2010/09/bogus_trend_of_the_day_nyc_criminals_wear_yankee_caps.html.

Stossel, Sage. "It's Not Easy Being Mean," theatlantic.com, April 25, 2002, accessed December 18, 2013, at http://www.theatlantic.com/past/docs/unbound/interviews/int2002-04-25.htm.

CHAPTER 10

Enterprise Reporting

As reporters gain experience and confidence, they are ready to move beyond the reactive mode of beat coverage and start to act on the insights they have gained from their regular study of and writing about the news on a particular topic. This chapter explains how DOT applies to large reporting projects by analyzing the process by which major stories get reported.

As described in Chapter 2, enterprise stories are based on reporting that is initiated by a journalist as opposed to reporting that is driven by specific events. Enterprise stories can arise from events, when reporters take the initiative to move beyond the obvious facts to look for underlying causes or explanations. They may also arise solely from a reporter's response to a situation that has not yet made it into the news. For many news organizations, and individual reporters, enterprise reporting becomes a mark of distinction that helps to create their reputation. *The New York Times* will always be associated with the Pentagon Papers, for example, just as *The Washington Post* will be associated with Watergate. Rachel Carson, Hunter Thompson, Barbara Walters, Ed Bradley and many other well-known journalists made their names with their own highly personalized approach to stories that to a large degree arose out of their individual choices of whom or what to cover. For those who know to look, and how to look, enterprise stories can be found anywhere, from Wall Street to the White House, and from the locker room of a major league team to the laboratories of medical researchers.

There are many contradictions associated with enterprise reporting. On the one hand, it can be the most glamorous part of journalism, leading to recognition by peers and the public. However, it also can involve almost excruciating tedium as records are assembled and information is double- and triple-checked. Successful enterprise reporters typically play to their personal strengths, and, as a result, there is no single approach that is recognized as foolproof or necessarily superior. At the same time, most enterprise stories do move through distinct phases that can be studied and adapted for use by student journalists. Oftentimes the stories are said to arise out of sheer determination and hard work, but in other cases coincidences and lucky breaks are critical.

Sometimes things just fall into place. For example, Nate Blakeslee's prize-winning investigation into sexual abuse by officials of the Texas Youth Commission started as a tip from a source, who said she thought the case had been investigated and there was a report available. It was better than that.

"The report was about 100 pages and had been conducted by the Texas Rangers," Blakeslee said in an interview with the Association of Alternative Newsmedia. "The stuff the report documented was far worse than what my source had described," he said. "It also had all the contact information listed in it" (Stoker, 2008).

Blakeslee still had significant work to do, getting in touch with those involved and persuading them to talk to him. But having the detailed report meant that he was well on his way to a blockbuster story. "Reporters don't often run into documents like this one," Blakeslee added. "In fact, a person can go a whole career without a case like this. This story was just waiting out there to be found" (Stoker, 2008).

Sometimes journalists get breaks in other ways, with assistance coming from unexpected quarters. A coincidence can lead to surprising new information as well. Both of those factors came into play in the investigation of Boys Town by *The Sun Newspapers of Omaha* in the early 1970s. As described in more detail below, the paper had assembled an extensive file on the charity and had strong suspicions that something was amiss in the way that it continued its aggressive fundraising past the point that it needed to finance its operations. But the big break in the investigation came, thanks not to anyone on the editorial staff but thanks to the paper's billionaire owner, the famed investor Warren Buffett.

It was Buffett who realized that the way to get specific information about Boys Town's financial condition was to obtain its tax returns, filed on Form 990, which thanks to a new law were being collected by the Internal Revenue Service and being made available for public inspection. Buffett recalled, "I was sitting there in the family room doing the Form 990 for the Buffett Foundation, and it just hit me—if I had to file a return, maybe they did too" (Schroeder, 2008, 359).

It was the Boys Town tax return that showed it had a net worth greater than that of Notre Dame University and was taking in money at a rate four times greater than what it needed to run on. There was still more work to do, interviews to conduct and information to collate. But the needed boost for the investigation came from Buffett, an old-fashioned newshound who still remembered his days running a paper route for *The Washington Post*.

What these anecdotes demonstrate is that there is a certain amount of serendipity in successful journalism. Some tips turn out to be better than expected; sometimes crucial information is just sitting there waiting to be picked up; sometimes an unrelated chain of events leads to the big break you were looking for. But experienced reporters know that these kinds of things happen rarely and that they won't get very far without a systematic approach for finding and developing big stories.

These stories also show why there is no such thing as a step-by-step guide to reporting and writing a major piece of investigative or explanatory journalism. Enterprise reporting can go in many different directions, as the Pulitzer Prize listing of winners in the investigative category makes clear (Columbia, "Investigative," n.d.). Some of the topic areas include:

- Bribes paid by a major international retailer.
- A program of spying on Muslim communities by the New York Police Department.
- A dangerous expansion in the use of methadone in the state of Washington.
- Faults in Florida's regulation of property insurers.
- Questionable drug enforcement in Philadelphia.
- Medical decisions in one New Orleans hospital after Hurricane Katrina.
- The role of retired generals in helping the Pentagon promote the Iraq War.
- The contamination by toxic substances of medical and other products imported from China.
- Problems in federal regulation of hazardous products used in raising children.
- Corruption in Alabama's system of two-year colleges.
- The corrupt dealings of a Washington lobbyist.
- A long ago story of sexual misconduct by the governor of Oregon with a 14-year-old girl.

A similar pattern, or rather lack of a pattern, can be seen in the stories that were listed in the explanatory category (Columbia, "Explanatory," n.d.):

- The business practices of Apple and other computer companies.
- The ways the wealthy avoid taxes.
- A 4-year-old with a genetic disease.
- Food safety issues.
- Wildfires in the West.
- The ethics of DNA testing.
- Ocean pollution.
- Yemen's move toward democracy.

- Stem cell research.
- Aneurysms.
- The fallout from corporate scandals.

As these topics suggest, stories arise out of different events and take shape in different ways. Nonetheless, there are certain phases that all investigations go through, from the initial idea for a story all the way through to production and publication of the finished report.

These phases are not necessarily sequential. Some of them may occur simultaneously, and some of them may have to happen repeatedly. On different stories they may occur in different order. As reporters move through these phases, they are analyzing documents, making observations and talking with sources. At several points in the process, they also look back over the information they have gathered, testing its validity and whether it still points to a publishable story.

Paul N. Williams, who led the prize-winning Boys Town investigation, outlined a detailed process for conducting an enterprise reporting project in his book *Investigative Reporting and Editing,* which was published in 1978, two years after his death, and since has gone out of print (Williams, 1978). Williams, a longtime journalist turned journalism professor, was looking for a way to standardize a form of reporting that was most often pursued by journalists who were disinclined to acknowledge the existence of an intellectual discipline at the core of their work. It was true that their work ranged across many different fields and often proceeded in an unorderly fashion, filled with fits and starts, frustrations and setbacks. But Williams argued that in reviewing how enterprise reporters pursued their stories, a pattern could be seen. "What is found is a definite order of activities arranged in such a way that no lead was passed up, no bit of information unevaluated" (13).

This method, now known as the "the Paul Williams Way," has been included in subsequent works, such as *The Investigative Reporter's Handbook* (Houston et al., 2009), because it represents an approach that provides a practical way of conducting large-scale projects while also establishing benchmarks for thoroughness and care. The Paul Williams Way is perhaps more of an idealized description of how an investigation can unfold rather than a recipe that has to be followed exactly. But it is a useful way into the investigative reporting process for a student journalist, and this chapter will consider how it was applied in the Boys Town case and can be applied, at least with modifications, in other contexts. The outline included here does not begin to capture all of the insights and advice about the reporting process that Williams offered in his book, and anyone who is serious about this kind of journalism would do well to seek out a copy in a library or used bookstore.

Williams identified 11 steps that would take a reporter or a reporting team from story idea to publication and argued that each one was a necessary part of the progression. But students should not be put off by this admonition or by the apparent intricacy of the Paul Williams Way. His approach, much like the approach of this textbook, emphasized the contingent nature of journalism and the importance of sifting, checking, evaluating (and re-evaluating) the information a reporter acquires.

Here are the 11 steps that Williams outlined (14):

1. Conception.
2. Feasibility study.
3. Go/no-go decision.
4. Planning and base-building.
5. Original research.
6. Reevaluation.
7. Go/no-go decision.
8. Key interviews.
9. Final evaluation.
10. Final go/no-go decision.
11. Writing and publication.

What should be immediately apparent is that Williams put a lot of emphasis on repetition. Notice that three of the stages of his investigative process are the same—making a go/no-go decision. Also notice that there are two evaluations and a feasibility study. Williams knew that for a successful enterprise reporter, there is no such thing as being too diligent. While Williams was careful to say that this process was not a recipe that had to be followed exactly, the number of steps and the apparent intricacy of this method can be a little overwhelming, especially for student journalists. As an alternative, journalists who are contemplating their first enterprise project may find it easier to break the process down into just three steps: the beginning, the middle and the end.

THE BEGINNING

The beginning of an enterprise story is when you get an idea for a story and decide to do something about it. Both parts of this formula are important—catching a glimpse of a potential story and then pursuing it. You may think that the key to being a successful reporter is being in the right place at the right time or having sources who slip you secret documents or tip you off to upcoming controversies. Such factors can contribute to your success, but they are to a certain degree beyond your control. What is under your control is how you react to a potential story, whether you are willing to deal with the uncertainty and possibly the hostility that you will encounter as you develop an idea for a story into a finished report.

Where do stories come from? The only honest answer is not very helpful because the reality is that story ideas can and do come from all over. There can be anonymous tips and hints from trusted sources. A throwaway comment from an official or an enigmatic footnote in a report can start reporters on their way. Sometimes an event story leaves unanswered questions begging for further study, and sometimes a promising story idea doesn't pan out but may allow a reporter to stumble across a situation that is worthy of review.

Consider the case of the Pulitzer Prize that Walt Bogdanich won in 1988 for specialized reporting, in his case on medicine. His articles in *The Wall Street Journal* spotlighted the errors that laboratories frequently make in evaluating medical tests with consequences that range from minor inconveniences to the preventable deaths of patients. His reporting showed that the underlying problems ranged from simple incompetence to outright illegalities, and his work led to congressional investigations as well as reform of industry practices. What set all of this in motion? The reporter's personal experience, getting bad results from a routine cholesterol test (Pearlstine, 1988). It's unlikely that Bogdanich was the first journalist to have such an experience, but he certainly was the first to go from this starting point on to such an extensive exploration of the issue.

An incomplete, and unscientific, review of accounts of prize-winning journalism reveals several things. First, big stories often have humble beginnings as small, even routine requests for information turn into much bigger issues. The second point is perhaps more important, that the key in many cases is the reaction of the reporter, and especially the ability to consider that something might be amiss, that it is not the way it is supposed to be, which was the definition of news outlined in Chapter 2.

"Finding the piece in the puzzle that doesn't fit, the extraneous fact in all of the collection of data, is what starts the investigator on the trail," Williams wrote. "Comparing and contrasting as the reporter sifts through the accumulation of records, he develops nerves closer to the surface than most people, an instinct for the telltale clue—the fact unlike in all the facts alike" (1978, 28).

Using as a guide the awards program of Investigative Reporters and Editors, the nonprofit organization that promotes in-depth journalism that is also known as IRE, let's take a look at some student reporting projects that began small but turned into something bigger. For J. David McSwane the starting point was a conversation he overheard at his high school in suburban Denver. A couple of his fellow students were discussing their plans to join the military even though they lacked high school diplomas and had an abiding fondness for illegal drugs. Their confident talk about making it through the enlistment process aroused his doubts, which he decided to resolve by going undercover (McSwane, 2006). "After seeing how military recruiters at my high school fished for students willing to fight a war, I began to wonder just how far they'd go to get one more finger on the trigger," McSwane wrote in a follow-up article for *Westword,* an alternative weekly and website in Denver. "I decided to find out for myself" (McSwane, 2005).

McSwane went to an Army recruiting station, where he presented himself as a high school dropout and drug addict. Two recruiters tried to help him through the process, by telling him how to obtain a fake diploma and how to get through a drug screening. When he was asked to sign an affidavit that his diploma was genuine, McSwane brought the undercover operation to a halt and wrote up his experience for the Arvada West High School newspaper, *The Westwind,* which published his story in March 2005. Other media outlets, including the *The New York Times,* picked up on his findings, and within a matter of months the Army ordered a stand-down, a one-day suspension of operations, in its recruiting command so that personnel could review the legal and ethical dimensions of the enlistment process (Cave, 2005).

In its reporting the *Times* found that recruiters were aware of problems with the enlistment process in at least 10 states, and the Army itself said it had investigated and documented several hundred cases of improper recruiting practices. It would seem, then, that the conversation McSwane overheard was not an isolated case, and it's unlikely that he was the only student journalist, either in high school or college, who had heard of irregularities in the recruiting process. What was different in his case was his decision to look further.

In 2006 IRE cited McSwane's work as a top example of student journalism (IRE, 2006), but McSwane is not the only example of award-winning student work that got its start with a conversation. Chelsea Boozer (see Figure 10.1), a staffer at *The Daily Helmsman,* was in the process of turning down a story pitch from a fellow student at the University of Memphis when the student, a member of the Student Government Association, mentioned the university provided scholarships for SGA members (Boozer, 2011).

To Boozer the idea that the university would provide scholarships for student representatives didn't sound right—and in fact it wasn't quite true. But instead of dismissing this comment out of hand, she decided to follow up. What she found was that scholarships did not go to all student members of the SGA—only to the officers, and to the officers of another student group, the Student Activities Committee. As she dug further, she was able to document the full extent of this financial support, which included not only tuition but also parking and stipends for six student leaders, at a total cost of almost $70,000 a year. She also discovered that student fees were the source

FIGURE 10.1   *Reporter Chelsea Boozer. Credit: Larry Kuzniewski*

of this money and that the fees also were being spent in other questionable ways. Like McSwane, Boozer was cited by IRE for her reporting (2011).

Successful enterprise stories get started in other ways, too—from roadblocks that you encounter, class assignments you may get, brainstorming discussions you are part of. Not all passing comments or overheard conversations or class projects will result in stories or are worth weeks or months of investigations. But some are. And you can't tell the difference until after you have taken some steps and asked some questions. The biggest stories are often the ones that seem most unbelievable at first.

A tip that isn't followed up on because it sounds too improbable or outlandish (or possibly upsetting) is like the proverbial tree falling in the middle of the forest that makes no sound because no one is there to hear it. Following up on tips is not always a simple task, and reporters can expect to experience various forms of pushback, everything from noncooperation to pleas to keep things quiet to outright threats. Especially at the beginning of a complex story, you are unlikely to know where your reporting will lead or whether it will lead you anywhere at all. This lack of certainty can produce some anxiety. When you are cold-calling sources to try to find out even simple background information, you shouldn't be surprised to hear a note of a suspicion in their voices. Again, this kind of response can make you uncomfortable. Whatever you do, don't let this low-level stress deter you. It's often a necessary start for getting going on a story.

Since an enterprise story is one that, by definition, isn't driven by the news, reporting such a story means moving out of regular routines and rhythms. An enterprise story is optional; it doesn't have to be written, and in many cases there is only one reporter or one news organization pursuing it. As a result, the success of an enterprise story will depend heavily on a reporter's news sense and curiosity. But there is more to it than that, because an enterprise story can also require a degree of personal resilience, depending on a reporter's tolerance for uncertainty and, ultimately, criticism. Part of the recipe for success in enterprise reporting is a willingness to be viewed as an outsider, a nonconformist.

This approach may come naturally to some people, but for most people, and even for most reporters, it is a difficult step to take, to move outside one's comfort zone. We all want to be liked, but as the scholar Michael Schudson has argued, "democracies need an unlovable press" (2008). There are at least two good reasons to follow an independent path as a reporter. First it will lead to good journalism, and second it is a major part of the responsibility of reporters in a free society.

"Zig when everyone else zags," was the mantra of Gene Roberts when he came to *The Philadelphia Inquirer* in the early 1970s. Over the 18 years of his tenure as editor the paper won 17 Pulitzers. Long after he left Philadelphia, his advice is still quoted by some of the reporters who worked for him there, including Buzz Bissinger, who went on to write *Friday Night Lights,* a book about high school football in Texas (LaFrance, 2012), and Mark Bowden (2004, 8), whose books include *Black Hawk Down,* an account of the Battle of Mogadishu that became an Oscar-winning film. Zigging instead of zagging sounds easier than it is. It requires being out of step and out of place.

Schudson is one of many scholars and critics of the press who believe that reporters work too hard to be insiders, with negative consequences for their profession and for the country as a whole. Some studies have tied the news media's weak performance across a range of measures—including audience size, profitability and public perceptions—to its inability to provide a counterweight to conventional wisdom, especially in the sphere of government and politics. The mainstream press is too often a mouthpiece for those in power, and clear examples abound across the political spectrum. The way the administration of President George W. Bush manipulated public opinion in advance of the invasion of Iraq has been called "the media's greatest failure in modern times" (Kurtz, 2013). But the news media has also been accused of going easy on his successor, Barack Obama (Farnsworth and Lichter, 2012), although they increased their criticism after discovering they themselves were the subject of secret surveillance (Downie, 2013).

Schudson believes that journalism education itself needs to be reformed to help students cope with the difficulty of being an outsider. "The idea would be to disorient rather than orient the prospective journalist," he writes. "Disorientation—and ultimately alienation of journalists—helps the press to be free" (2008, 60). In his view, journalists who are doing the greatest service for democracy do not always behave in ways that would be seen as positive or uplifting, such as when they are the troublemaking outsider. You don't have to be a troublemaker to be a successful reporter, of course, but you do have to develop a bit of a thick skin.

Alex Stuckey (see Figure 10.2), then the assistant managing editor of Ohio University's student newspaper, *The Post,* was working on a story about drug usage in Athens County, where the school is located. But her story, which appeared in 2012 and won an award from IRE the following year, ended up being about something else. Instead of writing about the way drug laws were being broken, she wrote about the way local law enforcement

FIGURE 10.2   *Reporter Alex Stuckey. Credit: Courtesy of the* Post Register *(Idaho)*

agencies were breaking state laws that required them to maintain records and report on the seized and forfeited property they were holding in their evidence rooms. Her story took this detour because the local sheriff wouldn't give her information about the amount of drugs confiscated, even though she had already gotten similar data from city and university police. She discovered that he couldn't give her this information because he wasn't keeping track of it. Her research eventually showed that 69 percent of the 670 law enforcement agencies in the state that were supposed to report this information were not doing so.

When she was initially rebuffed by the sheriff, Stuckey could have given up, but as she said in an interview with IRE, she knew that the sheriff's office "prides itself on its drug task force." As a result, she filed public records requests to get the information she wanted—not that this approach was all that successful. "He'd deny my records request with either no reason attached or a reason that would not stand up in a court of law, and I'd walk down to his office and wait outside his door. I called him several times a day, showed up there all the time" (Harkins, 2013).

Unsolicited tips from unidentified sources can lead to breakthrough articles, but so can sitting around and talking through ideas. In 2008 student journalists at the University of Georgia, following up on a tip, found that professors who had been violating the school's sexual harassment policy were still allowed to teach. These reports roiled the campus and led to a full-scale review of campus procedures (O'Neil, 2009). The Boys Town series that Williams coordinated, by contrast, got started in a much less dramatic way. His paper held weekly staff meetings to brainstorm story ideas, looking for ones that would, among other things, scoop the competition. Based on those discussions, Williams would develop every January a list of stories that might be investigated over the course of the year. That list would in turn be the subject of more discussions with the paper's publisher and its owner. It was at one of these periodic meetings, as the three newspaper executives discussed the state of their publication over soft drinks, that they decided to turn their attention to Boys Town (Williams, 1978).

In the Williams approach to in-depth reporting, the beginning of a project involves the idea stage and then two other stages: a feasibility study and a go/no-go decision. In an idealized world, reporters do have to consider the feasibility of whether they can bring back a story and decide whether to go forward, but it isn't always necessary to do so in such a formalized way. Many times one piece of information leads to another, and the project is either rolling ahead, or if a dead end is reached right away, the idea is discarded without this kind of formalized review.

But even if you don't take your story idea through one phase called "feasibility study" and another one called "go/no-go," there are some considerations that Williams cites worth paying attention to. One aspect of feasibility, of course, is whether you or your colleagues have the skills and time to bring the story in, but another aspect of feasibility is what happens after the story is published. A critical story may bring unwanted consequences from readers and advertisers. A campus publication may have the additional problem of dealing with school administrators who may be unhappy with your story.

Journalists should not engage in self-censorship, but they should be clear about what they are reporting and why. Just because some powerful individual or institution doesn't want you to publish a story doesn't mean that you shouldn't. But just because you are within your legal rights to publish something doesn't mean that you should.

Developing an enterprise story requires judgment, both about whether to pursue a story at all and about how to proceed. Enterprise stories don't always end up in the place that they look like they are headed when you first get started, which is one of the main reasons why it's usually a good idea to do some preliminary research on a story idea before deciding to reject it or pursue it full force.

Consider the case of a player on one of your school's athletic teams who is caught in a relatively minor incident with the campus police, say underage drinking. Such an incident would be documented in a police report and possibly in a court document. A student newspaper would be well within its rights to report such a story, and some might do so as a matter of routine. A star athlete at a Division I school would certainly expect to be the subject of media scrutiny.

But under other circumstances, the question of whether to publish may not be so clear-cut. Say the incident happened at a Division III school, where the athletes are not on scholarship. Or maybe the player isn't a starter, or plays in a "minor" sport that normally attracts little attention. The player's teammates, his coach and possibly top school administrators might rise up in the player's defense, and readers, and even some members of the newspaper staff, may take offense at publication of the story. It is not uncommon, after all, for college students to commit minor infractions or to be caught with banned substances.

The easy thing at this point would be to walk away from the story. But letting a story drop without giving it further consideration is a recipe for inferior journalism. The traditions of journalism say that reporters should stick to the facts (and they should), but there is also a place in the reporting process for imagination, and good reporters use their imaginations to think about alternatives to how their stories may turn out. In this case, a single-shot story about an unknown player may not be worth pursuing. But there are some questions that should be answered first. For example, is this the student-athlete's only run-in with the law? Are there other student-athletes who have been ticketed or arrested? Is there any indication of favoritism, such as a deferred prosecution agreement? In many jurisdictions, all of these questions could be investigated with simple online searches.

It's also necessary to turn things around, and look at the possibilities from a completely different angle. If you do find that student-athletes are regularly getting into legal scrapes, you should at least consider the possibility that they are drawing extra attention, perhaps because of their size or perhaps because of other physical attributes, from the police. This concept, of looking at alternative possibilities for your finished story, is another key piece of the Paul Williams Way. Stories may be bigger than you think initially, but they may also turn out to be smaller. Where there is smoke, there may only be smoke—and no fire.

That's why Williams recommended that reporters identify a minimum story that they would find even if the bigger story they are after doesn't materialize (1978, 24). In the scenario outlined above, the biggest potential story would be possible police misconduct, and questions have been raised on several college campuses in recent years about whether student-athletes are singled out for arrests (Hawco, 2001; Mayrer, 2012). But even if that story didn't pan out, there might be less explosive ones, perhaps about a particular team, or even an individual athlete. The point that Williams was making was that journalists need to have a fallback position before they decide to commit a lot of time and energy into an enterprise story. They need to have a minimum story that they know they can publish if they expect to be able to convince an editor to let them devote significant resources to a project.

Once you have gotten the green light to proceed with your reporting project, you are still not quite ready to begin your research, which is, without a doubt, the most important phase of your work. Before you get started picking up the phone or filing public records requests or wandering around to look at someone else's property, you need to spend some time planning out your actions, envisioning the steps you will need to take to gather information as well as the process of developing a suitable publishable presentation, which will often include multimedia elements.

Inexperienced reporters may be tempted to dive into the research phase, but this is usually a mistake. For one thing, depending on the story topic, it's possible to sink your project before you get underway by tipping off sources about what you might be hoping to find out, scaring them and prompting them to ask their associates not to cooperate with you. In the long run, your efficiency as a reporter and the impact of your research will depend on your willingness to take some time out to get a feel for the lay of the land and to identify the steps that will need to be taken to make sure the project will be a success.

Your reporting plan, which may evolve from your original project proposal, needs to include the following elements:

- **Documents.** What data sources will you use, and where will you get them? Are there background reports you can use to familiarize yourself with your topic? A successful enterprise story is almost always going to be based on some deviation from the standards and norms that apply in a given subject area. Reporters have to make sure they understand what the norms are so that they can see where the deviations are.

- **Observation.** Where will you go? What will you look for?

- **Talk.** Identify by name, or at least by general type, the people you will need to interview.

- **Presentation Material.** Still photography, videos, sound clips, interactive graphics and searchable databases have all become common elements in enterprise projects. You cannot afford to wait until all of your reporting is done to think about these things. You may not have time to sit on your findings while you pull these aspects of your project together. In addition, depending on how your reporting proceeds, you may not be able to recreate interviews or gain access to places for photographs or video if sources decide they will no longer cooperate. (See Chapter 11 on technology for more details on digital tools you can use in reporting.)

- **Timeline.** Try to describe the tasks that need to be accomplished and specify target dates. Set some intermediate goals and checkpoints so that you can make sure your project is proceeding appropriately— or to take corrective action to get back on track if you start to fall behind.

- **Support.** Can you do this alone, or will you need help? For example, do you need help in obtaining a dataset and analyzing it? Are you prepared to conduct interviews that may turn adversarial? Do you need access to specialized equipment or software? Perhaps you need to try to put a team together.

THE MIDDLE

The middle of an enterprise project is the most important phase, since it consists of the period when you are doing most of your research. Although Williams did not use a phrase like "connecting the DOT," it's clear that he prized the use of different kinds of information gathering techniques and, even more important, recognized the importance of looking not so much for convergence between different pieces of information as for the gaps that are inevitably there. It is through the process of closing those gaps, making connections between different datapoints, that journalists strengthen their stories and come closer to a true version of events.

At the heart of any enterprise project is the skillful application of the DOT methodology, with a special emphasis on documents. The Boys Town investigation is a good illustration of this point.

Documents. Documents don't have to be secret or arcane or even hard to get to prove useful to a reporter. In this case one of the first things that the paper did was to gather up Boys Town's promotional material, which included the claim that it did not get any form of government funding. This seemingly innocuous statement was repeated routinely, but it turned out to be false, since the organization did receive relatively small amounts of state and federal aid through school and welfare subsidies. Williams recalled, in an article published in the *Columbia Journalism Review,* that the discrepancy "was a chink in Boys Town's publicity armor," making him and his staff wonder about other statements the organization had made (1975, 32). Throughout the investigation, documents were uppermost in the minds of Williams and his staff. Because of Boys Town's stature in the community and its past refusal to discuss its financial operations, the newspaper reporters knew they couldn't just start asking question but instead would have to work from the outside in until they had enough solid data to ask hard questions.

In addition to the organization's promotional materials, Williams (1975) described how his staff identified six kinds of records the reporters needed to get their hands on:

- Boys Town was an incorporated village, which meant that it had to file a budget and a report of operations with the state.

- Boys Town operated its own post office, which meant that it had to file reports with the postmaster general of the United States.

- Boys Town operated an accredited school, which meant that it had to prepare reports of attendance, staffing, curriculum and regulatory compliance.

- Boys Town was a nonprofit corporation, which meant it had to file reports, corporate documents and lists of officers with the state.

- Boys Town was licensed to provide child care, which meant there were other reporting requirements to the state Welfare Department.

- Boys Town was a landowner, which meant that there were records of deeds, debts, prices and dates of ownership transfer.

By identifying these records and tracking them down, the newspaper was able to put together extensive background information on Boys Town without ever asking a direct question. To top it all off were the tax returns that the paper obtained based on Buffett's suggestion.

Observation. Although direct observation played a relatively small role in the Boys Town story, it was a key element that provided reinforcement to the reporters that they were on the right track. In the Boys Town case, it was the size and appearance of the Boys Town property that was the clearest evidence the organization enjoyed robust finances. In the past, Boys Town had claimed it needed to raise funds because of the large, but unspecified, expenses it incurred. "But it was obvious that Boys Town was not going broke," Williams wrote. "The physical plant (a huge green campus dotted with brick and stone buildings, a 1,000 acre farm using boys as hired hands) and the size of the payroll (some 600 employees) were enough to tell us that" (Williams, 1975, 31).

Talk. As in almost any story, talking with human sources will yield the most, and the most significant, information. But not all interview subjects are created equal, and reporters typically save the best for last. In the middle stage of the enterprise story, you may conduct large numbers of interviews but you may not be talking yet with the people who are at the heart of your story. Those interviews will most likely come in the final phase of the project, when you have assembled as much information as possible.

Williams recommends a systematic approach to interviews, not only transcribing your material but also adding statements about the nature of the interview and noting questions that were not answered (1978, 27–28). This may be especially important in complicated stories that take months to investigate since your memory may have faded from the time when you spoke to your source.

Connecting the DOT. Williams emphasizes the importance of going beyond the information you have gathered and actively analyzing what you have learned—and what you still do not know. On a regular basis, at least once a week on an extended project, Williams recommended that you review what you have discovered and determine whether it raises new questions or calls for further clarification. Williams called this phase "gap-closing" and explained it as a process of reconciling inconsistencies (1978, 28). The goal is to understand why you have gaps—are there inconsistencies in the records you consulted? Does the timing of a process or series of events differ in the retelling by different sources? Does a comment conflict with your recollection of the physical layout of a place you have visited? It is through this process of examining the information you have collected and seeing how it connects, or does not connect, that you will achieve a highly credible account.

Gaps can also arise when you are unable to find the information you need to allow you to reach a definitive conclusion about a person, institution or situation. In the Boys Town case, Williams reached this point when his staff had assembled information from state records and from interviews that pointed to a problem with the nonprofit but did not definitively prove that it was engaging in excessive fund-raising. This is when Buffett's recollections about the new tax return filing requirements for charitable organizations allowed the paper to get Boys Town's tax records.

THE END OF THE ENTERPRISE PROJECT

The last phase of the enterprise project includes the major interviews, final double-checking of information, production and publication, and then follow-up. The major interviews are, clearly, the most important, whether they are hostile or friendly, and they have to wait until you have as full a picture as possible about your reporting subject. Going into a final interview without having done the homework is inexcusable. But there may be situations when you may choose to gamble and see if you have enough information to bluff you way to the point where you provoke a confirmation from a source. This was the situation the Omaha paper faced before it obtained the Boys Town tax returns (Williams, 1975, 34). Fortunately, it did not have to adopt this strategy, which is highly risky.

All of the information in an enterprise story, down to the smallest detail, bears on the credibility of the overall thrust of the piece. An important, but factually flawed, story will get drowned in criticism if details, even ones that are arguably inconsequential, are not correct. Unfortunately many smaller news organizations have reduced their editing capacity, which means that it is up to individual reporters to do much of their own editing themselves. If this is not a strong suit of yours, and even if it is, it is probably a good idea to take a systematic approach and use an accuracy checklist, an itemization of mistakes that are frequently made in news copy. Use the checklist to go through your piece and satisfy yourself that all of your facts are accurate.

At larger news organizations, there might be the necessary support staff to help with the editing and final production of multimedia elements of your project. On the other hand, there may not be.

Once your project is ready for publication, you may think it's time to sit back and relax. But it's not. In today's overcrowded media environment, it is quite possible that an outstanding piece of journalism will be overlooked because it is crowded out of the public's field of attention by all the other news and information of the day. Unless you work for a marquee news organization with an international reputation, you are going to have to do some promotion on your own using social media. In addition you should gear yourself up for reaction stories and other kinds of follow-up.

EXERCISES

1. Several of the prize-winning stories mentioned in this chapter came out of more or less casual conversations. Think back about conversations you have had over the last week and make a list of at least 10 topics that you covered. On each topic, try to think of something that was said that has the makings of a news story, something that is potentially out of place, something, to quote Paul Williams, that

is a "fact unlike in all the facts alike." Try to formulate three story ideas from this list, and then identify the first step you would take to look into these further, such as an informal discussion with a source, the filing of a public records request or backgrounding using the Internet.

2. One way to think of an enterprise story is that it is an answer to a question that no one else has yet thought to ask. It follows then that framing your story and organizing your research around a question is a good way to get started on an enterprise story. Try to think of some questions you do not have the answers to regarding your campus or your community.

3. Do an Internet search on the term "accuracy checklist." Look over some of the versions that have been developed and identify the 10 items you think are most important to double-check.

4. Review some examples of reporters who talk about how they developed enterprise stories. You can find several resources on the Internet, such as http://howigotthatstorywebinars.com/. Come up with three tips you can share with fellow students.

REFERENCES

Boozer, Chelsea. "Official Entry Form," Investigative Editors and Reporters, January 12, 2011, accessed (with password) December 19, 2013, at http://www.ire.org/resource-center/stories/24887/.

Bowden, Mark. *Road Work: Among Tyrants, Heroes, Rogues, and Beasts,* New York: Atlantic Monthly Press, 2004.

Cave, Damien, "Army to Spend Day Retraining Recruiters," *The New York Times,* May 12, 2005, accessed December 19, 2013, at http://www.nytimes.com/2005/05/12/national/12recruit.html?pagewanted=print&_r=0.

Columbia University. "Investigative Reporting," *The Pulitzer Prizes,* undated, accessed December 19, 2013, at http://www.pulitzer.org/bycat/Investigative-Reporting.

———. "Explanatory Reporting," *The Pulitzer Prizes,* undated, accessed December 19, 2013, at http://www.pulitzer.org/bycat/Explanatory-Reporting.

Downie, Leonard. "The Obama Administration and the Press: Leak Investigations and Surveillance in Post-9/11 America," Committee to Project Journalists, October 10, 2013, accessed December 19, 2013, at http://www.cpj.org/reports/2013/10/obama-and-the-press-us-leaks-surveillance-post-911.php.

Farnsworth, Stephen J., and S. Robert Lichter. "News Coverage of New Presidents in *The New York Times,* 1981–2009," *Politics & Policy* 40, No. 1, February 2012, 69–91.

Harkins, Sarah. "Behind the Story: Student Investigation Wins IRE Award," *IRE News,* June 5, 2013, Investigative Reporters and Editors, accessed December 19, 2013, at http://www.ire.org/blog/ire-news/2013/06/05/behind-story-student-investigation-wins-ire-award/.

Hawco, Stephanie. "N.C. State Linebacker Arrested on Domestic Violence Charges," WRAL.com, February 7, 2001/updated January 4, 2012, accessed December 19, 2013, at https://www.wral.com/news/local/story/136565/.

Houston, Brant, and Investigative and Reporters and Editors Inc., *The Investigative Reporter's Handbook: A Guide to Documents, Databases and Techniques,* 5th ed., Boston: Bedford/St. Martin's, 2009.

Investigative Reporters and Editors, "2005 IRE Awards Winners," 2006, accessed December 19, 2013, at http://www.ire.org/awards/ire-awards/winners/2005-ire-awards-winners/#army.

———. "2010 IRE Awards Winners," April 8, 2011, accessed December 19, 2013, at http://www.ire.org/awards/ire-awards/winners/2010-ire-awards-winners/.

Kurtz, Howard. "Media's Failure on Iraq Still Stings," *CNN Opinion,* March 11, 2013, accessed December 19, 2013, at http://www.cnn.com/2013/03/11/opinion/kurtz-iraq-media-failure/index.html.

LaFrance, Adrienne. "Buzz Bissinger: Newspaper Editors Are 'Very Cautious—Too Cautious,'" Nieman Journalism Lab, May 21, 2012, accessed December 19, 2013, at http://www.niemanlab.org/2012/05/buzz-bissinger-newspaper-editors-are-very-cautious-too-cautious/.

Mayrer, Jessica. "Former Griz Player, Family Threaten Lawsuit Over Controversial Arrest," *Missoula Independent,* August 19, 2012, accessed December 19, 2013, at http://missoulanews.bigskypress.com/missoula/the-other-side/Content?oid=1892046.

McSwane, J. David. "An Army of Anyone," Westword.com, September 29, 2005, accessed December 19, 2013, at http://www.westword.com/2005-09-29/news/an-army-of-anyone/2/.

———. "Official Entry Form," Investigative Reporters and Editors, January 1, 2006, accessed (with password) December 19, 2013, at http://www.ire.org/resource-center/stories/22504/.

O'Neil, Carey. "Red & Black Reporters Win National Investigative Award," *The Red & Black,* April 1, 2009, accessed December 19, 2013, at http://www.redandblack.com/news/red-black-reporters-win-national-investigative-award/article_3782cccf-eb8e-5a53-ac3f-51891460ffd0.html?mode=jqm.

Pearlstine Norman. Letter to Pulitzer Prize Board, January 29, 1988. Microfilm from Columbia University Lehman Library, the Pulitzer Prizes in Journalism Archives.

Schroeder, Alice. *The Snowball: Warren Buffett and the Business of Life,* New York: Bantam Books, 2008.

Schudson, Michael. *Why Democracies Need an Unlovable Press,* Malden, Mass.: Polity Press, 2008.

Stoker, Sam. "How I Got That Story: Nate Blakeslee," Association of Alternative Newsmedia, November 4, 2008, accessed December 19, 2013, at http://www.altweeklies.com/aan/how-i-got-that-story-nate-blakeslee/Article?oid=678230.

Williams, Paul N. "Boys Town: An Expose Without Bad Guys," *Columbia Journalism Review,* January/February 1975, 30–38.

———. *Investigative Reporting and Editing,* Englewood Cliffs, N.J.: Prentice-Hall, 1978.

PART THREE

21st Century News Reporting

CHAPTER 11

Technology

The Pulitzer Prize Board made its first award in the category of feature writing in 1979, to science writer Jon Franklin for his account of a surgical operation on a woman with a tangle of malformed blood vessels in her brain. His articles appeared in *The Evening Sun,* a Baltimore broadsheet that, like most newspapers of its day, published almost exclusively in black and white. The two-part series was accompanied by a simple illustration, the outline of a person's head with the brain highlighted and a short phrase superimposed: "Tales from the Gray Frontier" (Franklin, 1978, C1).

Franklin is a recognized master of nonfiction narrative, and it was clearly his ability to tell the story of the medical procedure by means of such literary techniques as foreshadowing and conflict that caught the judges' attention. It was Franklin's polished prose—words on the page, carefully chosen and artfully arranged to turn a highly complex topic into a thrilling account of a medical doctor fighting, but ultimately losing, a battle against one woman's disease—that won him the Pulitzer. Franklin had editors who looked over his copy and made improvements, but no one would argue that the Pulitzer belonged to him alone.

In 2013 the Pulitzer Prize for Feature Writing went to John Branch of *The New York Times* for his story of an avalanche that killed three people (Branch, 2012). The citation for his award began by praising "his evocative narrative about skiers killed in an avalanche and the science that explains such disasters." But few people doubted that what really made his work so distinctive was described in the last part of the citation: "a project enhanced by its deft integration of multimedia elements" (Columbia, 2013).

Branch's article, which appeared both in print and on his paper's website, was beautifully written and relied on many of the same literary techniques that Franklin employed three decades earlier. But it wasn't the writing alone that had many journalists wondering if Branch's piece was "the future of journalism." That's because on the Web his text had been skillfully woven with multimedia elements to form what was described as an "experience-based feature" (Greenfield, 2012).

When site users arrived at the online version of the story, they were greeted with an eerie video of snow blowing across the side of a mountain.

As they scrolled down, they encountered images, slideshows, videos (including footage from helmet cameras) and full-screen animated graphics, starting with a flyover map of the mountains where the story was set. Creating this multimedia extravaganza took six months and involved a team of 16, including 11 people working on graphics and design, three who shot video, a still photographer and a researcher (Branch, 2012).

In some ways Branch's work was a classic application of the DOT methodology. It began with documents, the initial report of the accident and "the examination of reports by the police, the medical examiner and the Stevens Pass Ski Patrol, as well as 40 calls to 911 made in the aftermath of the avalanche" (Branch, 2012). He traveled to Colorado so that he could make direct observations. In a Q&A posted on the *Times* website, Branch recalled, "I hiked up the lower portion of the avalanche path with [survivor] Tim Carlson, and was with him when he found one of the skis of the victims" (*The New York Times*, 2012). The story quoted only those survivors and rescue workers who were on the scene the day of the avalanche, but Branch ended up talking with many more: "every survivor, the families of the deceased, first responders at Tunnel Creek, officials at Stevens Pass and snow-science experts" (Branch, 2012).

Clearly, digital technology allowed Branch to go far beyond the kind of story he could have produced if he had been working, like Franklin, primarily with words. The sights and the sounds and the animated graphics provided a layer of rich auditory and visual sensations in a way that words alone cannot do. But while his article demonstrated the promise of technology when applied to journalism, it also demonstrated the peril. As noted, the project took six months to complete, and it seems unlikely that there are many other news organizations besides the *Times* that could afford to do such a thing.

For the individual reporter, Branch's prize-winning story offers contradictory views of the future. On the one hand, we can see that it is possible to report for the Web and produce stories that go far beyond a print-only article, no matter how well written or well told. But, on the other hand, the range of possibilities is almost equally matched by the scale of the effort it will take to achieve them.

The Branch story was a pioneering effort, and it's likely that future work in this vein will go more quickly and get accomplished with less of an investment in time and energy. That's because digital technology continues to improve on an almost daily basis, both in terms of capability and in terms of ease of use. This is the rub for most reporters. Since technology is available and is getting easier to use, there is an expectation that journalists will be able to learn how to use it and put it to work in their regular routines. But adopting technology in this way is not a trivial task, for a couple of reasons. First of all, there is a big gap between using simple tools to record sound or shoot video and then having the software and editing skills to produce a quality report, particularly at the warp-drive pace of the mobile news culture.

Some news organizations have decided that their reporters should be able to produce a solid written account of a news event as well as multimedia elements, such as sound, images and video (Hopkins, 2011). From a dollars-and-cents standpoint, the attraction of this approach is understandable. But it is rare to find a journalist who is equally equipped to write for a newspaper and to produce audio reports for a radio network. Even if you can do both, it's hard to do them both in the same constrained timeframe.

Current technology does allow for the rapid production of multimedia elements, such as short videos or photo galleries. But getting the most out of multimedia requires a far more significant investment of time. Consider the case of David Isay, an award-winning radio documentarian. One of his best-known works is "The Sunshine Hotel," which is an exploration of the flop-house culture of New York's Lower East Side. It was broadcast on National Public Radio in 1998, and print versions of it appeared in the *Times* and as part of a subsequent book. To gather material for the project, Isay spent two full months going to the hotel and recording at all hours. The radio version of the story runs for 23½ minutes, but it was edited down from 70 hours of raw recordings (Stewart, 2001).

The other complicating factor is that technology is changing not just one aspect of journalism. It is changing the entire process, from story generation through reporting and analysis all the way to production. It is not one multimedia skillset or software application that a journalist needs to know; it is many. At this point many students, and working journalists, could reasonably decide to give up, to say that the task is too broad and too big. But that would be a mistake. The key is to remember that technology is not there to control you, but for you to control it. It is powerful, and it can be used to create powerful, dynamic journalism, the kind that can make a difference.

You also have to be reasonable in your expectations about your mastery of technology. You are not going to be equally good at all of the tools that are now available to you, tools for number-crunching and for creating interactive graphics and for telling a story with sounds and pictures. Every journalist, and every journalism student, will be expected to know the basics—to use word-processing and content management software and to capture images and sound. After all, these functions can be found on the smart phones that have become a near-necessity on most campuses. Where you go from there, perhaps developing specialized skills in data analysis or Web presentation, is up to you.

But under any circumstances all journalists will have to have two things—at least a passing knowledge of the kinds of technological tools that are available and a willingness to keep on top of digital evolution. Technology will get easier to use and more powerful, but it will also get applied in new ways and in new situations. You need to be prepared for that to happen and to be willing to keep taking on new challenges.

How deep does your knowledge need to be? That's a question without a clear answer. If you have a knack for writing code as well as a knack for uncovering stories, you almost certainly will have a leg up in a competitive job market. But it is unreasonable to expect all journalism students, while trying to master the skills of that discipline, also to develop a mastery of another field, namely computer science. Computer code is hard to write, and it's unforgiving (see Figure 11.1). A comma or a semicolon that is out of place in a sentence of English prose will probably not render it incomprehensible (although it could give it a meaning you did not intend). But when you are writing computer code, a misplaced punctuation mark will not just degrade what you are trying to create, it will cause your project to seize up, like a gasoline engine that runs dry of oil. The animation will not run, or the Web page will not load.

You will be a better journalist if you have some acquaintance with the underlying mechanisms of the digital world. Web pages are dynamic and they present possibilities that are not available in print. This is obvious to anyone who has used a Web browser, but the important questions are what are those possibilities and how can they be accessed.

This chapter is not intended to make you a multimedia expert or to forecast what new technologies will shape your work. Instead it will examine the main uses of digital technology throughout the reporting process. It will

```
href="/web/20070210233836/http://www.oshkoshnews.org/sponsors.html"
onMouseOut="MM_swapImgRestore()"
onMouseOver="MM_swapImage('sponsorsnav','','navbuttons/sponsors_over.gif'
,1)"><img
src="/web/20070210233836im_/http://www.oshkoshnews.org/navbuttons/sponsor
s_up.gif" alt="sponsors_button" name="sponsorsnav" width="110"
height="16" border="0"></a></td>
        </tr>
        <tr>
          <td><a
href="/web/20070210233836/http://www.oshkoshnews.org/contactus.html"
onMouseOut="MM_swapImgRestore()"
onMouseOver="MM_swapImage('contactnav','','navbuttons/contact_over.gif',1
)"><img
src="/web/20070210233836im_/http://www.oshkoshnews.org/navbuttons/contact
_up.gif" alt="contact_button" name="contactnav" width="110" height="16"
border="0"></a></td>
        </tr>
        <tr>
          <td><a
href="/web/20070210233836/http://www.oshkoshnews.org/index.html"
```

FIGURE 11.1 *Although most reporters will not be full-fledged programmers, they need to have some familiarity with the use of computer code and how Web pages are structured.*

then describe specific ways that this technology can be incorporated into the DOT methodology.

It may be helpful to think of technology not as a completely different part of the reporting process but rather as an extension of that process, a way to take key functions and improve on them, by making them more powerful or more flexible or more accessible. As you delve more deeply into the matter, you will likely come to agree with those, like Neil Postman, who say that seeing technology this way is an overly simplistic view. But this notion provides a place to start.

Postman, a pioneer in the field of media ecology, was a longtime professor at New York University, who wrote insightful criticism about the news business, especially television. He recognized the power, and inevitable advance, of digital technology. But he also urged caution, noting, for example, that the introduction of technology always involves tradeoffs and that not everyone benefits from change. "We need to proceed with our eyes wide open so that we may use technology rather than be used by it," he warned (1998).

With that advice in mind, let's start with some fairly straightforward applications of digital technology. Consider three basic reporting tools that journalists have long kept on paper: lists, calendars and contact information. Lists are a simple but extremely powerful organizational tool. They are easy to overlook because they are so elementary. But smart reporters keep lists of all kinds of things: story ideas, documents to review, sources to contact, follow-ups to make. The importance of the list is that it helps you focus and use your time wisely. It reminds you of things you need to do and helps you avoid careless mistakes. As the Boys Town investigators came down to the wire in their work, they recognized that they had assembled a mass of information that was going to raise a lot of eyebrows when it was published. It needed to be as accurate and as airtight as possible. The newspaper staff developed a list of 175 specific tasks that had to be done—everything from double-checking data to planning the layout—before they would be ready to publish (Williams, 1978).

Once the list was completed, the editor, Paul N. Williams, transferred the list to a calendar, showing when the tasks had to be done and by whom. The calendar is a second important tool that reporters have long used, relying on paper versions. Like a list, a calendar is a great organizational tool that will keep you on schedule and help you avoid embarrassing oversights. Students may think that lists and calendars contain information that can be easily stored in their human memory cells. This may be true as long as your life is simple and your responsibilities are few, but those conditions do not hold for a serious journalist.

A third reporting tool that all journalists maintain is a list of sources with contact information (home, office and cell phone numbers as well as email addresses) and other important details, such as exact titles and areas of expertise. For decades reporters kept this information in books or on the rotating file devices called Rolodexes. Source lists are open-ended, constantly being updated. The most important thing about them is that they have to be easy to use—so that on deadline you can get to just the right person as quickly as possible.

All three of these tools have proven their worth to reporters—but all of them can be even more useful if implemented with digital technology. For example, consider creating a list as a Word document, which then becomes easier to keep up to date. It's also possible to share your list with your editor or with collaborators by including it as an email attachment. And it's also possible to go further using digital technology, by putting your list on a cloud storage service such as Google Drive. You are then able to access it no matter where you are, and you can also allow colleagues to access it as well. A list on a cloud computing platform can also be updated by you (or others), and you can also recover previous versions if you want to throw out changes that you, or others, have made.

Even with these basic examples of technology applied to journalism, we can see two processes at work. We are, initially, simply transferring existing practices into a new environment, typically with advantages in speed, scale and productivity. But then we are also changing those practices in a way that will change the journalism we produce. Let's see how this plays out in the three main areas of the reporting process: gathering information, analyzing information and presenting information.

GATHERING INFORMATION

Reporters have always gathered information in two basic ways, pushing and pulling. They push for information by, for example, knocking on doors, making phone calls and consulting official documents. They pull for information by letting people know that they are interested in certain topics, leaving business cards with potential sources and getting on official distribution lists for press releases and other announcements. The push for information is like using a shovel, where reporters are looking for specific pieces of information. The pull is like being a magnet, where information is drawn in without being specifically targeted.

Both of these processes can be enhanced by technology. Journalists need to use technology, but they should also be aware of how their work is shaped by the technological choices they make. Take email, for example, or other electronic messaging services. Email is a great way to push for information. It is fast and efficient. You can pepper a dozen sources at once in just about the same amount of time it would take you to contact just one. But email is not simply another way to conduct an interview or to get information.

There are, as Postman warned, tradeoffs involved with using a technology like email. In an electronic conversation you will be cut off from some of the visual cues that you get if you were talking to a source face to face. Similarly, you may lose the spontaneity of response that you can get with a telephone conversation. It will typically take your sources longer to respond to an email query just because typing is more complex than talking. In writing back to you, sources will have more time to consider the ramifications of what they are saying and may decide to leave out certain information or to phrase it in a less direct manner.

Another way that reporters push for information is by looking for documents, a process that has been revolutionized by the World Wide Web. A search engine like Google can almost instantaneously put a vast array of information in front of a reporter. No reporter working today can afford to work without Internet searches. But for all the power of a search engine, there are also shortcomings, a fact that reporters need to keep in mind and work to mitigate. Search engines can be great for helping you find a specific piece of information that you are looking for, but they may also take you right past other information that may be useful but that you have not specified in your query. Consider for a moment the old-fashioned way of looking for information, which might involve working through a library bookcase full of printed material. To be sure this can be a slow, cumbersome process, but it can also allow for the unexpected find, the stumbling upon of a valuable bit of information you wouldn't have known to look for because you didn't know it existed.

As discussed in Chapter 3, another, and perhaps more serious, drawback of search engines is that many users don't know how to get the most out of them. Google is, by far, the dominant choice for search, but it is not the only search engine available. You will get different results if you use different search engines, such as Bing or one of the lesser known alternatives. (How to find other search engines? Google the phrase "alternative search engines.") Google itself can also be tweaked to give you more precise results. You can, for example, search for an exact term or exclude a specific term from your search. You can also focus your search on a specific site, or make sure that Google includes in its search the kind of common terms (like "and" or "of") that it typically excludes.

Social media, such as Facebook and Twitter, are information-gathering tools that reporters can use in either push or pull mode. Both Facebook and Twitter are frequently used as a way of finding sources or contact information for sources. Twitter has proven to be an especially useful way to follow breaking news. In some contexts and on some stories, social media can be invaluable tools for reporters, but don't forget their limits. Not everyone uses social media, and users of social media may skew toward certain demographic characteristics, such as age or social background. By all means use social media to find sources, but don't limit your source pool to users of social media. News organizations also use social media to pull in information, by, for example, sending out alerts that they are looking for sources who may have particular experience with or insights on a news topic. This can be an effective tool, especially on deadline stories, but here again you may be limiting yourself to certain kinds of sources. You also run the risk of alerting your competitors to what you are working on.

Social media, as well as other online tools, also play an important role in the relatively new phenomenon of "crowdsourcing." One of the earliest examples of this kind of Web-enabled reporting, in which ordinary citizens are invited to take part in a news organization's coverage of an event or an issue, occurred in 2006 in Fort Myers, Florida, when the local Gannett paper, the *News-Press,* assembled what it called "Team Watchdog," a 20-person team of readers. According to a report from *Wired* magazine, this experiment in crowdsourcing began with the paper receiving complaints of high sewer connection fees for new homes (Howe, 2006).

When the paper turned to its readers for help in analyzing the situation, it was overwhelmed by the response. People with specific technical knowledge, in engineering and accounting, for example, provided expert analysis of documents, and an insider leaked information that indicated bid-rigging. Based on the investigation by the paper, and its readers, the city government cut its sewer hookup fees by 30 percent and one official resigned, wired.com reported. Based on this and other experiences, Gannett decided to adopt the crowdsourcing approach as part of its corporate strategy for all of the newspapers it owned across the country.

Some Gannett staffers were not enthusiastic about this shift, as they feared that the crowdsourcing approach would be a way for the company to cut costs by eliminating the jobs of professional journalists. While not all of the crowdsourcing efforts led to such dramatic results, the approach has become a standard part of journalism.

For all its potential for improving the quality of reporting, however, crowdsourcing comes with no guarantee of accuracy, and the unintended consequences of the technique can be quite damaging. This point was clearly illustrated in April 2013 when Reddit, a website that allows contributors to post content and to vote on whether a particular item should have more or less prominence, became involved in the effort to identify the persons who had placed bombs near the finish line of the Boston Marathon. One site user created a page called "findbostonbombers" that was intended to organize the information being posted to the site. But the situation soon got out of control, as photos from the bombing scene were posted and innocent people were falsely identified as likely suspects in the attack. While many photographs of the bombing scene were available on the Internet, none of them had images of the men who were eventually accused of the attack, until after authorities posted the pictures of the individuals they were looking for.

The situation was particularly painful for the family of a missing university student who was wrongly accused of taking part in the bombing. The family had set up a Facebook page to help find the student, who had suffered from depression and, at the time of the bombing, may have already been dead. The incident prompted the general manager of Reddit to publish an apology (Martin, 2013), and the Reddit user who set up the bombing thread said that he had made a big mistake in thinking that technology-enabled community sourcing would lead to the bombers. In an interview with *The Atlantic Wire* website (now known as *The Wire*), he said: "When someone on Reddit says something is suspicious, it's no different from someone on the street saying it. There's a big difference between journalistic integrity and the opinion of some guy on Reddit. Reddit should never ever ever be used as a source, unless there's actually some proof there. It's no different from a newspaper printing 'a guy on the street said, "My mate told me that this guy is a bomber"'" (Abad-Santos, 2013).

ANALYZING INFORMATION

One of the first times that digital technology played a role in news reporting was in the wake of the Detroit riots of 1967 (Houston, 2004), which claimed the lives of 43 and proved to be the most violent of the civil disturbances of the 1960s. For white residents of the city, the riots came as a great surprise. *The New York Times* reported that "Detroit probably had more going for it than any other major city in the North," including available union jobs in local auto plants, sympathetic police commissioners who had tried to improve relations with the black community, a white mayor who had worked to direct federal anti-poverty funds into blighted neighborhoods, and a well-established network of black political leaders who had helped make Detroit the only city in the country with two black representatives in Congress (Flint, 1967, 19).

A local paper, the *Detroit Free Press,* won a Pulitzer Prize for its coverage, and in its submission to the competition, its managing editor described the difficulty of covering the riot. "The first casualty of the Detroit riots was truth," wrote Frank Angelo. "Official voices" could no longer be counted on, and "rumor and falsehood and fear were freely used as substitutes for accuracy and reason." To a large extent the paper relied on the old-fashioned approach called shoe-leather reporting, particularly in its effort to investigate every one of the 43 deaths that were tied to the disturbance, which required an "endless, foot-slogging search for witnesses in the disrupted, apprehensive and mobile Negro community" (Angelo, 1968).

But the paper decided to supplement traditional approaches with more modern ones, as reporters applied social science survey techniques to try to answer the question of why Detroit, with its thriving black political class and active community development programs, erupted into so much violence and destruction. The *Free Press* conducted surveys of city residents to test several theories about the causes of the riots and then subjected the results to statistical analysis. Intriguingly the results were consistent with what the paper had found through traditional interviewing techniques, but the computerized analysis seemed to lend the pen-and-paper findings greater weight (Meyer, 2001).

For computer analysis, journalists have a range of software tools to choose from: spreadsheets, databases, mapping tools and statistical analysis packages. Some of them have similarities and overlapping functionalities, but they also have some specialized capabilities that make the choice of one over another fairly clear-cut in most cases. For example, spreadsheets, which are the simplest to use, can perform statistical tests, but depending on the size of the dataset and the complexity of the analysis, you may find it easier to use a program dedicated to statistical analysis. Learning the specifics of how to use these programs is beyond the scope of this textbook, but there are numerous printed and online resources that you can turn to if you wish to explore this aspect of technology further. Let's take a look at the two simplest kinds of programs to use, spreadsheets and databases, and how they can help you pull stories out of raw information.

Electronic spreadsheets, which evolved from the paper ledgers that bookkeepers traditionally used to keep track of accounts, consist of vertical columns that are subdivided by horizontal rows. The result is a tabular array made up of individual rectangles called cells. Either numerical or textual information can be placed in a cell. Although the spreadsheet can be used to store and sort text, its most common use is for fast calculations and manipulation of data. Spreadsheets are ideal for figuring percentages and making comparisons and can allow you to reach conclusions that might not otherwise be available to you. For example, a reporter covering the maritime industry in Baltimore wanted to identify the largest customers of the port, but the agency in charge of running the marine terminals said this was confidential commercial information and refused to answer the reporter's question. This could have been the end of the story, but the reporter had access to routine reports that contained the information he needed. These reports tracked the port's specialized cargo cranes and recorded the amount of time they were rented each month by each of the steamship lines that used the port.

While the information was contained in the report, the report was on paper and could not be deciphered just by looking at it. This was where a spreadsheet came into play. In the first column of the spreadsheet, the reporter listed the names of those steamship lines. In the next column, he entered the number of minutes that each line had rented the port's cranes. Using one of the functions built into a spreadsheet, he was able to quickly add up those times to arrive at a total number of minutes that the cranes had been in use. Then he was able to calculate percentages of the total crane usage for each of the steamship lines, this time using a function that makes it easy to write simple formulas. In the end, he had a list showing all of the steamship lines using the port ranked by how much use they had made of the port's cranes (Maguire, 1984, C1).

A database is a program that is used to organize information in powerful ways so that it is possible, for example, to compare information from different sources and draw inferences. It shares some overlapping functionality with a spreadsheet in that both kinds of programs can be used to capture and sort data and to perform calculations. Databases are much more difficult to learn to use than spreadsheets, and, as a result, some reporters prefer to stick to spreadsheets. More experienced journalists, however, say this is a mistake, pointing out that spreadsheets are especially good for some tasks while databases are especially good for others. The tasks that spreadsheets are especially good at involve analysis based on mathematical and statistical formulas. They are also good at producing graphical displays of information in chart form. Databases, by contrast, are better at handling large amounts of data and finding connections within that mass of information. Databases are sometimes known as *relational* databases because they can be used to relate different kinds of information, for example, place-based information with time-based information. Once a database has been created, it can be posted online so that site users can do their own individualized searches to find information that falls within particular parameters, such as a period of time or relating to a particular organization or location. Without going into all of the details of how a database works, the following example, drawing on the reporting project that won the 2013 Pulitzer Prize for Public Service, illustrates how databases can be used to explore and convincingly document situations that might otherwise prove elusive to cover (Kestin and Maines, 2012).

The series of articles, published by the *Sun Sentinel* in Ft. Lauderdale, Florida, demonstrated beyond a shadow of a doubt something that most local motorists knew at an anecdotal level—that police officers frequently violated traffic laws by driving at excessive speeds. Some of these cases broke into the news, but only when they were attached to particularly extreme outcomes, such as fatal accidents or arrests of officers driving well in excess of 100 mph. To document the story the newspaper developed a database consisting of 1.1 million toll records created by police vehicles as they passed through. This database showed when an officer drove past a particular location, but this information was not enough to calculate speed.

The paper then used a GPS device to measure the distances between different toll plazas, driving 2,500 miles to do so. The paper's findings were dramatic—that 800 officers, many of them off duty at the time, had driven at speeds between 90 mph and 130 mph on the highways of South Florida (Saltz, 2013).

The paper's project was extensive, including a photo gallery of victims and video of officers being pulled over by other officers. At the core of it, however, was the database of specific instances of speeding. The information was presented in a table, listing the vehicles involved, identified by transponders they were carrying and showing the toll plazas they drove through and what the average speed was. This kind of information theoretically could have been developed and presented using a spreadsheet. The power of a database program, however, is demonstrated by an advanced search feature that the paper included on its website. On a separate page, site users could specify the particular police agency they wanted to look at, individual transponder numbers, the timeframe, the locations and the length of travel time between locations (*Sun Sentinel*, 2012). With the click of a mouse, users could then get the results of searches defined by their specific criteria of interest—information that could be extracted from a spreadsheet but only through multiple cumbersome steps.

PRESENTING INFORMATION

The previous section of this chapter emphasized the ways that technology can help you work with the document part of the DOT methodology. But technology clearly has had just as big an impact on way reporters carry out the observation and talk phases of their work. In many organizations reporters are expected to do far more than just come back with observations they can incorporate into their writing—they are also supposed to come back with still images and/or video that can be posted on the Web. Depending on the project, they may also be expected to capture sound, including interviews they conduct.

There was a time when a reporter might get sent to cover a story armed with no more than a pencil and a wad of scrap paper to jot down notes. Those were the days that when street reporters, known as legmen, would call the newsroom and dictate their stories to the rewrite desk. Then their job was done. News production is a much more complicated task these days, as reporters need not only to gather quotes and images and sound but also to figure out how to put them together.

Perhaps the biggest hurdle you will face in using technology is simply getting accustomed to using it, incorporating it into your regular routines. Two of the exercises below are simple activities that you can repeat until you get more comfortable working with sound, image and video files.

Once you have captured these files, you will then need to learn how to organize and present this content. To do so you will need to rely on two tools that are probably familiar to you if you have worked in broadcast but that may be new to you if your interests lie with print: the storyboard and the story script.

Storyboards are a visual outline of how a multimedia presentation will work online. You might, for example, create one to show how photo galleries or sound clips or background documents might be embedded and linked from the main page. Another use of the storyboard concept is to plan out the sequence of images or video clips that will make up a report. It is possible, of course, to work without a storyboard using simple editing software, but the storyboard gives you a chance to try out different variations of your story.

Once you start working in multimedia, the importance of a story script, which is the voiceover narration for your piece, will become immediately apparent. That's because the length of your script will determine the length of your multimedia presentation, and the script also provides the timing marks for when you will include a given image or video sequence. If, for example, you introduce a person or a scene 8.3 seconds into the script, that's when you will want to introduce a photo of that person or location. The story script functions as the roadmap that will take you through your story as you edit in media files.

GOING FORWARD—DIY LEARNING

No one expects the pace of technological innovation in journalism to slow down, which means students cannot make the mistake of thinking that what they have learned in the college classroom will be enough. Instead students need to recognize that it will be their responsibility to continue to expand their skills through do-it-yourself learning. Fortunately they will find there is an abundance of resources available to them. Here are some suggestions:

- If you hear about a new program or a new technique that you want to know more about, you can likely find either a print or video tutorial online. YouTube is an excellent resource for such materials.

- Several organizations have developed extensive collections of Web courses and tutorials. Check out the Poynter Institute, the Knight Digital Media Center and Codeacademy. Many, though not all, of these resources are free.

- Other resources are available from journalists and journalism educators, such as Mindy McAdams of the University of Florida (2013), who are generous in making available on the Web information about software programs that they are using and updates about new tools and techniques.

EXERCISES

1. Try your hand at crowdsourcing by picking some event or issue that lends itself to this kind of coverage. Possibilities might include an appearance on your campus of a headline entertainer who is expected to draw a large crowd or some perennial issue, such as the quality of food at campus dining halls or shortages of parking spaces. Here are points to keep in mind as you carry out this project:

   • Once you have selected your topic, you will need to enlist members of the "crowd" to contribute. How will you do this? If you are working with a campus-based media outlet, such as a newspaper or a radio station, you can use its website. Otherwise you may want to set up a blog site or a Facebook page. You should also use a Twitter account and create a hashtag.

   • Before you recruit crowd members to contribute, you need to think about what it is you want them to contribute. News organizations that have experimented with this technique warn that people may be reluctant to participate if the assignment is too open-ended. Some projects that have been successful were narrowly focused and asked for limited kinds of input, such as obtaining a specific phone number or other datapoint.

   • A related issue is what you want people to send you. Just text? Images? Video? Sound files?

   • You also need to think about how to encourage participation. Some journalists encourage the use of a technique called "gamification," which essentially is a way of adding a competitive element to the process. Possible methods include awarding badges to active participants or creating a leaderboard, showing who has made the most contributions or which aspects of your topic have drawn the most interest. This approach may not be appropriate in all circumstances, and there is a danger that you will skew the results by incorporating these techniques.

   • You cannot ignore the possibility that some members of the crowd will try to disrupt your efforts by sending bogus information or that they may just be incorrect in their observations and conclusions. You need to create some kind of editorial filtering process to ensure the validity and accuracy of your crowdsourced report.

   • How will you present your findings? If you are doing this as a class exercise without affiliation with an existing news outlet, you can easily establish a blog or build a site using a free service.

- Don't forget to close the loop by using your original social media channels to alert contributors that your project has been published.

2. Data journalism can be intimidating as there are many challenges that you will encounter in obtaining data and then organizing it in the appropriate software so that you can analyze it. A good way to get a taste of the power of data journalism while you are still learning the mechanics of data manipulation is to use an existing database to do some research and write some stories. Here are some possibilities:

    - Some states have started posting searchable online databases of day care centers, nursing homes or other specialized providers. You can typically search to find such services in a specified geographical area and then check to see if there have been violations or fines associated with any of them.

    - In May 2013 the Association of Health Care Journalists opened a website called hospitalinspections.org, putting in searchable form information that previously was available only on paper following Freedom of Information Requests. In its initial version the database was incomplete, in part because the source for the data, the U.S. Centers for Medicare and Medicaid Services, had only recently started gathering the information. Still it could be a good starting point for research and point you to potentially newsworthy information about hospitals in your area.

    - Various federal agencies also put vast amounts of information online. The Department of Education, through the National Center for Education Statistics, provides information on student achievement down to the school level. The Environmental Protection Agency has a range of databases that you can use to research, for example, air and water quality in your areas. The Bureau of Labor Statistics can provide background information on such topics as wages and comparative growth rates of different professions.

    In many cases you can download the results from one of these online searches into a spreadsheet format. Alternatively you can create a spreadsheet of your own design and transfer your results there to do basic analysis.

3. Audio. For this assignment, you will post 10 minutes of audio in an mp3 file based on an interview that you conduct in conjunction with the "National Day of Listening." The purpose of this assignment is

to expose you to some of the possibilities and challenges of working with audio.

- Select someone to interview.

- Develop a list of interview questions. Refer to the question generator or list of great questions on the Storycorps website.

- Once you have your questions, find a quiet place to talk with your interview subject.

- Record your interview. If you have a smartphone, you can use it to capture sound.

- From the interview, select a particularly interesting segment, edit out distracting side comments and then match it up with some introductory and closing sound, using Audacity.

- For your soundtrack, try GarageBand, public domain music from the Internet Archive (https://archive.org/details/audio) or http:/wwww.inbflat.net/.

4. In our cross-platform, multimedia world, every reporter is also expected to be able to handle a camera—or at least to come back from an assignment with some images that can be posted to the Web. In this assignment you will take some pictures in a couple of standard patterns that could be used to help provide a narrative arc to a story.

The first pattern that you will follow is called a "three-shot sequence," and it is probably already familiar to you because it is a fairly standard way of introducing a story on television news. In this assignment you will be shooting still images and not moving ones, but the same concepts apply. Essentially you are trying to create a sense of movement and progression by capturing a series of images taken from different distances.

The three shots are:

1. A long-range, "establishing" shot.

2. A medium-range shot, starting to focus the viewer's attention on the subject, shown from a different angle.

3. A close-up, perhaps of a face or perhaps a different part of the body (hands for a musician, for example, or feet for a dancer).

The second pattern is slightly more elaborate and is called a five-shot sequence.

The five shots are:

1. Hands.

2. Face.

3. Medium shot (hands and face both).

4. Over the shoulder.

5. Something else: creative framing or angled or low/high shot.

These links may help you visualize what you are supposed to do here:

- From the Poynter Institute: http://www.poynter.org/how-tos/digital-strategies/183861/how-journalists-can-improve-video-stories-with-shot-sequences/.

- From Mu Lin: http://www.mulinblog.com/2012/05/22/how-to-shoot-photos-for-an-audio-slideshow/.

- From Mindy McAdams: http://www.jou.ufl.edu/faculty/mmcadams/video/five_shot.html.

REFERENCES

Abad-Santos, Alexander. "Reddit's 'Find Boston Bombers' Founder Says 'It Was a Disaster' but 'Incredible,'" April 22, 2013, accessed December 23, 2013, at http://www.thewire.com/national/2013/04/reddit-find-boston-bombers-founder-interview/64455/.

Angelo, Frank. Letter to the Pulitzer Prize Advisory Board, January 17, 1968, included in the *Free Press* prize submission, microfilm, Columbia University Library Archives.

Branch, John. "Snowfall: The Avalanche at Tunnel Creek," *The New York Times*, December 20, 2012, accessed December 20, 2013, at http://www.nytimes.com/projects/2012/snow-fall/#/?part=tunnel-creek.

Columbia University. "The 2013 Pulitzer Prize Winners Feature Writing," *The Pulitzer Prizes*, accessed December 20, 2013, at http://www.pulitzer.org/citation/2013-Feature-Writing.

Flint, Jerry M. "Detroit Leaders Were Optimistic," *The New York Times*, July 26, 1967.

Franklin, Jon. "Frightening Journey Through Tunnels of the Brain," *The Evening Sun*, December 12–13, 1978.

Greenfield, Rebecca. "What *The New York Times*'s 'Snow Fall' Means to Online Journalism's Future," *The Atlantic Wire*, December 20, 2012, accessed December 20, 2013, at http://www.thewire.com/technology/2012/12/new-york-times-snow-fall-feature/60219.

Hopkins, Jim. "GCI Buys 'Thousands' of iPhones and Other Devices, Memo Says, in Ramp-up of Mobile Newsroom Tech," *Gannett Blog*, December 21, 2011, accessed December 20, 2013, at http://gannettblog.blogspot.com/2011/12/memo-gci-buys-thousands-of-iphones.html.

Houston, Brant. *Computer-Assisted Reporting: A Practical Guide*, Boston: Bedford/St. Martin's, 2004.

Howe, Jeff. "Gannett to Crowdsource News," *Wired*, November 3, 2006, accessed December 23, 2013, at http://www.wired.com/software/webservices/news/2006/11/72067?currentPage=all.

Kestin, Sally, and John Maines, "Above the Law: Speeding Cops," *Sun Sentinel*, February 11–13, 2012, accessed December 23, 2013, at http://www.sun-sentinel.com/news/local/speeding-cops/.

Maguire, Miles. "High Tariffs at Port Cause Concern for Businessmen," *The Baltimore Sun,* November 11, 1984.

Martin, Erik. "Reflections on the Recent Boston Crisis," Reddit.com, April 22, 2013, accessed December 23, 2013, at http://blog.reddit.com/2013/04/reflections-on-recent-boston-crisis.html.

McAdams, Mindy. "Required Reading: How Open Source Makes You Better," *Teaching Journalism Online,* January 4, 2013, accessed December 23, 2013, at http://mindymcadams.com/tojou/2013/required-reading-how-open-source-makes-you-better/.

Meyer, Philip. "Precision Journalism and Narrative Journalism: Toward a Unified Field Theory," *Nieman Reports Online Exclusives,* Fall 2001, accessed December 23, 2013, at http://nieman.harvard.edu/reports/article-online-exclusive/100044/Precision-Journalism-and-Narrative-Journalism-Toward-a-Unified-Field-Theory.aspx.

New York Times. "Q. and A.: The Avalanche at Tunnel Creek," December 21, 2012, accessed December 20, 2013, at http://www.nytimes.com/2012/12/22/sports/q-a-the-avalanche-at-tunnel-creek.html.

Postman, Neil. "Five Things We Need To Know About Technological Change," speech to New Tech 98 conference, Denver, Co., March 27, 1998.

Saltz, Howard. Entry letter to Pulitzer Committee, undated, accessed December 23, 2013, at http://www.pulitzer.org/files/2013/public-service/sunsentinelentryletter.pdf.

Stewart, David. "Audio Producer David Isay: Curiosity . . . Respect . . . Trust," *Current,* April 23, 2001, accessed December 20, 2013, at http://www.current.org/wp-content/themes/current/archive-site/people/peop0108isay2.html.

Sun Sentinel. "Database: Speeding Cops in South Florida," February 11, 2012, accessed December 23, 2013, at http://databases.sun-sentinel.com/news/broward/ftlaudCopSpeeds/ftlaudCopSpeeds_list.php.

Williams, Paul N. *Investigative Reporting and Editing,* Englewood Cliffs, N.J.: Prentice-Hall, 1978.

CHAPTER 12

Public Relations and News Management

In many countries around the world, the way that powerful people and institutions work to influence the press is far from subtle. Reporters are sometimes sued and slapped with huge financial judgments, jailed, kidnapped, and even hunted and killed (Phillips, 2013). By contrast, reporters working in the United States face far less serious overt pressures, although a handful were arrested covering a protest in California in 2012 (Aronsen, 2012), others have been subject to judicial subpoena and search warrants (Horwitz, 2013), and many fear that federal investigations of sources who leak confidential information will make it far more difficult to do the job of journalists (Royce-Bartlett, 2013).

While American journalists are much less likely than their overseas counterparts to encounter retaliation either in the form of legal or lethal actions against them, they should not pretend they are operating in a neutral environment. People and organizations in the news are constantly seeking to exert influence over journalists, in ways that range from more-or-less friendly types of guidance up to certain forms of intimidation and even outright restrictions on coverage. As a result, reporters need to be clear-sighted about the way their sources have become increasingly media savvy and sophisticated in their dealings with the press. Journalists who are not sensitive to the ways that their contacts are attempting to shape their reporting face a compromise of their independence that will necessarily degrade the quality and accuracy of their articles.

To be sure death threats, lawsuits, arrests and other forms of intimidation have been a part of American journalism and will continue to be a possibility for American journalists, particularly for those who venture into highly charged areas of the news. But for most reporters the greatest significant challenge to their ability to discharge their professional responsibilities will come in a much more nuanced form, through the practice of perception management.

Reporters who have not worked on the "other side," that is in a media relations capacity on behalf of individual newsmakers or organizations that are frequently in the public eye, would be shocked to learn how much time and energy public officials and other public figures put into worrying about how they are portrayed in the press. While they may say that they don't care what the media report about them, they do—and often to an obsessive degree.

The concept of perception management, which can be defined as the systematic manipulation of information and images to achieve a particular result, is said to have originated with the Department of Defense, although the term cannot be found in the current versions of reference documents such as the official Department of Defense dictionary. An earlier version of the DoD dictionary defined it this way:

> Actions to convey and/or deny selected information and indicators to foreign audiences to influence their emotions, motives, and objective reasoning as well as to intelligence systems and leaders at all levels to influence official estimates, ultimately resulting in foreign behaviors and official actions favorable to the originator's objectives. In various ways, perception management combines truth projection, operations security, cover and deception, and psychological operations. (Department of Defense, 1994, 287)

Reporters should be aware of how each of these elements—truth projection, operations security, cover and deception, and psychological operations—come into play in the practice of perception management.

Truth projection. This term suggests two different considerations that public relations practitioners keep in mind as they seek to influence the media. The first is that there needs to be some measure of truth at the heart of a successful perception management campaign. According to Edward L. Bernays, whom we met in Chapter 2 in connection with pseudo-events, "the engineer of consent should be powerfully equipped with facts, with truths, with evidence, before he begins to show himself before a public" (1947, 116). These truths may be twisted and distorted as they are presented to the media, but they cannot be completely false. Facts carry weight with the public, while a complete falsehood will almost certainly be found out and eventually undermine the credibility of any perception management campaign. Projection is the other key term to be considered, and what it suggests is that truth cannot be allowed to be found out on its own. Rather, a particular truth, or a particular version of the truth, has to be raised up and given greater prominence.

Operations security. Sometimes in retrospect it comes to light that key aspects of a perception management campaign were in fact false. But as long as the falsehoods do not come to light during the campaign, the campaign can still be successful. In other words, operations security—maintaining control and protecting key information from becoming known on a contemporaneous basis to the media and therefore to the public—is a critical part of perception management. What happens after the operations are over is not so important. A good example of this can be found during the period before the first Iraq War, in 1990, when Hill & Knowlton, the global public relations firm, was working on behalf of the Kuwaiti government. At the time, the Kuwaitis were anxious to win support in the United States for a military effort to force Saddam Hussein to pull his troops out of their country and return to Iraq. A key moment came when a young woman, identified only by her first name to protect her family, testified to members of Congress about seeing Iraqi soldiers enter a hospital and dump hundreds of newborn infants from their incubators onto the floor, leaving them to die. This horrific story was repeated in television interviews and included in a report by Amnesty International, a respected human rights organization. After the war, however, no corroborating evidence could be found, and the story was eventually dismissed as a hoax. At that point it didn't matter because the story had had its desired effect—turning public opinion against Hussein and in support of the Kuwaiti government. After the war, another key detail about the young female witness emerged—she was a member of the Kuwaiti royal family and the daughter of the Kuwaiti ambassador to the United States, facts that had to be kept under wraps during the course of the perception management campaign (Rampton and Stauber, 2003).

Cover and deception. The testimony described above is an example of cover and deception, since the identity of the young woman needed to be kept under cover and her story was pure deception. But the cover and deception aspect of perception management extends further, as media relations practitioners work to distract reporters and to keep certain facts from being reported. One of the reasons why it was important to provide this woman's account of baby killing by Hussein's soldiers was to draw attention away from the fact that Hussein had previously gassed thousands of civilians—while receiving financial support from the United States. The gas attack killed an estimated 5,000 civilians in the village of Halabja in 1988, just two years before the United States was gearing up to attack Hussein (Rampton and Stauber, 2003).

Psychological operations. The term "psychological operations" has been scrubbed from the most recent Defense dictionary and replaced with the phrase "military information support operations" (2010, 180). But the meaning of the new term tracks with the old definition, referring to activities that are intended to influence the "emotions, motives, objective reasoning, and ultimately . . . behavior" (1994, 304). Because of the nature of news reporting, journalists are especially susceptible to these kinds of ploys, a fact that is often lost in the accounts either of reporters as heroes or reporters as goats. On one hand, reporters are supposed to be independent, hard-boiled cynics who, like Clark Kent's alter-ego, Superman, possess some kind of X-ray vision that allows them to see straight through to the truth. On the other hand, when the press does break down, failing to challenge statements by powerful officials or buying into a compelling but not completely true narrative told on behalf of a sports star or celebrity, reporters are pictured as the helpless pawns of corporate media conglomerates. Neither of these extreme visions of how reporters operate is accurate.

The German scholar Wolfgang Donsbach (2004) is one of the few academic media critics to explore the psychological dimensions of journalism. Getting the story straight is hard enough in and of itself, but reporters have to face five factors that further complicate their situation. The first is time. Working on a deadline means that reporters don't have the luxury of checking out every possibility or thinking through every possible complication. The next issue is competition. Reporters hate to be scooped, missing a story that some other news organization got to first. There's a flip side to this problem as well—since it can be very uncomfortable for a reporter to be the only one pursuing a particular angle when all the other reporters are focusing their attention elsewhere. The fourth factor that Donsbach discusses is a lack of the kind of objective standards that exist in other fields, such as medicine or engineering, to allow reporters to evaluate their conclusions. As a result, reporters are always in danger of isolation, of having to fall back on their personal opinions of what is news or whether something is news. The final factor that complicates the life of reporters is that the work they do is out in public, for everyone to see and to criticize. Workers in other professions make decisions that affect other people, to be sure, but these decisions are not nearly so visible and their mistakes are not nearly so easy to obscure.

These five factors—the difficulty of the work itself, time constraints, competitive pressures, the absence of objective standards and the public nature of their output—lead inevitably to insecurity and anxiety, emotions that are the essential levers in a successful propaganda effort. In fact Harold D. Lasswell, a pioneering political scientist of the 20th century who was one of the first to conduct detailed studies of propaganda, viewed anxiety as the key motivator to be used in trying to affect public opinion through mass psychology (Ascher and Hirschfelder-Ascher, 2005, 78).

If anything, the situation that Donsbach described has only gotten worse over the last few years because of continuing changes in technology and the uncertain business prospects for serious journalism. Whether they admit it or not, reporters cannot help but feel a large measure of anxiety about the future of their field as well as their personal place in it. It's no wonder, then, that they are often easy targets for press aides, political consultants and public relations practitioners.

Most working reporters would likely reject the idea that they are unduly anxious about their work or that their independence, which they highly prize, can be easily compromised by psychological appeals, subtle or otherwise. Independence is a core journalistic principle, enshrined in places like the code of ethics promoted by the Society of Professional Journalists (1996). But the clearest evidence of a lack of independence and a need to deal with insecurity can be found in the phenomenon known as "pack journalism," in which large numbers of reporters working for ostensibly competitive news outlets end up producing stories that share remarkably similar qualities, including perspectives, human sources and even quotes.

The problem of pack journalism is not new, and it is not trivial. *The Washington Reporters,* published in 1981, revealed that journalists found it to be the most serious problem they faced. Reporters surveyed in the book said that pack journalism led to mistaken coverage, as incorrect impressions were picked up by one journalist and then repeated by others. In addition, pack journalism led to gaps in coverage, as reporters concentrated their efforts on a limited number of topics and ignored other ones that might be equally newsworthy. According to this analysis, pack journalism persists because there is safety in numbers. "What occupation wishes to maximize risk?" writes the book's author, Stephen Hess. "Even Hollywood stuntmen take precautions to survive" (131).

One way to understand the power of perception management is to look at several examples of its application by one of its leading practitioners, John Rendon. He is the founder of a Washington consulting firm called The Rendon Group that was described in the book *Weapons of Mass Deception* (Rampton and Stauber, 2003). The book recounts a speech Rendon gave in 1996 at the United States Air Force Academy. In his remarks, Rendon described the arrival of U.S. Marines in Kuwait City in February 1991 after they routed Saddam Hussein's invading army and sent it back to Iraq.

"If any of you either participated in the liberation of Kuwait City, five years ago this week, or if you watched it on television you would have seen hundreds of Kuwaitis waving small American flags," Rendon (1996) said. He went on to ask the audience members if they had ever thought about the unlikeliness of this scene—"how the people of Kuwait City after being held hostage for seven long and painful months, were able to get handheld American flags."

The answer, Rendon told them, was simple: He had arranged for the flags to be shipped to Kuwait so that they could be a part of the media images beamed back to the United States. "I am an information warrior and a perception manager," Rendon said. Getting those flags into the hands of Kuwaiti citizens "was one of my jobs" (1996).

This anecdote is telling in at least two ways. First, it shows the way that professional communications managers like Rendon think about how to project certain kinds of emotions and ideas through the media. The artificiality of the image he hoped to create was not a drawback in his view in any way. The second aspect of the anecdote that is worth considering is that it may not even be true. Contemporaneous newspaper accounts suggest that many of the flags the Kuwaitis were waving were of their own country, flags that had been banned during the occupation. *USA Today,* for example, reported that the Kuwaitis were asking the Marines for American flags while offering up their own national flags. The crowd "threw candy, cigarettes and Kuwaiti flags at the Marines and begged for American flags," the newspaper reported (Spitzer, 1991).

According to *Rolling Stone* magazine, Rendon was also behind the successful effort to get *The New York Times* to report in late 2001 that an Iraqi defector was able to identify locations where Saddam Hussein was hiding weapons of mass destruction. At the time of the newspaper's report, the defector had failed a CIA lie detector test and was not considered a credible source by U.S. intelligence. But members of a front group that Rendon had helped to organize, the Iraqi National Congress, facilitated a meeting between the defector and a *Times* reporter. The resulting article provided ammunition for those in the Bush administration who were arguing for invading Iraq (Bamford, 2005).

A third way that Rendon was involved in perception management of U.S. activity in the Mideast has been through monitoring the work of individual war correspondents on behalf of the Pentagon. In August 2009, *Stars and Stripes,* a newspaper that covers the U.S. military, reported that the Rendon Group was developing profiles about individual reporters to help commanders decide whether a reporter should be allowed to embed with U.S. forces. After the newspaper articles appeared and reporters complained that they were being blacklisted based on what they considered to be fair and neutral accounts, Rendon's contract was canceled (Baron, 2009).

The Rendon Group profiles included information about reporters' past work and also suggestions about how to steer the reporter toward providing positive coverage of military operations. This kind of effort to manage public opinion through the media is part of a long tradition in the field of public relations.

In a chillingly titled essay, "The Engineering of Consent," PR pioneer Bernays laid out his vision for how the media can be used to alter public opinion and lead to collective action (Bernays, 1947). Although Bernays insisted that public relations professionals should use his techniques only for positive objectives, he acknowledged that the same tools and strategies could be used by demagogues. Bernays explained that a successful PR campaign had to go through several phases, including studying the current state of public opinion, establishing specific objectives, putting together a plan and assembling the necessary organization, including the appropriate staff with the necessary equipment. The primary focus of all this activity is one thing: creating news—because it is news that "shapes the attitudes and actions of people" (Bernays, 1947, 119).

Bernays used a definition of news very similar to the one used in this text. "A good criterion as to whether something is or is not news is whether the event juts out of the pattern of routine," he wrote (1947, 119). Thus the engineer of consent, whether operating as a corporate spokesman, a political campaign consultant or the development officer for a nonprofit organization, recognizes that the key to success is the "developing of events and circumstances that are not routine" (119). The next step for the engineer of consent is to get reporters to project these events through the media in a way that will connect with those who are not there themselves.

Some journalists are, unfortunately, content to serve as conduits for information that is conveyed in this way, pretending that the news they report is spontaneous and acquiescing to the idea that they are not being manipulated. Reporters who are not interested in participating in such charades rarely have the option of ignoring stage-managed news events, for the simple reason that they usually involve powerful people and institutions whose actions need to be covered. The option that reporters do have, however, is to make plain the manipulation that is occurring and the devices that are being used. Journalists have choices in how they cover the news, and there are steps they can take to contextualize the news they are reporting and minimize the distortions associated with it.

Journalists and commentators are reluctant to use the word "propaganda" to describe current forms of political communication, but in the early decades of the 20th century, when the profession of public relations was taking shape, the term was employed more freely. Bernays titled one of his books *Propaganda* and made the argument there that shaping public opinion through media messages was critical to the survival of a free society. "The conscious and intelligent manipulation of the organized habits and opinions of the masses is an important element in democratic society," Bernays wrote, adding that "those who manipulate this unseen mechanism of society constitute an invisible government which is the true ruling power of our country" (Bernays, 1928, 9). Bernays went on to acknowledge that propaganda had an unsavory reputation, but not before arguing for its central role in modern society: "Whatever of social importance is done today, whether in politics, finance, manufacture, agriculture, charity, education or other fields, must be done with the help of propaganda. Propaganda is the executive arm of the invisible government" (20).

In the United States, propaganda is most often associated with totalitarian regimes and the widespread dissemination of false information. But political scientists who have studied propaganda understand that its workings are usually more subtle, relying not on outright lies but rather consisting of "the management of collective attitudes by the manipulation of significant symbols" (Lasswell, 1927, 627).

A symbol is an object that has a meaning beyond itself. An American flag, for example, is a tri-colored banner consisting of stars and stripes. But it is also a signifier of the United States, its people, culture, history, armed forces and values. Because symbols have multiple levels of meanings, they present a challenge to reporters, who generally try to control the content of their stories through careful selections of details and quotes and by arranging this information in a particular order. Because of the way that they resonate with a variety of meanings, symbols, while they can be captured and included in reports, cannot be controlled in the way that other kinds of information can be controlled. Reporters need to be conscious of how symbols are used in a media campaign, whether for a commercial or a political product, and consider ways to present them so as to minimize their manipulative effect on news audiences (see box below).

A special subclass of symbols is language, and public figures have become increasingly careful about using words in market-tested ways to shape perceptions of controversial subjects. Instead of using phrases that convey a plain meaning or that have been used as traditional labels for an issue, politicians, corporate leaders and others have been encouraged to employ new formulations that can evoke specific responses and shift public opinion. Perhaps the leading figure in popularizing this approach is Frank Luntz, whose personal and corporate slogan is "It's not what you say, it's what they hear" (2007).

The Mistake of "Mission Accomplished"

In retrospect, even George W. Bush came to agree that the pseudo-event he used in May 2003 to announce that "major combat operations in Iraq have ended" was a mistake. At the time, however, his press handlers and other staffers were hailed as geniuses of political communication (see Figure 12.1).

They arranged for the president to land in a jet warplane on the flight deck of the *U.S.S. Abraham Lincoln*, a nuclear powered aircraft carrier that was returning to the United States after helping to support Operation Iraqi Freedom, the invasion of Iraq. President Bush emerged from a four-seat Viking S-3B in full flight suit regalia and, after mixing with members of the ship's crew, appeared before a massive "Mission Accomplished" sign to state, "In the battle of Iraq, the United States and our allies have prevailed" (Sanger, 2003).

Within a few months, as it became clear that the Iraq War was far from finished and as the casualty toll continued to mount, Bush tried to separate himself from that event. He hadn't meant that the war,

FIGURE 12.1 *President George W. Bush is saluted by sailors aboard the USS Abraham Lincoln after arriving by jet. Credit: Photographer's Mate 3rd Class Tyler J. Clements/U.S. Navy*

which would last another eight years, was almost over, he said at an Oct. 28, 2003, news conference. The idea for the "Mission Accomplished" sign came from the crew of the *Lincoln*, not from the White House, he maintained. "I know it was attributed somehow to some ingenious advance man from my staff," Bush said. "They weren't that ingenious, by the way" (Canellos, 2003).

But initially the aircraft carrier speech seemed perfect, and it got a glowing reception in the media. On the right, naturally enough, there was strong praise. Said Anne Coulter: "It's stunning. It's amazing. I think it's huge. I mean, he's landing on a boat at 150 miles per hour. It's tremendous. It's hard to imagine any Democrat being able to do that" (Media Matters, 2006).

A similar reaction came from the other side of the partisan spectrum. Chris Matthews, a longtime Democratic operative who went on to host a political talk show said, "He looks for real. What is it about the commander-in-chief role, the hat that he does wear, that makes him—I mean, he seems like—he didn't fight in a war, but he looks like he does" (Media Matters, 2006).

Supposedly objective news anchors joined in. "Picture perfect. Part Spider-Man, part Tom Cruise, part Ronald Reagan. The president seizes the moment on an aircraft carrier in the Pacific," said Gwen Ifill of PBS (Silverstein, 2008). "He looked terrific and full of energy in a flight suit.

He is a former pilot, so it's not a foreign art farm—art form to him. Not all presidents could have pulled this scene off today," said Brian Williams of NBC (Media Matters, 2003).

An aircraft carrier, cheering sailors, a jet plane, the victory banner—the White House skillfully deployed these symbols of the triumphant warrior to convey an overwhelmingly positive, and misleading, message, that the war was over and that the rest of the military in Iraq would soon follow the crew of the *Lincoln* back home.

In its coverage *The New York Times* was careful to include some words of caution, including a report from Baghdad explaining that combat was continuing, albeit at a reduced level. But its front page was dominated by a photo of Bush speaking from a presidential podium, giving a thumbs-up salute to sailors whose arms were raised in applause.

In a column labeled "News Analysis," the paper even helpfully provided the three-pronged interpretation of the event that White House aides were shooting for: that U.S. forces were moving from combat to police operations, that countries that had not been willing to provide military aid could now step in with other forms of assistance and that the president himself was "coming home" by turning his attention to domestic issues (Bumiller, 2003).

The *Times* was clearly caught up in the moment, a point that was underlined when it had to issue a pair of corrections about its coverage to clear up some exaggerations it had made (Bumiller, 2003). The paper had named Bush as the first president to land aboard an aircraft carrier (others had done it by helicopter) and indicated that no president had spent the night aboard a warship since World War II (President John Kennedy had done so during the 1960s).

This example demonstrates how easy it is for reporters, even highly experienced ones, to be influenced by the skillful use of symbols. Fortunately, it also suggests some ways that reporters can guard against this kind of influence.

First, reporters need to learn to recognize the use of symbols as part of a media strategy and be especially careful in how they present them. Lesson No. 1 is to get the facts straight and resist the temptation to embellish with the kind of details that the *Times* later had to retract.

A second lesson is to provide as full a description of the symbol itself, because symbols are rarely as perfectly suited as they are presented. British news coverage of the event, for example, showed that Bush was not flying the kind of "Top Gun" fighter plane that Tom Cruise piloted in the movie of that name. It turns out the Secret Service had vetoed the idea of the president flying even in a two-seater plane and had insisted that a bodyguard go along, which meant that Bush was in a relatively unglamorous craft used primarily for anti-submarine warfare and refueling (Borger, Burkeman, and MacAskill, 2003).

As was later reported, the rationale for Bush arriving by fixed-wing aircraft had also been misstated. He was originally described as having to use the plane because the *Lincoln* was too far out at sea. But by the time of his arrival on the aircraft carrier, the ship was close enough to shore to be reached by a helicopter (Stevenson, 2003).

A third lesson in dealing with symbols is to be aware of how they are framed—and to try to view them from alternative perspectives. That's what the *Independent*, a left-leaning London newspaper, did. In its coverage of Bush's speech, it pointed out that Iraqis were unlikely to share Bush's view that the war was winding down, noting that American soldiers were still killing civilians on a regular basis.

"Hatred is taking hold here," the paper reported. "And as the Americans prepared to move from a war footing to beginning the enormous task of rebuilding and reconstruction, public disillusionment and simmering violence is growing. It threatens to undermine the prospects of a peaceful future and wreak havoc with the plans for a democracy in Iraq" (Reeves, 2003, C1).

By refusing to be caught up in the symbolic communication of the Bush White House, the *Independent* was able to provide an unfortunately accurate and prescient view of the true state of the war.

Luntz knows that the words he tells his clients to use will have an effect on audiences. That's because he tests the language out in advance with large focus groups using "people meters," wireless-enabled dials that participants turn to signal their positive or negative reactions to what they are hearing and seeing. This mechanism, which Luntz likens to an electrocardiogram, "measures a combination of emotional and intellectual responses and gets inside each participant's psyche, isolating his or her emotional reaction to every word, phrase and visual" (2007, 78). He painstakingly analyses the results because he knows that the American people "will often come to diametrically opposite conclusions on policy questions" just based on the words that are used (46). Examples that he cites are the *estate tax* versus *the death tax, drilling for oil* versus *exploring for energy* and *crime* versus *public safety* (see Figure 12.2).

The popularity of the idea that "perception is reality" is often attributed to Lee Atwater, a political strategist who is perhaps best known for his role in the 1988 presidential campaign that saw George H.W. Bush overcome a 17-point deficit in the polls to win a resounding victory over Massachusetts

FIGURE 12.2 *How Americans respond to news events like the Deepwater Horizon blowout can be shaped by the language that is used to create context, whether, for example, an activity is called "drilling for oil" or "exploring for energy." Credit: Spc. Casey Ware/Mississippi Army National Guard*

Gov. Michael Dukakis. That turnaround is credited to the infamous "Willie Horton" ad, which Atwater arranged for and which featured a mug shot of a black convicted killer who committed additional violent crimes after escaping from a temporary release. Horton's actions were horrific and raised legitimate questions about Massachusetts penal policies, but Atwater's goal was not to argue policy but to tie a black felon to the Democratic candidate. In one famous quote, he said, "By the time we're finished, they're going to wonder whether Willie Horton is Dukakis' running mate" (Simon, 1990, 203).

While Atwater is remembered for the Horton ad, it was actually his ability to manage the perceptions of the press that was the key to Bush's victory. The ad was risky—because it was so clearly a race-based appeal that could have backfired against candidate Bush. The solution to the problem was to ensure that Bush was depicted as a reluctant race-baiter, someone who didn't want to use the Willie Horton material but was convinced by his staff to go along. "Anecdotes his aides recounted always had the same point. You had to twist Bush's arm to get him to attack" (Simon, 1990, 230). This was the story that eventually stuck, that there was a "Good George" and a "Bad George" and that the "Bad George" only surfaced after his advisors told him there was no other way to win.

In other words, the key to making sure that the attack ad would work was to make sure that the news coverage went in a certain direction. If Bush were presented as racist and negative in news accounts, then the ads could have backfired. An associate of Atwater's, Turner Eskew, later noted how his friend "knew how to control media narratives." In a PBS documentary, Eskew remarked, "Now it's kind of rote in politics, but Lee was saying early: Perception is reality. He was ahead of his time" (Forbes, 2008).

During the presidency of George W. Bush, the idea took hold that perceptions could be used to create realities at will. As one White House aide told a reporter in 2004, "We're an empire now, and when we act, we create our own reality. And while you're studying that reality—judiciously, as you will—we'll act again, creating other new realities, which you can study too, and that's how things will sort out. We're history's actors . . . and you, all of you, will be left to just study what we do" (Suskind, 2004).

As we have seen, the basic tools of perception management are symbols—words, objects and images that are deployed to influence the public both emotionally and intellectually. Reporters should be conscious of their use and prepared to balance their effects. Reporters also need to be aware of the three common techniques that are used to draw the public's attention in particular directions: agenda setting, priming and framing (Scheufele and Tewksbury, 2007).

All three phenomena, agenda setting, priming and framing, regularly surface in discussions of media effects and have to do with the way the public's attention is directed in a particular way. Agenda setting refers to the process by which certain topics take on greater significance within society, setting the stage for some kind of action. A public official whose economic policies are not having the desired effect may use agenda setting to turn voters' attention in another direction, by declaring a war on drugs, for example, or calling for new education policies. Framing refers to the process in which a particular issue is presented, emphasizing some aspects and de-emphasizing others. A focus on illegal drugs, for example, could be framed as part of an anti-crime campaign, or it could be framed as a way of providing treatment for addicts. Finally, priming is the process by which the public's attention is drawn to one issue as opposed to another, perhaps by offering a major news outlet an exclusive interview with a top official or a celebrity endorser.

It's easy to see how all three processes work together and how reporters can easily be drawn into their workings. In many cases, these are legitimate methods public officials use to communicate their plans and priorities. But reporters owe it to themselves and to their readers to recognize that these processes are occurring and that there are tradeoffs involved. An anti-drug campaign that promises tough sentences for habitual users may have great appeal to certain elements of the electorate, and a reporter needs to report on such a campaign if it is coming to the forefront of the public agenda. But reporters also need to keep in mind that alternative frames are available and that a politically attractive solution to a problem may not work as intended.

One of the most insidious ways perception management works is to take the conventions, values and work routines of journalism and distort them to arrive at a desired outcome. For example, one of the best ways for a political figure or a corporation to minimize the effect of some piece of bad news is to time its release. This is the tactic known as the "Friday afternoon document dump," in which the release of negative news is timed to coincide with times when reporters and news audiences will be inclined to pay relatively less attention. Friday afternoons are used because reporters are often busy wrapping up their work weeks and perhaps preparing special reports for the weekend and because news audiences are typically less attentive to news that comes out at the beginning of the weekend.

Because of the way that journalists value the qualities of fairness and balance, perception managers have discovered that they can pressure journalists into providing a distorted view of the facts. This problem, as noted in Chapter 6 and Chapter 8, is sometimes referred to as "false equivalency," and it occurs when reporters, out of a desire to present opposing views of an issue, give equal weight to both sides of an argument even when one side of the argument is notably weaker. A commonly cited example of this phenomenon is climate change, and another example has been the controversy over the role of childhood vaccines in causing autism. This claim, which has been thoroughly debunked by medical researchers, has not been fully accepted by parents in many places, and much of the blame has been placed on the media, which covered the debate as if there were two opposing camps of scientists. In fact, the charge that the vaccine led to autism was the pet cause of a single researcher, whose findings were officially retracted by the journal that published them (Harris, 2010).

Yet another popular practice in journalism that has been co-opted by perception managers is the idea of narrative. Narrative journalism, with its emphasis on characters and storyline, has become a popular tool for news organizations to take on complex topics. Organizing information into stories can be a way to engage news audiences in a deeper way than the traditional inverted pyramid structure. For more than a decade starting in the late 1990s, the Nieman Foundation at Harvard worked to promote narrative journalism and for a while hosted an annual conference. While narrative has taken hold at many major news organizations, it can be a problematic technique because of the way it employs artistic devices that may depart from a strict factuality. But it has been successful, because it works. The human mind is apparently conditioned to organize information according to narrative accounts. Perception managers have recognized this as well and have begun to present ideas and candidates in the context of a narrative. Rather than providing a litany of facts about a person or a topic, perception managers are more likely to arrange them according to a storyline that seems to make sense and to provide a persuasive case. Stories are compelling, but just because they sound good or seem to fit together into a coherent whole doesn't mean that they are true. As a result, journalists have to be careful when they are urged to make their reporting conform with a particular narrative.

A good example of the power of narrative to propel individuals and events is President Barack Obama. As *Politico* described him, "No contemporary American politician has benefited more from the power of good storytelling than Barack Obama. He vaulted from obscurity to the presidency on the power of narrative—invoking his biography and personal values to make a larger point about how he would lead the nation" (Burns and Harris, 2013). But as Obama's approval ratings sank in his second term to well below 50 percent, at least some political journalists had to be wondering about the dangers of being seduced by a compelling personal story.

Many aspects of perception management can be described as mind games, but there are also strategies that seem designed to intimidate. At the trial of Bradley Manning, the soldier behind the release of classified documents to the website WikiLeaks, armed military guards in camouflage uniforms paced behind the rows of reporters and looked over their shoulders (Savage, 2013). Even more elaborate plans to disrupt reporters' activities at the trial were also documented, although it is not clear how fully they were executed (Ludlow, 2013).

MAINTAINING YOUR PERSPECTIVE

Since we live in a media culture that puts a premium on how perceptions of reality are transmitted through the news, you can expect to find yourself under near constant pressure to conform your reporting to someone else's agenda. Fortunately, there are things you can do to maintain your perspective and your independence in the face of these efforts to shape your reporting. Here are some specific steps you can take:

1. **Recognize the pervasiveness of the problem.** People lie. All the time. "One researcher after another has confirmed that lying has become as common as scratching itches" (Keyes, 2004, 4). Estimates about the frequency of lies that an average person is exposed to range from 13 a week to 200 a day. While many of these may be minor deceptions for the sake of being polite, there is little question that people under pressure will say something deceptive if they think they can get away with it. What's worse is that people will sometimes lie when there is no apparent reason to. It's not that no one will ever tell you the truth—it's just that you can't assume a trusted source has been entirely accurate. Not everything you hear will be a lie, necessarily, but even statements that may be technically true are likely to be pitched your way covered with spin. Try to keep in mind the

motto of the Chicago News Bureau: "If your mother says she loves you, check it out" (Royko, 1983, xi).

2. **Connect the DOT.** You will be far less susceptible to perception management if you don't rely on just one way to get information. Listen to your sources, but check what they tell you against direct observation and documents. Speaking of documents, don't automatically believe what they say, or seem to say. Just because something is written down doesn't mean it's true. But if you are able to use different kinds of information sources to arrive at a particular conclusion, chances are good that your conclusion is accurate. Learn to trust your judgment, making sure that your judgment is based on looking at a situation through multiple lenses. The more knowledgeable you are, the less likely that someone will be able to spin you into a misleading story.

3. **Watch for the telltale signs.** Pay attention to the words your sources use, and weigh carefully if the choice of words will have a misleading effect on readers. Is it more accurate to call waterboarding "torture" or an "enhanced interrogation technique"? Are students getting "private school vouchers" or "opportunity scholarships"? If your sources are reluctant to use common terminology or insist upon using one particular phrase over another, chances are that your sources are trying to use you to manipulate public opinion in a very specific way (Johnston, 2003).

4. **Consider the context.** Just as you learn to listen carefully to language, be alert to the framing and priming techniques that sources use to exert control over how issues are presented to the public. Consider alternative ways to think about a topic and how to include them in your reports. Maintain your independence, and don't fall into the trap of advancing a partisan agenda.

5. **Call people out.** The ultimate power that journalists have to shape the world is their ability to put together a story that illuminates a situation and affects public opinion. Instead of simply being on the receiving end of perception management, especially when it crosses the line from shaping the news to distorting the truth, reporters should not be reluctant to tell news audiences what is going on.

EXERCISES

1. How often do you lie—perhaps more often than you think? Keep a diary over the course of a couple of days, and try to make note of all of the times you are tempted to shade the truth—and how often you give in to this temptation.

2. Think about the five factors that Wolfgang Donsback identified as adding to the stress reporters face. Which ones do you think would be the hardest to deal with? How would you try to offset the effect of these conditions?

3. Review a recent major address of a political leader, such as the State of the Union, and try to pick out the ways that perception management techniques have been employed.

REFERENCES

Aronsen, Gavin. "Journalists—Myself Included—Swept Up in Mass Arrest at Occupy Oakland," *Mother Jones,* January 29, 2012, accessed December 23, 2013, at http://www.motherjones.com/mojo/2012/01/journalists-arrested-occupy-oakland.

Ascher, William, and Barbara Hirschfelder-Ascher. *Revitalizing Political Psychology: The Legacy of Harold D. Lasswell,* Mahwah, N.J.: Lawrence Erlbaum Associates, 2005.

Bamford, James. "The Man Who Sold the War," *Rolling Stone,* December 1, 2005, 53–62.

Baron, Kevin. "Military Terminates Rendon Contract," *Stars and Stripes,* August, 31, 2009, accessed December 23, 2013, at http://www.stripes.com/news/military-terminates-rendon-contract-1.94400.

Bernays, Edward L. "The Engineering of Consent," *The Annals of the American Academy of Political and Social Science* 250, No. 1, March 1947, 113–120.

———. *Propaganda,* New York: Liveright Publishing Corporation, 1928.

Borger, Julian, Oliver Burkeman, and Ewen MacAskill. "Bush Makes Carrier Landing for TV Address," *Guardian,* May 2, 2003, accessed December 24, 2013, at http://www.theguardian.com/world/2003/may/02/usa.iraq2.

Bumiller, Elisabeth. "Cold Truths Behind Pomp," *The New York Times,* May 2, 2003, A1.

Burns, Alexander, and John F. Harris. "Obama's Dangerous New Narrative," *Politico,* May 15, 2013, accessed December 24, 2013, at http://www.politico.com/story/2013/05/obamas-dangerous-new-narrative-91390.html.

Canellos, Peter S. "Bush Distances Himself From Sign Aboard Carrier," *Boston Globe,* October 29, 2003, accessed December 24, 2013, at http://www.boston.com/news/nation/articles/2003/10/29/bush_distances_himself_from_sign_aboard_carrier/.

Department of Defense. *Dictionary of Military and Associated Terms,* Washington: U.S. Government Printing Office, 1994.

———. *Dictionary of Military and Associated Terms,* Washington: Department of Defense, 2010 (amended through November 2013), accessed December 24, 2013, at http://www.dtic.mil/doctrine/new_pubs/jp1_02.pdf.

Donsbach, Wolfgang. "Psychology of News Decisions: Factors behind Journalists' Professional Behavior," *Journalism* 5, No. 2, May 2004, 131–157.

Forbes, Stefan. "Boogie Man: The Lee Atwater Story," *Frontline,* November 11, 2008, accessed December 24, 2013, at http://www.pbs.org/wgbh/pages/frontline/atwater/etc/synopsis.html.

Harris, Gardiner. "Journal Retracts 1998 Paper Linking Autism to Vaccines," *The New York Times,* February 2, 2010, accessed December 24, 2013, at http://www.nytimes.com/2010/02/03/health/research/03lancet.html.

Hess, Stephen. *The Washington Reporters,* Washington: Brookings Institution, 1981.

Horwitz, Sari. "Obama Calls for Review of Rules on Subpoenas to the Media," *The Washington Post,* May 23, 2013, accessed December 23, 2013, at http://articles.washingtonpost.com/2013–05–23/world/39472622_1_president-obama-media-organizations-justice-department.

Johnston, David Cay. *Perfectly Legal: The Covert Campaign to Rig Our Tax System to Benefit the Super Rich—and Cheat Everybody Else,* New York: Penguin Press, 2003.

Keyes, Ralph. *The Post-Truth Era: Dishonesty and Deception in Contemporary Life,* New York: St. Martin's 2004.

Lasswell, Harold D. "The Theory of Political Propaganda," *The American Political Science Review* 21, No. 3, August 1927, 627–631.

Ludlow, Peter, "The Real War on Reality," *The New York Times,* June 14, 2013, accessed December 24, 2013, at http://opinionator.blogs.nytimes.com/2013/06/14/the-real-war-on-reality/?hp.

Luntz, Frank. *Words That Work: It's Not What You Say, It's What People Hear,* New York: Hyperion, 2007.

Media Matters Staff. "Mission Accomplished: A Look Back at the Media's Fawning Coverage of Bush's Premature Declaration of Victory in Iraq," Media Matters for America, April 27, 2006, accessed December 24, 2013, at http://mediamatters.org/research/2006/04/27/mission-accomplished-a-look-back-at-the-medias/135513.

New York Times, "Corrections," May 3, 2003, A2.

Phillips, Karen. "CPJ Risk List: Where Press Freedom Suffered," Committee to Protect Journalists, February 22, 2013, accessed December 23, 2013, at http://www.cpj.org/2013/02/attacks-on-the-press-cpj-risk-list.php.

Rampton, Sheldon, and John Stauber. *Weapons of Mass Deception: The Uses of Propaganda in Bush's War on Iraq,* New York: Jeremy P. Tarcher/Penguin, 2003.

Reeves, Phil. "The War Is Over (Except for Iraq)," *Independent,* May 1, 2003.

Rendon, John W., Jr. Speech to the Olin Foundation Information and National Security Conference, Colorado Spring, Co., February 29, 1996, accessed December 23, 2013, at https://web.archive.org/web/19970622154146/http://www.rendon.com/docs/airforce.html.

Royce-Bartlett, Lindy. "Leak probe has chilled sources, AP exec says," CNN, June 19, 2013, accessed December 23, 2013, at http://www.cnn.com/2013/06/19/politics/ap-leak-probe/.

Royko, Mike. "Introduction," in A. A. Dornfeld, *Hello Sweetheart, Get Me Rewrite: The Story of the City News Bureau of Chicago,* Chicago: Academy Chicago Publishers, 1983.

Sanger, David E. "Bush Declares 'One Victory in a War on Terror,'" *The New York Times,* May 2, 2003, accessed December 24, 2013, at http://www.nytimes.com/2003/05/02/world/aftereffects-the-president-bush-declares-one-victory-in-a-war-on-terror.html?pagewanted=all&src=pm.

Savage, Charlie. "In Closing Argument, Prosecutor Casts Soldier as 'Anarchist' for Leaking Archives," *The New York Times,* July 25, 2013, accessed December 24, 2013, at http://www.nytimes.com/2013/07/26/us/politics/closing-arguments-due-in-manning-leaks-case.html.

Scheufele, Dietram A. and David Tewksbury. "Framing, Agenda Setting, and Priming: The Evolution of Three Media Effects Models," *Journal of Communication,* 57, no. 1, 2007, 9–20.

Silverstein, Ken. "Ifill on George Bush: 'Part Tom Cruise, part Ronald Reagan,'" The Stream (blog) *Harper's,* October 2, 2008, accessed December 24, 2013, at http://harpers.org/blog/2008/10/ifill-on-george-bush-part-tom-cruise-part-ronald-reagan/.

Simon, Roger. *Road Show: In America Anyone Can Become President. It's One of the Risks We Take,* New York: Farrar, Straus, Giroux, 1990.

Society of Professional Journalists. "SPJ Code of Ethics," SPJ.org, 1996, accessed December 24, 2013, at http://www.spj.org/ethicscode.asp.

Spitzer, Kirk. "Freed Kuwaitis Shower Troops With Gratitude," *USA Today,* February 28, 1991, 2A. LexisNexis Academic.

Stevenson, Richard W. "White House Clarifies Bush's Carrier Landing," *The New York Times,* May 7, 2003, accessed May 6, 2014, at http://www.nytimes.com/2003/05/07/politics/07CARR.html.

Suskind, Ron. "Faith, Certainty and the Presidency of George W. Bush," *The New York Times Magazine,* October 17, 2004, accessed December 24, 2013, at http://www.nytimes.com/2004/10/17/magazine/17BUSH.html?_r=0.

CHAPTER 13

Journalism That Makes a Difference

In the polarized political context of the 21st century—where science has lost the power to command consensus and journalists are routinely accused of taking sides—what happened on April 15, 1970, seems almost unimaginable. On that day the Department of Defense announced that it was suspending immediately the use of Agent Orange (*The New York Times,* 1970, 29). At the time, the United States military had been spraying millions of gallons a year of the herbicide over the Southeast Asian jungle (Stellman et al., 2003), and commanders viewed it as a critical tool in fighting the Vietcong (Whiteside, 1971). But questions raised in news reports had prompted a series of Senate hearings that focused uncomfortable attention on the effects of the chemical. The active ingredient in Agent Orange was also widely used domestically, and on that same day in April 1970 the surgeon general announced that the Department of Agriculture would move to curtail the use of this chemical both on farm fields and in residential neighborhoods (Senate Committee on Commerce, 1970).

The announcements came in the face of a rising tide of environmental activism, just a week before the first Earth Day demonstrations were expected to sweep through Washington and other major cities. But the issue of Agent Orange was complicated and full of uncertainty, and the country's paper of record, *The New York Times,* had been keeping its distance (Whiteside, 1971). Still the role of the press in bringing the issue to a head was large, as the surgeon general, Dr. Jesse L. Steinfeld, made clear in disclosing the new policy on Agent Orange. "Great public fear of the possible implications for man has followed reports of harm in laboratory animal tests," he said in testimony to the Senate Subcommittee on Energy, Natural Resources, and the Environment (Senate Committee on Commerce, April 1970, 168).

The chair of that subcommittee was Philip A. Hart, Democrat of Michigan, a low-profile legislator who was held in such high regard by his colleagues that they would vote to name a new Capitol Hill office building in his name and inscribe a dedication over the entrance that read in part: "His humility and ethics earned him his place as the conscience of the Senate" (U.S. Senate). It was Sen. Hart who called the hearings that focused attention on Agent

Orange and that brought about the restrictions on its use. At one of the hearings, Sen. Hart in turn made clear what it was that spurred him to action. Speaking at the start of a session on June 17, 1970, he took a moment to praise the "thoroughness and care" of Thomas Whiteside, "whose *New Yorker* article entitled 'Defoliation' was in large part responsible for our earlier hearings." The senator then said he wanted to place a copy of that piece in the subcommittee's record and "again to express gratitude to Mr. Whiteside and to the *New Yorker* for their respective contributions" (Senate Committee on Commerce, June 1970, 1–2).

Media critics, political scientists and other scholars have long debated the role of the press in affecting government action. As numerous scholars have noted, many of the most celebrated examples of press coverage leading directly to political or governmental action do not stand up to close scrutiny (Schudson, 1996). But in the case of Agent Orange, there is little question that a single reporter, Thomas Whiteside, through a series of conventional and unconventional magazine articles and some personal intervention in Washington, brought the issue into the spotlight in a way that led to changes in policy. One of the most striking aspects of the Agent Orange decision was the speed with which it was made, compared, for example, to the decade of debate over DDT that followed the publication of Rachel Carson's *Silent Spring* before the chemical was banned in the United States, although it's also true that the restrictions announced to the Senate subcommittee were not as definitive as they first appeared.

At first glance it would appear that Whiteside's reporting on Agent Orange would stand as a singular example of impact journalism. The application of Agent Orange in Vietnam has created considerable medical and financial consequences both in Southeast Asia and in the United States. Without his work and the follow-up Senate hearings, the use of Agent Orange would have continued for longer and led to greater human suffering and monetary costs. But the path from a news account to a change in policy is not always direct. A closer look at the Agent Orange coverage reveals a complicated backstory, illustrating the limitations that journalists face in trying to get a story out as well as reinforcing the critical role that the media can play in fostering public debate and creating the circumstances in which decisive actions are taken. Journalists need to be aware of these complications because these are the kinds of challenges they will face as they go about addressing news topics and deciding how to evaluate the impact of their work.

Whiteside was a crusader against Agent Orange, engaging in what is known as advocacy journalism. Many journalists have come to the conclusion that taking an overt position on a controversial issue is ultimately self-defeating, and it is rare to find reporters today at mainstream news organizations who are so clearly tied to one side of a debate, although the rules are somewhat looser at magazines such as *The New Yorker*. Other journalists and media critics, however, scoff at the idea that reporters are ever truly objective about the topics they research and question whether it is even a good idea for journalists to maintain a front of objectivity (Keller, 2013).

In any case the effort to curtail the use of Agent Orange, which included other reporters besides Whiteside, belongs to a long tradition in American journalism, a tradition of trying to bring about change by raising public awareness. Scholars have identified numerous examples of journalists whose work contributed to improvements in society, in areas as varied as food safety, the integration of professional sports and the right of women to vote. Reporters have contributed to the creation and preservation of parks and wilderness areas, to the lowering of consumer prices and to the indictment of war criminals. Indeed, "the chance to make a difference has historically been, and continues to be, one of the attractions that draws people into journalism" (Serrin and Serrin, 2002, xx).

But it is difficult to draw a direct connection between a piece of journalism and any subsequent social reform. As observers and analysts of a situation, journalists may set in motion a series of actions, but they themselves do not carry out those actions. It was four cabinet secretaries who issued orders to limit the use of Agent Orange, not a reporter for *The New Yorker.* The connection between an article and a governmental action is not always easy to document because there are often many intervening steps and other players involved—working under shifting circumstances that can make it easier or harder for change to happen.

As J. Edward Murray, a former executive editor of the *Arizona Republic,* once said, "Investigative reporting, no matter how excellent, cannot accomplish much all by itself" (Wendland, 1977, 251). Reporters and news organizations serve to contextualize, amplify and repeat information that might otherwise be ignored. They can focus attention on a problem, but they cannot fix it just by reporting about it.

While working journalists are well aware of the limitations built into their profession, an extensive mythology has developed about the power of the press, a mythology that media scholar W. Joseph Campbell examined in his 2010 book, *Getting It Wrong: Ten of the Greatest Misreported Stories in American Journalism.* Some of the myths Campbell has attempted to puncture include the story that Walter Cronkite's reporting in Vietnam convinced President Johnson that he had lost public support on the war and the one about Edward R. Murrow ending that career of Wisconsin's red-baiting senator, Joseph McCarthy.

One of Campbell's recurring targets, perhaps because it has grown so large and is repeated so often, is the Watergate myth, the notion that two inexperienced but intrepid reporters from *The Washington Post,* Bob Woodward and Carl Bernstein, were able through the sheer force of their journalism to drive Richard Nixon from the White House. No one can argue that Woodward and Bernstein didn't play a role by writing stories about the Watergate burglary pointing to political shenanigans. But the disclosures that proved to be Nixon's undoing were beyond the scope of hard-working journalists to discover. The reporters lacked the subpoena power and the ability to threaten jail terms that federal prosecutors and judges used to gather information. The reporters lacked the capacity of congressional committees to hold public hearings and to make administration officials provide testimony under oath. Perhaps most importantly the reporters lacked the legal authority of the U.S. Supreme Court, which issued the order forcing Nixon to hand over damaging tapes of his conversations in the Oval Office. Without the undeniable evidence of hush money and cover-ups, Nixon would likely have ridden out the storm and stayed in office (Campbell, 2010).

Communications scholars have developed an entire field of research devoted to what they call "media effects," in which they try to trace out the ways that news stories, and other forms of communication, influence the public. While some of this research can provide useful insights for journalists, much of it is highly theoretical and focuses on relatively narrow questions, such as whether survey respondents think differently about nanotechnology based on whether they get their news from newspapers, the Internet or television (Lee and Scheufele, 2006).

Since the turn of the century, however, professional journalists and journalism organizations have begun to study the question of impact more closely and with a focus on how to track and measure the way that news can affect citizens and society. There have been at least three factors at work here. First is a concern about the disconnect between journalism and its intended audience as the economic underpinning of news reporting has been greatly eroded by declines in readership and viewership while the volume of news and information has expanded greatly. The second factor is the emergence of digital tools for tracking news consumption as information is distributed over the Internet. The third development is a shift toward alternative funding for news, away from the cross-subsidy approach of advertising revenue supporting newsgathering. Instead news organizations are turning to other sources, such as foundations making donations or users paying for access to websites. While nonprofit groups often have large sums of money at their disposal, they are also insistent on seeing tangible outcomes from their giving, whether to news organizations or elsewhere. Similarly, individual readers who are now paying a greater percentage of the costs of news reporting are unlikely to maintain either print or digital subscriptions unless they perceive that their payments are being rewarded with valuable information.

The decline of the news media, both as an economic engine and as a mechanism for information dissemination and debate, is easy to observe and has been well documented in numerous ways. In March 2013 the Pew Research Center's 10th annual report on the state of the news media reported on continuing declines in newspaper advertising revenues, newsroom staffing and audience attention (Pew, 2013).

Meanwhile other kinds of information sources, including ones that are promoting specific political views or commercial products, have expanded their activities. News has become a commodity that can be produced and distributed by a far larger number of individuals and institutions than in previous eras. As a result, news organizations are facing a situation in which "distinguishing between high-quality information of public value and agenda-driven news has become an increasingly complicated task, made no easier in an era of economic churn" (Pew, 2013).

As news organizations struggle to make this distinction, they are finding that they have a previously unimagined wealth of information about how news consumers respond to the various types of content that are available to them on the Web. Analyzing this audience information has become a priority for many news organizations based on the belief that journalists can overcome the value erosion that results from the sheer volume of information by producing news that carries a measurable impact. At *The New York Times,* an effort was started in 2012 to sort through the "metrics" of the Internet to look for the kinds of content that reflect positive reader reactions.

Unlike the print environment, the Web generates vast amounts of data about the news audience. News organizations can track what stories draw the most readers and which ones draw the longest looks. They can also see what kinds of stories and which formats are most likely to become "viral," spreading across the Internet through social media and email. When news organizations relied mostly on print or broadcast, they could either guess at this kind of information or use surveys to gather some approximations, but the Internet allows for the measuring of specific kinds of impact in real time.

"We are awash in metrics, and we have the ability to engage with readers at scale in ways that would have been impossible (or impossibly expensive) in an analog world," says Aron Pilhofer, who works on digital strategy and interactive news at the *Times* (2012). On his website Pilhofer describes his job at the *Times* as leading a newsroom team "that blends journalism, social media, technology and analytics." The team's challenge is to figure out what to do with all that data and find the elements that are worth acting on, a task that is complicated by recent instability in the news industry.

Traditionally, news operations have been funded by means of various subsidies, the most important one of which has been advertising. While this arrangement created the possibilities of conflicts of interest as reporters were sometimes kept from pursuing stories that might offend major advertisers, in most settings newsroom personnel did not concern themselves with the effect of their work on ad sales. In almost all cases, advertisers pay news organizations for access to a target audience, and as long as the connection is made, advertisers are not overly concerned with news content or its impact, at least as long as it does not have a negative effect on the advertiser's image or sales (Anderson, Bell, and Shirky, 2012). But in an era of more direct funding of journalism, either by news consumers or sponsoring organizations, this dynamic is changed. News that does not generate an impact of some kind, either on a personal or society-wide level, may fail to capture the attention of funders and thus lose their support.

Scholars predict that quantitative ways of assessing the reaction to news reports will become a part of newsroom culture and that "measures for the aims and outcome of journalism will be routine, and public" (Anderson et al., 2012, 43). The idea that impact needs to be a regular part of reporting has indeed taken hold among journalists, and one online news organization went so far as to trademark the term "impact journalism" (U.S. Patent and Trademark Office, 2011).

But for the foreseeable future, the question of how to define impact will likely remain open. In fact some wonder whether defining and measuring impact is even appropriate. The concern is that journalism has a broad responsibility to present information and that a focus on high profile stories with obvious kinds of impact will mean that reporters and news organizations will prioritize coverage of "gotcha" stories while ignoring important, but routine, events. Without denying the validity of these concerns, proponents of focusing on impact in journalism argue that tracking and measuring outcomes is not at all incompatible with traditional values of accountability and broad public service. They also argue that the digital environment has changed journalism in a way that makes measuring impact a crucial tool for survival as news consumers are no longer passive recipients of information but rather engaged participants in the media ecosystem.

Richard J. Tofel served as an assistant managing editor at *The Wall Street Journal* and general counsel of the Rockefeller Association before becoming the founding general manager and later president of ProPublica, a nonprofit journalism site that started operating in 2008. He has written an extensive review of his organization's efforts to achieve impact that is a mixture of useful insights and unanswered questions. This analysis concludes with three "tentative lessons": that impact is relatively rare, that it is hard to prove and that there is no single reliable measurement of impact (Tofel, 2013). These are all worth further consideration.

THE RARITY OF IMPACT

ProPublica, like many though not all nonprofit news organizations, has made impact a central aim. Its mission statement includes an explicit goal of achieving impact: "Our mission is to expose abuses of power and betrayals of the public trust by government, business and other institutions, using the moral force of investigative journalism to spur reform through the sustained spotlighting of wrongdoing" (ProPublica, n.d.). Right from the start the organization has put a great deal of effort into tracking the impact of its work and making regular public reports on the results it has achieved.

For ProPublica impact occurs when change occurs, and for a news article to count as having an impact the organization has to be able to identify "a clear causal link" (Tofel, 2013, 14) between its reporting and the ultimate change. Significantly, ProPublica does not count as impact an official statement or a promise of a policy review. Similarly it does not count as impact the mere fact that oversight hearings are convened or a commission is formed to delve into a problem. Given this high standard, it is probably not surprising that Tofel acknowledges that ProPublica has rarely achieved impact. Over three years from 2010 to 2012, the organization documented impact only 27 times, even with a staff of about 20 reporters working full time. But, as Tofel notes, the frequency of impact is only one of the quantitative measures that could be applied, the other being magnitude. One case, the group's financial reporting on Wall Street practices before the crash of 2008, "has already resulted in the levying of more than half a billion dollars in fines and settlements to the federal government by financial institutions" (20).

It's also important to note, as Tofel does, that investigative reporting is inherently difficult and time-consuming. Reporting and writing a major investigative story can take many months, and a further complicating factor is that many story ideas do not pan out. To get stories with impact, reporters often have to be willing to take risks with their time, following up on tips or hunches. But there is no guarantee that further reporting won't lead to results that aren't all that interesting or to the conclusion that what looked like a story really doesn't matter or just isn't true.

HARD TO PROVE

While ProPublica takes a conservative approach to attaching impact to its work, it also acknowledges that even these judgments may not stand up to the most rigorous kinds of scrutiny. News stories are often about complicated subjects and involve many different actors. A close examination of how change comes about may well show a central role for journalism, but such a review is unlikely to show that a story or group of stories led directly to change without intervening factors. Reporting can catalyze change, but there will always be other factors at work.

NO SINGLE MEASURE

In the 27 instances that ProPublica has cited as examples of impact, the outcomes vary and are hard to compare or rank. The impacts include the conviction of New Orleans police officers, the enactment of a new law governing psychotropic drugs in Illinois nursing homes, restrictions on sales of wild horses and the dissolution of a charitable foundation. Which one is the biggest impact, or the most significant? As Tofel notes, there is "no single algorithm that can be devised, no magic formula to load into a spreadsheet or deploy in an app" (2013, 21) to evaluate these outcomes and measure their relative worth.

That's not to say that ProPublica does not apply quantitative measures where it can. Because its content is distributed over the Internet, ProPublica can track reader response using a variety of tools and over a variety of different platforms, including Facebook, mobile apps and the websites that reprint its work. Tofel argues that the most useful approach to tracking impact would involve a combination of narrative tools, describing stories and the changes they prompt, with datapoints captured through Web tracking and by manual counts of media appearances by ProPublica reporters or citations of their work by other news outlets. In the end, each news organization may have to devise its own approach, based on the nature of its work and of its audience, but without allowing impact measurement to overshadow the core purpose of original reporting and public service, a point that has been made by one of the pioneers of nonprofit journalism, Charles Lewis (Lewis and Niles, 2013).

The challenges of evaluating impact can be illustrated by looking at specific cases, including instances in which high quality reporting has failed to make a difference. Let's start by returning to the case of Agent Orange that was discussed at the beginning of this chapter. We'll first analyze Whiteside's work in the context of the documents-observation-talk methodology of this textbook and then examine the sequence of events that led to the restrictions on the use of Agent Orange.

A close look at Whiteside's article makes clear the role of documents, observation and talk in his reporting, including an interesting decision about what his story was about and what it was he needed to observe. More significantly, it is possible to see how Whiteside wielded the information that he found, not simply adding one piece to another but rather comparing one against another to indicate inconsistencies and even contradictions. He did all of this while working at a distinct disadvantage: Unlike many of his sources who held advanced degrees and were well grounded in the technical issues surrounding Agent Orange, Whiteside was a scientific layman who did not hold even a high school diploma (see Figure 13.1).

The documents Whiteside used ranged from public material found in books, newspaper articles and official statements to a lab report that at one time had been held very closely among a select group of government officials and contractors. At several points in his article, he showed how statements that seemed reasonable enough on the surface were actually misleading when put in the proper context by using information drawn from

FIGURE 13.1   *Reporter Thomas Whiteside. Credit: Photo courtesy of Thomas Whiteside family*

other sources. For example, White House officials attempted to downplay the significance of a report that indicated toxic effects from Agent Orange by noting that the lab tests on which the report was based involved "relatively small numbers of laboratory rats and mice" (Whiteside, 1970, 50). A lesser reporter would have, of course, included this cautionary point, as Whiteside did. But *The New Yorker* writer went further, researching the issue of lab protocols. What he discovered was that the White House statement, while factually correct, could obscure the truth that the Agent Orange tests were actually far more extensive than the standard tests that were then in use for chemical substances. Rather than making citizens feel more comfortable about Agent Orange, the circumstances surrounding the Agent Orange tests, when properly understood, actually suggested either the apparent danger of Agent Orange was greater than the White House was letting on or that the U.S. government was routinely using extremely low standards for testing new chemical products. In Whiteside's view both conclusions were justified.

Whiteside's use of human sources was similarly extensive, including college professors, medical doctors and toxicologists. Not all of these conversations went well, and Whiteside describes being put off by several people he talked to. One, an official of the lab that had conducted the Agent Orange tests under a contract with the federal government, told the reporter that he was "asking sophisticated questions that as a layman you don't have the equipment to understand the answers to" (1970, 38). Whiteside's finished article, of course, proves the inaccuracy of this statement. Another scientist, who ended up not cooperating with Whiteside and not being quoted in the article, told the reporter, "To be blunt, I don't think that you know what you are talking about" (1971, 15). Whiteside offered to have the scientist improve his understanding, but the scientist refused to do so over the telephone, and the reporter went on to other sources. Some of these sources are quoted directly. Others provided information on background and are not named in the article as it was published in *The New Yorker*.

Whiteside's 1971 book on the topic, *The Withering Rain: America's Herbicidal Folly*, includes an introduction in which the journalist provides insights into his reporting process. One of the more notable ones has to do with Whiteside's direct observation of the effects of Agent Orange. As it turns out his reporting includes no such observations, but for a very good reason. As Whiteside started his research, it occurred to him that he should travel to Vietnam to see firsthand what the chemical was doing to that country. But as he thought about the issue further, he realized that his story was not really about Agent Orange as a chemical but about Agent Orange as an illustration of the policy issues surrounding the use of a toxic compound in a military context. "What needed to be investigated most were the government and industry standards—or lack of them—that had made the defoliation and herbicidal programs in Vietnam possible in the first place, and that had permitted these programs to grow to their present huge size," he explained. "And I concluded that these problems could most profitably be explored in this country by an examination of the circumstances through which potentially dangerous chemicals could be approved for such widespread use without adequate testing" (16). The reporter wanted to write about something that could not be seen, because it did not exist, a mechanism for thorough government review of dangerous chemicals. He ended up describing this problem by identifying gaps in communications and instances where agencies with joint responsibilities did not work together.

Although Whiteside's writings on Agent Orange were credited by Sen. Hart as key influences that prompted the hearings on the chemical, it is a little hard to trace out the trajectory of how these pieces worked their effects. To begin with, Whiteside was not the one who "broke" the story of Agent Orange's most serious side-effect, namely its teratogenicity, its ability to cause malformations in a developing fetus. He said he read about a government study that indicated this problem in October 1969 in the London *Sunday Times* (1971, 11), and by the end of that month the *Los Angeles Times* had also reported on the study (Nelson, 1969, 11). A fuller report, making many of the same points Whiteside would make in his articles, appeared in the January 1970 issue of *The New Republic* (Haseltine, Cook, and Galston, 1970), a publication that, because of its focus on politics and policy, could be expected to have a greater readership and more influence on Capitol Hill than *The New Yorker*.

To Whiteside's dismay and disappointment, his article outlining the dangers of Agent Orange and the inadequacy of government testing regimes landed with a resounding thud among major news organizations, both print and broadcast. "Up to then, I had taken the attitude that somehow, once a writer brings out facts that need to be brought out, he's done his job and he can move on to his next project," he wrote in the introduction to *The Withering Rain*. "But the unpleasant fact now confronted me that just *writing* wasn't enough, and that unless I took some sort of personal action the impact of this journalistic investigation would be quickly dissipated by other issues coming to public attention" (1971, 17).

His first step was to see if he could drum up some interest among fellow journalists by contacting "various friends at newspapers, news magazines, and broadcasting networks." But these efforts came to naught, and he was even told that the *Times* wouldn't go near the story because it "made a practice of staying away, where it possibly could, from such issues if the paper hadn't actually uncovered and developed the story itself" (1971, 17).

At this point Whiteside decided to cross the line that separates the detached observer from the engaged participant, although it's important to keep in mind that this line may be drawn more clearly in textbooks about journalism ethics than in the world of actual practice, where reporters and sources routinely engage in exchanging gossip and bartering information, actions that are not publicly acknowledged but that can affect news coverage. In Whiteside's case he "put in a couple of telephone calls to people I know in Washington" to share the information he had and to suggest that some kind of formal investigation was warranted (1971, 17).

One of those calls went to Michael Pertschuk, then the chief counsel and staff director of the Senate Committee on Commerce and later chairman of the Federal Trade Commission. Pertschuk and Whiteside had both professional and personal connections. Both men had worked, for example, on tobacco control issues, Whiteside as a journalist covering especially the marketing and advertising aspects of the matter and Pertschuk as one of the key figures shaping legislation and federal policy. In addition they had a family connection, in that Whiteside's wife, the former Marie Pertschuk, was Michael Pertschuk's cousin. Pertschuk today says he cannot recall the precise sequence of events but thinks it highly likely that he was the one who brought Whiteside's article to the attention of Sen. Hart, who at the time was looking for issues to bring before the relatively new environmental subcommittee (Pertschuk, 2013).

Over the weeks and months after his first story on Agent Orange appeared, Whiteside kept the public pressure up, with ongoing articles in *The New Yorker* that continued to point out contradictions between official promises to deal with the issue and a lack of concrete action. The work he did behind the scenes may have been even more instrumental in the outcome of the Agent Orange hearings. He worked closely with Sen. Hart's staff, helping to identify potential witnesses and to plan their testimony (Whiteside, 1981). The journalist also enlisted his French-born wife, who was known for her extraordinary cooking skills, in his lobbying efforts. The Senate staffer who was assigned to Agent Orange was invited to lunch with the Whitesides at their Greenwich Village apartment and later wrote a personal note to Mrs. Whiteside, telling her, "Your lunch may well have been the best I've had since I left Europe" (Bickwit, 1970).

Whiteside was an extremely meticulous reporter who had a reputation for not exaggerating his facts or shading their meaning. He was careful to include in his articles information that might undercut his overall point, and in that spirit it's important to acknowledge, as Whiteside himself did, that his articles about Agent Orange were not the immediate cause of the government taking steps to impose limits on the use of the herbicide. The story is a little more complicated than that since the executive branch agencies initially testified to Sen. Hart's committee that they did not see a need to impose further restrictions on Agent Orange despite what *The New Yorker* had reported. As the Senate hearings continued, however, they changed their minds, based on a new study, the analysis of which was completed during the week between the first and second hearings on the chemical's toxicity (Whiteside, 1977).

Making note of this development, however, does not diminish Whiteside's role, for it was his reporting and related activities that forced the issue into the public eye. The government had many years of testing data already available to it, and it could have acted to restrict Agent Orange before Sen. Hart's hearings. Further, there is no way of knowing whether the new testing would have had an impact within the federal bureaucracy absent the Senate hearings. One indication that the new lab results that supposedly prompted the government's turnabout were not so clear-cut is that the debate over the safety of Agent Orange went on for another 15 years before the Environmental Protection Agency finally banned its distribution and sale (Wagner, 1986).

In today's media environment, a reporter who worked as intensely on an issue as Whiteside did on Agent Orange would likely come under heavy criticism for crossing the objectivity barrier that supposedly exists between journalists and their stories. Hammering home his points in print would be one thing, but calling on family connections to advance his case and getting involved in the details of staff preparations for hearings on a public controversy would be viewed as improper behavior. But it's doubtful that this kind of criticism would have dissuaded Whiteside from doing what he did, especially given what was at stake with the continued use of Agent Orange.

FIGURE 13.2   *A four-plane formation sprays defoliant over the South Vietnamese jungle. Credit: United States Air Force*

The compound has been linked to a range of health problems, including cancer, diabetes, heart disease and birth defects (see Figure 13.2). As many as 3 million Vietnamese, including children and other noncombatants, suffer serious toxic effects from Agent Orange, and close to 3 million American service members may have received some degree of exposure to the chemical (U.S.–Vietnam Dialogue Group on Agent Orange/Dioxin, 2010). The cost of repairing the environmental damage done by Agent Orange has been estimated at $300 million (Dialogue Group), and the U.S. government has been paying $2 billion a year to veterans with medical conditions related to Agent Orange (Grotto and Jones, 2010). Given the magnitude of the danger posed by the compound, and how much worse if could have been, it's hard to find fault with Whiteside's efforts to effect change.

Whiteside's extraordinary actions led to a specific change in federal policy, an impact. But sometimes extraordinary work comes up short and does not have the desired impact. A review of these kinds of stories can also help shape our thinking about journalism impact, and perhaps one of the most dramatic examples relate to the catastrophic consequences of Hurricane Katrina on the city of New Orleans.

The storm hit New Orleans in August 2005 and left behind tens of billions of dollars in property damage. More than 1,100 people died, and more than 400,000 fled for their lives. At least 80 percent of the city was flooded, to a depth of 10 feet in places, after levees and floodwalls failed at more than 50 locations, according to an authoritative report that put much of the blame for the destruction on a series of engineering mistakes (American Society of Civil Engineers, 2007).

Although President George W. Bush famously said in the aftermath that "I don't think anyone anticipated the breach of the levees" (Sawyer, 2005), the dangers that the city faced from weakness in the flood control system were well known. Three years earlier the local newspaper, *The Times-Picayune,* had published a five-day series that outlined the shortcomings in the city's flood defenses. "It's only a matter of time before South Louisiana takes a direct hit from a major hurricane," the newspaper warned. "Billions have been spent to protect us, but we grow more vulnerable every day" (2002).

Against this backdrop of warnings, one has to wonder what went wrong—what accounts for the lack of impact of these reports? A couple of possibilities immediately come to mind. Perhaps the articles focused on the wrong information. Or perhaps the information was correct, but the emphasis was misplaced. Maybe the tone was not strong enough.

Some analysts fault the media's coverage of natural disasters for focusing too much on institutions and the role of government agencies with less attention paid to the role of individuals and communities in preparing for disaster (Barnes et al., 2008). This pattern can be seen in *The Times-Picayune's* work, which included a piece on what individual residents should do in terms of developing a personal evacuation plan. But this article appeared on the last day of the series and likely got less attention than other stories describing, for example, the area's flood protection system or shifts in population patterns that had been exposing more people to risk.

After Katrina, the reporters who wrote *The Times-Picayune* stories, Mark Schleifstein and John McQuaid, were hailed for their accuracy and foresight. But they were careful about what they took credit for. In an interview with *Columbia Journalism Review,* Schleifstein sought to clarify this point: "When people ask me, 'Didn't you predict Katrina?' I answer, 'No, I didn't. I predicted what could have happened if a catastrophic event had hit us. But Katrina was not a catastrophic hurricane the way it hit New Orleans," with only Category 1 or 2 winds (Brainard, 2012).

Even if the reporters had known about the engineering problems and reported them, it's not clear that inclusion of such information would have made a difference. In their book about the hurricane, the two journalists described their concerns about how to pitch their newspaper articles. They feared that if they were too alarmist, they would simply turn readers off. As a result, they chose to focus on the ways soil erosion was increasing the likelihood of a hurricane catastrophe as opposed to how the worst-case scenario would play out. The risks that New Orleans faced were no secret. "The question was no longer Did anyone know but Did anyone care?" the journalists wrote (McQuaid, and

Schleifstein, 2006, 127). Schleifstein, who ended up losing his home in Katrina, acknowledged that even he had grown complacent. "Unlike his neighbors, he never boarded up his windows when a storm menaced the city. To him, the yearly hurricane gamble was just the price of living in New Orleans" (125).

A key difference between the Agent Orange and New Orleans reporting examples is that the former was responding to events while the latter was trying to predict effects. Reporters, as in Whiteside's case, have a greater chance of having an impact if they can point to actual consequences as compared to those journalists, like Schleifstein and McQuaid, who are warning about something that may happen but has not yet come to pass.

Hindsight is always perfect, of course, and second-guessing is usually unfair, but it is still useful to look back over *The Times-Picayune*'s reporting to see if an approach based on connecting documents, observation and talk might have yielded a different result. The paper correctly reported that the safety standards adopted by the federal government were relatively low, with flood protection designed to withstand a Category 3 hurricane that passed quickly. But the paper did not report, until after Katrina spurred several investigations by engineering experts, that there were deeper problems with the government's flood protection plan. The Army Corps of Engineers had discovered back in the mid-1980s that there were potential design problems with the levees it was installing, meaning that the city was vulnerable to smaller and weaker storms. This point did not come out until after the hurricane disaster and was only grudgingly acknowledged by the Corps (McQuaid and Schleifstein, 2006).

As it turns out, there was a documentary "smoking gun" in the form of a report published in 1988 with the innocuous title "E-99 Sheet Pile Wall, Field Load Test Report" (Jackson, 1988). The report described the potential failure of the kind of steel floodwall that was blamed for some of the worst flooding that occurred in New Orleans. In theory, at least, this report could have been the basis for a different line of investigation, one focusing on unacknowledged flaws in the city's flood controls.

While this highly technical report does not state its findings in the clearest of terms and includes caveats about the need for additional study, it does provide the basis for the other two parts of the DOT methodology. It contains information about the location of the test site, an opportunity to collect some direct observations, as well as names and contact information for additional sources with whom to talk. To make the most of this information, it would also have been necessary to use some of the strategies that were described in Chapter 2 for making connections:

1. Search for patterns—and for the lack of a pattern.

2. Look microscopically—and see globally.

3. Break the story—and put it into context.

4. Probe the past—and imagine the future.

5. Accept every possibility—and doubt everything.

The examples of Agent Orange and New Orleans help to highlight why the journalism profession will continue to have trouble with the concept of impact. As in the case of Agent Orange, impact sometimes occurs because of factors that are beyond the scope of reporters' normal activities, and sometimes, as in the case of New Orleans, impact does not occur even when reporters have done an extensive job of assembling relevant information.

Clearly, there is no simple formula for creating journalism with impact. But it is fair to assume that for a story to have impact it must have qualities that allow, if not encourage, engagement by readers with the underlying topic. Journalists most often assume that these qualities relate to content, that stories are more compelling because of their subject matter or perhaps because of the emotions that they stir. These are issues that certainly belong in the forefront.

But news consumers must also have a reason to believe in the validity of the reports that they receive from journalists, and this is where the documents-observation-talk methodology set forth in this book can help to increase credibility. "Connecting the DOT" won't do it alone, but this approach is a way of expanding the impact of what you report. In addition to applying the documents-observation-talk methodology in news gathering, journalists can take the extra step of making explicit to readers the steps that were taken to verify and validate news accounts.

By focusing attention not just on their findings but on how they arrived at their findings, reporters would do a great service to readers, who might then more easily navigate through the great mass of news accounts that are available. News consumers could skip over, or put less weight on, those reports that were developed with fewer sources, fewer types of sources or without significant cross checking. News organizations that use a protocol to develop their stories and also explain this protocol in a transparent way would be taking important steps toward achieving greater impact. To be sure, journalists who use this methodology would not be guaranteed a payoff in impact. But higher reader confidence in news accounts would certainly lead to an increased likelihood that such accounts would inspire action and change.

EXERCISES

1. Definitions of journalistic impact ultimately will be based on individual responses to news accounts. What kinds of news stories have the most impact on you personally? What are the factors that contribute to their impact? Do certain news outlets, or kinds of outlets, generate more impact than others? Do certain kinds of stories, either

on certain topics or produced in certain forms or containing certain elements, produce more impact than others?

2. What are the different forms that impact can take? Which ones are most significant in the context of journalism?

3. What do you think is the best way to measure impact?

REFERENCES

American Society of Civil Engineers. "The New Orleans Hurricane Protection System: What Went Wrong and Why," Reston, Va., 2007.

Anderson, C.W., Emily Bell and Clay Shirky. *Post-Industrial Journalism: Adapting to the Present,* New York: Tow Center for Digital Journalism, 2012, accessed December 21, 2013, at http://towcenter.org/research/post-industrial-journalism.

Barnes, Michael D., Carl L. Hanson, Len M. B. Novilla, Aaron T. Meacham, Emily McIntyre, and Brittany C. Erickson. "Analysis of Media Agenda Setting During and After Hurricane Katrina: Implications for Emergency Preparedness, Disaster Response, and Disaster Policy," *American Journal of Public Health* 98, No. 4, April 2008, 604–610.

Bickwit, Leonard. Letter to Mrs. Thomas Whiteside, March 12, 1970, Thomas Whiteside Papers, box 10, folder 24; Rare Book and Manuscript Library, Columbia University Library.

Brainard, Curtis. "'Prophet of Katrina' Stays Put," *Columbia Journalism Review* Observatory blog, June 22, 2012, accessed December 21, 2013, at http://www.cjr.org/the_observatory/times_picayune_mark_schleifste.php?page=all.

Campbell, W. Joseph. *Getting It Wrong: Ten of the Greatest Misreported Stories in American Journalism,* Berkeley: University of California Press, 2010.

Grotto, Jason, and Tim Jones. "VA Laboring Under Surge of Wounded Veterans," *Chicago Tribune,* April 9, 2010, accessed December 22, 2013, at http://articles.chicagotribune.com/2010–04–09/news/ct-met-disabled-veterans-cost-20100409_1_veterans-groups-veterans-for-common-sense-persian-gulf-veteran.

Haseltine, William, Robert E. Cook, and Arthur W. Galston. "Deliberate Destruction of the Environment: What Have We Done to Vietnam?" *The New Republic,* January 10, 1970, 18–21.

Jackson, Richard B. *E-99 Sheet Pile Wall, Field Load Test Report.* Washington: US Army Corps of Engineers, 1988.

Keller, Bill. "Is Glenn Greenwald the Future of News," *The New York Times,* October 27, 2013, accessed December 21, 2013, at http://www.nytimes.com/2013/10/28/opinion/a-conversation-in-lieu-of-a-column.html?_r=0.

Lee, Chul-joo, and Dietram A. Scheufele. "The Influence of Knowledge and Deference Toward Scientific Authority: A Media Effects Model for Public Attitudes Toward Nanotechnology," *Journalism & Mass Communication Quarterly* 83, No. 4, Winter, 2006, 819–834.

Lewis, Charles, and Hilary Niles. *Measuring Impact: The Art, Science and Mystery of Nonprofit News,* Washington: Investigative Reporting Workshop, 2013, accessed December 21, 2013, at http://investigativereportingworkshop.org/ilab/story/measuring-impact/.

McQuaid, John, and Mark Schleifstein. *Path of Destruction: The Devastation of New Orleans and the Coming Age of Superstorms,* New York: Little, Brown, 2006.

Nelson, Bryce. "Studies Find Danger in Defoliation Herbicides: White House Removes One from Use after Tests on Mice Indicate Cancer," *Los Angeles Times,* October 30, 1969.

New York Times. "U.S. Curbs Sales of a Weed Killer," April 16, 1970.

Pertschuk, Michael. Telephone interview with the author, February 5, 2013.

Pew Research Center's Project for Excellence in Journalism. "The State of the News Media 2013: An Annual Report on American Journalism," March 18, 2013, accessed December 21, 2013, at http://stateofthemedia.org/2013/overview-5/.

Pilhofer, Aron. "Finding the Right Metric for News," aronpilhofer.com, July 25, 2012, accessed December 21, 2013, at http://aronpilhofer.com/post/27993980039/the-right-metric-for-news.

ProPublica. "Frequently Asked Questions," undated, accessed December 21, 2013, at http://www.propublica.org/about/frequently-asked-questions/.

Sawyer, Diane. "President George W. Bush Exclusive Interview," *Good Morning America,* aired September 1, 2005, transcript, LexisNexis Academic.

Schudson, Michael, Theda Skocpol, Richard M. Valelly, and Robert Putnam. "What if Civic Life Didn't Die?" *The American Prospect* No. 25, March 1996, 17.

Senate Committee on Commerce. *Effects of 2,4,5-T on Man and the Environment,* 91st Cong., 2nd sess., April 7 and 15, 1970.

———. *The Effects of 2,4,5-T and Related Herbicides on Man and the Environment,* 91st Cong., 2nd sess., June 17 and 18, 1970.

Serrin, Judith, and William Serrin. *Muckraking! The Journalism That Changed America,* New York: The New Press, 2002.

Stellman, Jeanne Mager, Steven D. Stellman, Richard Christians, Tracy Weber, and Carrie Tomasallo. "The Extent and Patterns of Usage of Agent Orange and Other Herbicides in Vietnam," *Nature,* 422, April 17, 2003, 681–687.

Times-Picayune. "Washing Away," June 23, 2002, accessed December 21, 2013, at http://www.nola.com/washingaway/.

Tofel, Richard J. *Non-profit Journalism: Issues Around Impact,* New York: ProPublica, 2013, accessed December 21, 2013, at http://s3.amazonaws.com/propublica/assets/about/LFA_ProPublica-white-paper_2.1.pdf.

U.S. Patent and Trademark Office Trademark Electronic Search System. "Impact Journalism," June 21, 2011, accessed December 21, 2013, at http://tess2.uspto.gov/bin/gate.exe?f=searchss&state=4803:e66day.1.1.

U.S. Senate. "Senate House Office Building," undated, accessed December 21, 2013, at http://www.senate.gov/pagelayout/visiting/d_three_sections_with_teasers/hart_senate_building_web_page.htm.

U.S.–Vietnam Dialogue Group on Agent Orange/Dioxin. *Declaration and Plan of Action,* Washington: The Aspen Institute, 2010, accessed December 22, 2013, at http://www.aspeninstitute.org/sites/default/files/content/docs/advocacy%20and%20exchange%20program%20on%20agent%20orange/2010–6-16USVietnamDialogueGroupDeclarationandPlanofAction.pdf

Wagner, Wendy. "Environmental Regulation and the Doctrine of Scientific Uncertainty: A Case Study of the EPA's Cancellation of 2,4,5-T," *Journal of the National Association of Administrative Law Judges* 7, 1986, 7–55.

Wendland, Michael F. *The Arizona Project: How a Team of Investigative Reporters Got Revenge on Deadline,* Kansas City: Sheed Andrews and McMeel, 1977.

Whiteside, Thomas. "Defoliation," *The New Yorker,* February 7, 1970, 32–69.

———. *The Withering Rain: America's Herbicidal Folly,* New York: E.P. Dutton, 1971.

———. "The Pendulum and the Toxic Cloud," *The New Yorker,* July 25, 1977, 30–55.

———. Letter to Gilbert Bogen, M.D., August, 24, 1981, Thomas Whiteside Papers, box 27, folder 35; Rare Book and Manuscript Library, Columbia University Library.

INDEX

CPSIA information can be obtained
at www.ICGtesting.com
Printed in the USA
FFOW04n0149160518
46695782-48784FF

9 780415 824286